In Search of Other Skies

REVIEWS

This engrossing story unveils raw and real emotions around vivid and detailed descriptions of barely known but beautiful parts of Mexico. What a delightful read!
—Alejandra Chiapa

I think In Search Of Other Skies is a fascinating book, and will become a treasure of Saltillo—a city practically unknown to the rest of the world. It's also very funny in places.
—Erick Tovar

The romance at the heart of the book between an older gringo and a very beautiful young Mexican woman is full of emotion and surprises. I had to keep reading!
—Judy James

In Search of Other Skies

A Story of Saltillo

Chris Steer

© 2019 Chris Steer. All rights reserved. No part of this book may be scanned, copied, uploaded or reproduced in any form or by any means, photographically, electronically or mechanically, without written permission from the copyright holder.

ISBN: 978-1-943492-74-9 (Hardback)
ISBN: 978-1-943492-75-6 (Soft Cover)

Cover painting, *Landscape Under a Stormy Sky*, 1888 by Vincent Van Gogh

Elm Grove Publishing | San Antonio, Texas | www.elmgrovepublishing.com
Elm Grove Publishing is a legally registered trade name of Panache Communication Arts, Inc.

To Evelyn, Erick, Ana, Patricia, Didi, and Benito.

CONTENTS

Preface to First U.S. Edition	8
Introduction	9
1. Lomas de Lourdes	11
2. Regarding Our House	14
3. In The Middle Of The Night	16
4. Some Definitions	28
5. A Little Background Information	29
6. The End Of The Middle Of The Night	43
7. Next Morning	44
8. Breakfast	49
9. A Phone Call	52
10. "What are you smiling at?"	56
11. A Feeling And A Circling	60
12. Widely Separated Areas	63
13. Ready To Go	66
14. Heading Out	68
15. On Our Way	69
16. Arrived	71
17. Enter Bertie	74
18. Enter Mike	76
19. Enter A Couple	81
20. Enter Paula	86
21. Dinner-1	88
22. Dinner-2	95
23. Dinner-3	99
24. Heading Back	102
25. When I Saw Grandma	107
26. Back Home	109
27. At The Alameda	110

28. Into Paula's Apartment	118
29. Lunch With Paula	125
30. Belinda Calling	132
31. So	135
32. The Days Before Thursday	136
33. Thursday-1	151
34. Thursday-2	156
35. Home Almost Alone	166
36. Goodbye Thursday	176
37. The Nightmare	177
38. Chris's List	181
39. Come Friday (YCTIWY)	184
40. Must Be A Cultural Thing	192
41. That Saturday	194
42. The Red Tricycle	201
43. Saturday Breakfast With Jasmine	203
44. Except Maybe Tahiti	205
45. The Beetle	210
46. The Sunday Before Monday	213
47. Monday-1	217
48. Monday-2 (The Gargoyle)	221
49. Monday-3	223
50. "You Ain't Nothin' But A Hound Dog"	230
51. "Thinkin' Cap Time"	234
52. The Conversation	236
53. Happenings	239
54. The Void	241
55. My Friend Benito	246
56. Like An Exile	251
57. Intuition	253
58. An Encounter	254
59. Stunned	256
60. The Finality Of A Friday	258
61. Cheerful	263
62. In Our Yard	265
63. The Bear	269
64. Ending In Arteaga	273

Preface to First U.S. Edition

I hesitate to call *In Search Of Other Skies* a "novel," though I suppose it more or less fits into that category. This is to say that most novels are made up of fictional characters speaking fictional dialogue, and moving about in a fictional (though sometimes real) setting. At the most, they may be based on real people. This is not the case with this book. All of the people in it are real people speaking their own words in a real place. If you were to come to Saltillo, Mexico today, in 2020, you could meet and talk to all of them (myself included), with the one exception of Paula, who moved to the United States around four years ago. Of course, I'm talking about the main storyline. There are autobiographical and historical anecdotes included in the story which deal with people who've passed on. One exception to this is the anecdote about the Beatles concert: as of this writing, Paul and Ringo are still living.

This book was first published in Mexico in March of 2019. It's my hope that republishing it in America, through Elm Grove Publishing, it will reach a wider, English-speaking audience. Plaudits must be given to Mick Prodger of Elm Grove Publishing who has been of great assistance in guiding me through this republishing process.

CS

INTRODUCTION

Doin' the Lampedusa

The following pages are just something I wrote; and the following story is set in the month of September in 2015. As for the actual writing of it, all I really did was just "let 'er rip." Oh, I had some general idea of what I wanted to say and where I wanted to go, but the pages pretty much just wrote themselves, one after another. As a matter of fact, as the pages started piling up, I kept saying to myself, "I'm doin' the Lampedusa," a phrase that came to me one night as I lay in my bed in the dark, before dropping off to sleep, wondering what in the world I was doin' typin' out words, words, and more words, at my age . . . Giuseppe di Lampedusa, a Sicilian aristocrat, wrote only one novel in his whole life, and a great one, *IL Gatopardo (The Leopard)*, based loosely on the life and times of his great-grandfather, Giulio Tomasi, Prince of Lampedusa. Giuseppe, himself, died, at sixty, in 1957; and his novel didn't see publication until 1958, when a willing publisher, thanks to the continuing efforts of his widow and friends, finally published it, after it had been rejected by two publishers during Lampedusa's lifetime, mainly for being considered too "old-fashioned."

The book was an immediate and astonishing success in Italy, and soon in the rest of the world; and it was made into a beautiful and majestic (though slow-moving) movie in 1963, starring Burt Lancaster; but, of course, none of this benefited its author, six feet underground. From what I've read, Lampedusa had entertained notions of writing this novel for decades; but he only sat down to actually do it in the last years of his life, only to find out, in early 1957, a few months after finishing it, that he had inoperable lung cancer. He was a heavy smoker, and most of the photos of him, of which there aren't many, show him with a cigarette. He died on July 22, 1957. *The Leopard* was, thus, his first and last gasp. He knew, once he received the diagnosis, that *The Leopard* would be the only novel that he'd leave behind him, even though he died without seeing it published. I can identify, to a degree, with him. I'm not any aristocrat—far from it—but am around the same age as Lampedusa was when he wrote his solitary book, and have also thought about writing a novel, (if that's what this is,) for decades. He was married to a woman from a foreign country and culture; and they never had any children. I'm married to a woman from a foreign country and culture, and we've never had any children, either. Most significantly, though I'm not dying of cancer—am relatively healthy—and may live to a ripe (or maybe rotten) old age, I know that *In Search of Other Skies* will be *my* solitary book, the only one to ever carry my name. Enough's enough. "The book stops here." I wrote *Other Skies*, basically, for myself; though I think it's a worthwhile read, and that there're good things in it, for anyone who wishes to turn its pages. In any event, *Other Skies* is my *Leopard*, my first and last gasp as well. "Doin' the Lampedusa."

CHAPTER 1

Lomas de Lourdes

Lomas de Lourdes (The Hills of Lourdes) is a residential colony (una colonia) situated on the southern edge of Saltillo ("SaulTEAyo") Mexico, a city of some million souls, located about fifty miles southwest of her big sister city, Monterrey, and about two hundred and fifty miles, as the crow (or buzzard) flies, south of the Texas-Mexico border at Laredo. Lomas, (as it's simply and popularly called) has, indeed, many large hills which are, in fact, foothills of the towering, pine-forested Sierra Madre, whose steep slopes soar up dramatically from them. From where the colony sits, this mountain range curves off to the east and west—Lomas being but one stop on its circuit—as it completes a great wide circle, and presents itself to the view, from the heights of Lomas, as an enormous blue bowl with the colorful city of Saltillo sitting down at its bottom in the distance, densely spread out across an immense plain. It's a spectacular view.

Though Lomas is still technically within the Saltillo city limits, it's at the very limit of those limits, there being nothing beyond it but the rising, uninhabited mountains. In the other direction, Lomas is a good five miles from the center of town (the centuries-old Cathedral Plaza, in about the center of the great plain) and the colony's separated by about half a mile of grassy fields from the southernmost reaches of the metropolis.

So situated, Lomas is a sort of sanctuary unto itself. Certainly, if you desire peace and quiet, it's the place to be, where most of the time it's so quiet and still you can hear a pinecone drop.

Lomas is essentially a "bedroom community" in the sense that it's necessary to go down into town for most of the things you need or wish to enjoy, whether it's to go to the grocery store or the bank, the doctor or the drugstore, or to a restaurant, a shopping center, or a movie. The same goes for getting gas, as there's not one gas pump in the whole colony.

Still, such inconveniences and lack of diversions aside, Lomas has many positive qualities. It affords breathtaking, panoramic views of the whole multicolored sea of a city in the distance, ringed in by the undulating, deep blue mountains. The air is fresher and cleaner—and, in the summer, cooler—than down in the city. You're surrounded by nature and wildlife, the latter of which includes birds of all kinds, (including hooting owls, at night,) squirrels, red foxes, skunks, possums, white-tailed jackrabbits, armadillos, raccoons, and coyotes. Concerning the coyotes, though they seldom make their presence known, they're sometimes faintly heard late at night spookily howling up in the mountains. On a rare occasion—by day, or in your headlights at night—in driving through the colony, you may come upon (or just miss) a tortoise slowly crossing the road. At night, too, in the colony, you can actually *see* all the stars in the sky, and how the Milky Way got its name. Cost-wise, your three basic utilities of electricity, gas, and water are much cheaper than down in town. And, last but not least, it's *quiet.*

If I may elaborate a little on what I just said about "The air ..." The city of Saltillo (founded in 1577) is celebrated as "La Ciudad de la Primavera Eterna" ("The City of Eternal Spring"). Though this is something of a typical Mexican exaggeration, it's not that far from the truth. Being at an official altitude of 5350 feet, Saltillo has, indeed, an agreeable climate, which is especially true in the summer when the daytime temperature rarely rises above the upper 70s Fahrenheit, out and about the city, it really does feel like springtime in summertime, and there's no "heat rising from the streets" like in sweltering Monterrey, which is pretty horrible in June, July, and August.

Since Lomas is at a higher altitude than the high altitude the mile high city is at, to begin with, summer days in the colony are even better—cooler, by about five degrees—than down in the city. Summer nights in the colony are deliciously cool, with the temperature hovering in the lower 60s.

Established only back in the 1970s on elevated land that was just empty, unnamed wilderness, Lomas de Lourdes incorporates a vast amount of territory. All of the housing in it (so far), on or between the hills, only takes up widely separated sections of this territory, (unlike your typical tightly-knit bedroom community,) and whole extensive areas of Lomas—wild and open countryside, hilltop, and hillside—have yet to see a shovel or a bulldozer. It's this openness and rural-like freedom that's one of the colony's chief charms.

One more thing. In speaking of this "rural-like freedom," Lomas is, in spite of its proximity to the city, very "country," both physically and mentally. Its residents, on the whole, are not like those who live down in town. It takes a certain kind of person to live up in Lomas on a full-time basis, year in and year out, someone who's able to endure its everlasting peace and quiet, its isolation, its "boringness," and its many inconveniences. Not to sound snobbish, most of the people who live in the colony are laid-back, unsophisticated folk, (which Lomas seems to attract,) who are, by and large, unprofessional (or, at least, not highly-professional) people, like the kind of people you'd find in any out-of-the-way, small country village. It really is the kind of place "where nothing much ever happens." In short, Lomas isn't for every John and Jane (or Juan and Juana), and even after forty years it's still only sparsely populated.

Well, one more thing, in speaking of the inhabitants of the colony—what they're like. Go into any home in Lomas and you won't see a book anywhere. Well—almost—for you may see the Bible conspicuously displayed on the coffee table or the mantel or somewhere. The Bible, thus, you could say, serves as "the Book of the House," (not that anybody ever actually *reads* it.)

CHAPTER 2

Regarding Our House

    I've read that the exciting, laughing, romantic actor—Robin Hood (1938), himself—Errol Flynn, whenever he answered the phone, his opening words invariably were, "Be brief." A good rule to follow, on most occasions, (though I wouldn't advise telling this to a woman.) I'd prefer to ignore, or just totally forget about describing the complicated physical layout of our street. Who cares? I don't even care. Still, I suppose, regarding our house, something must be said, if only for the benefit of what's-a-comin'. I'll try to "be brief" and get it over with. I'll do my best.
    Picture a high and wide, windswept foothill, covered in wild shrubbery, butting up against an ascending slope of the Sierras, at the southern edge of (and almost out of) the colony. A single residential street—really, just a block—cuts across the middle of the foothill, the Paseo de las Aves (Bird Drive). This street connects with a long, uninhabited street running down the eastern side and around the base of the foothill, the Paseo de los Pájaros (Bird Drive, also). Accelerating up or braking down the longer paseo, you turn onto its little brother over a speed bump right at its entrance, and on your left are five identical, white, one-story, cement row houses, built in the 80s, extending nearly to the end of the paseo, which dead ends at a deep ravine choked in wild shrubbery. These five rectangular houses, sitting at a right angle to the paseo, are perched up on an earthen embankment cut out of the foothill, some three feet up from the paseo. This great cut's faced, front and rear, by two stone'n mortar retaining walls running

all the way down the paseo to the ravine. If the front wall ("broken" by steps in five places) is some three feet high, the rear wall's some twelve feet high, with the descending foothill only inches from its top, (this top serving, on sunny days, as a favorite, long "promenade" for the dark-haired, shaggy and downright mean-looking, wild feral cats which inhabit the foothill and range across it like a loosely-united, savage gang.). On the right, two more identical, white, rectangular houses run, by contrast, lengthwise with the paseo, side by side, at street level, and only about two-thirds of the way down the block, these two houses being supported, on their foundations, by a thick and long cement wall digging into the face of the sloping foothill. Anyway, this means that, on the right, between the western wall of the second house (Baby Diego's house) and the ravine, for some fifty feet, there's an empty, open area which serves as the off-center, but better-than-nothing turnaround for the block. This turnaround's bordered by a low, white, L-shaped cinderblock wall.

Now that that's all clear I'll conclude this description by saying that the last (or fifth) house on the left (our house) has a bonus, a large backyard (or *side*yard) between the house and the ravine—large enough to put another house in—containing two huge pine trees, while the other six houses only have small, cement, back patios. And our house has another bonus—a bonus of bonuses, from our front windows or yard we have an unobstructed and absolutely incredible, jaw-dropping view, across the turnaround directly opposite us, of the whole colorful, sprawling city in the distance and the surrounding, sea blue, majestic mountains. Truly, it's a sight that has to be seen to be believed.

I mentioned that the foothill's "windswept." It often is; and there're times—usually, in the late afternoon—when the wind's ferocious, loudly howling, and tossing about the thick, heavy limbs of our pine trees as if they're so many sapling branches.

CHAPTER 3

In The Middle Of The Night

It was after one in the morning when the movie came to its startling conclusion. Evelyn had gone to bed around eleven; but I stayed up late watching TV in the living room—or, rather, watching one of my favorite videos on TV, the classic 1950 movie, *Sunset Boulevard*, starring Gloria Swanson and William Holden. I've seen it a number of times in my life, and this time was no different, I sat there totally absorbed in the dark and tragic, but fascinating story. (I'm a big fan of old movies, even if Evelyn isn't.) Lonely, forgotten, delusional Norma Desmond, faded movie queen of a bygone era, secluded in her creepy and over-decorated Hollywood mansion, living in the past while planning for a comeback that's never gonna happen. Then there's that bizarre and frightening, Dracula-esque close-up and fade-out of crazy Norma which ends the movie, to the sounds of crashing cymbals and pounding drums, surely one of the most powerful endings in film history.

A few minutes later, after having retired to my room, I said to myself, "They just don't make—they *can't* make—movies like that anymore," as I changed into my single pair of gray and white striped pajamas. I got into bed, switched off the lamp on the night table, pulled up the covers, and rested my head on the pillow, only to be made aware that Evelyn was snoring (or, rather, was *starting* to snore—again?) across the hall in her bedroom—was "sawing logs," as they say—though, from her somewhat distant bed, it sounded like she was cutting them with only a fine-tooth saw. It was loud enough to be irritating, just the same. Her snoring is why we sleep in separate bedrooms—have since very early in our marriage. Evelyn vehemently denies that she snores—always has—which explains why she's never done anything about it, including listening to any "medical suggestions" from me.

For the first few months of our marriage, I made a determined and heroic attempt to sleep beside her; but trying to do so under such a merciless barrage was like being stretched on the rack. Ear plugs didn't help, but only made the snoring sound deeper and weirder. Besides, Evelyn (the non-snorer) took the introduction of ear plugs into our marriage bed as a personal insult. Finally, I threw in the towel (or pillow.) I regretted the separation to some extent, though, at the time, not only because it was a pretty unfeeling thing to do, going to another room (—Evelyn certainly thought so—) especially as we were still truly just newlyweds, but also because there were some nights—some—when Evelyn wouldn't (or would barely) snore, and I'd wake up in the morning feeling refreshed and relaxed and, perhaps, ready for love. On the other hand, such nights were far outnumbered by the *long*, snoring-plagued nights of tossin' 'n turnin', after which I'd greet the new day like (and probably looked like) Adolf Hitler.

Well, I lay there patiently-impatiently for a bit, hoping her snoring would stop—at least long enough for me to drop off to sleep. No such luck. After maybe ten minutes, I reached over and switched on the lamp, climbed out of bed, and stepped over the few feet to close my door; but, on second thought, went over and closed her door first, for good measure. This done, I stood there in the hall for a moment. Then, instead of going back to bed, I went back and slipped into my ancient brown slippers and grabbed my green robe off its hook on the door. I put it on, tied the belt, and went down the hall to the kitchen. I wanted a cigarette. Grabbing the pack and lighter off the kitchen counter, I stepped out the kitchen door into the dark backyard (or *side*yard—its darkness somewhat diminished by a virtually full moon overhead—) and, looking to my right—"Sweet Delilah!"—what a bright sight splashed out of the darkness before my eyes! Spread out in the distance, the whole metropolis of Saltillo was a magical, sparkling sea of golden lights, dotted with some additional sparkling reds and greens, here and there, which was glorious beyond words.

I lit up a cigarette and stood there by the door smoking and drinking in the utterly beautiful view. As I did so, for some reason, the little house on Nicholson Drive drifted into my mind, probably because, just the day before, I'd been thumbing through an old photo album of mine I hadn't looked at for ages; and I was particularly affected by the various old photos of that house which was once so dear to me. A smile played across my face as it occurred to me, for the first time, that my whole life was anchored, so-to-speak, by two houses, the house on Nicholson Drive where I started from, and this house on the hill in Lomas, at the end of a dead end street, where I was now, a lifetime later; and all the other houses and apartments in-between faded into insignificance. Two houses. The beginning and the ending. Yes, it was from this house on the hill to the cemetery.

I thought about that small, white, two-bedroom frame house with the green shutters on Nicholson Drive, in the Oak Cliff section of Dallas, where I grew up in the 50s and 60s, and was living in when JFK was assassinated and The Beatles first appeared on The Ed Sullivan Show. I remembered how very happy I was there—my mother and sister and me—and little Bonnie, our highly temperamental, brown dachshund dog to end all dachshunds! How she loved the backyard! She knew every square foot of it. Maybe it was a simple *The Music Man* sort of world, but it'd been *my world* for so many years—and the only completely *my world* I'd ever known and loved—which was absolutely gone with the wind.

Yes . . . the house on Nicholson Drive . . . I remembered, especially, Christmastime each year, as my sister Carol and I were growing up—in particular, our Christmas tree. Always the real pine Christmas tree before the front window of our small living room, which filled the room with its aromatic fragrance for the whole holiday season. Pine trees aren't common in North Central Texas, like they are in East Texas; and to bring a pine tree into our house each year, for three weeks or so, always seemed to me to be a sort of exotic thing to do. It always followed the same pattern, I'd go with Mother on a Saturday or Sunday afternoon to some place where they were selling the trees. Selecting one we both liked, I'd help Mother put it in the trunk of the car, help tie the trunk down, and home we'd go. Before dinner, Carol and I would decorate the tree and string it with lights, (but not turn them on.) Then, later, after dinner, and after darkness had fallen, Mother would turn off all the lights in the living room, dining room, and kitchen, throwing this part of the house into total darkness. As Carol and I stood back expectantly in the dark, Mother would step over and plug the light cord into the wall, whereupon—presto!—abracadabra!—the lights would burst out of the darkness in a rich pyramid/fantasy of glowing blues, reds, yellows and greens before our delighted eyes. I remembered how Carol would usually let out a clap or two with her hands. It was like the tree was *instantly* more than alive.

    I was startled out of this memory by a series of rapid-fire explosions—well, mini-explosions. I frowned. "Oh, brother!" I didn't even bother to walk around to the front of the house to have a look-see, for I knew perfectly well what it was, it was Baby Diego starting/revving up his ancient Volkswagen Beetle on the curb across the block, which sounded like a couple of bazookas going off non-stop simultaneously. Baby Diego's lovingly restored his "classic car", not to its original condition, but to his conception of a "racing car"—if that's not a contradiction in terms applied to a Volkswagen Beetle. He's had it painted a bright cherry red; has had the chrome bumpers and running boards refinished so that they shine like new silver in the sun; and he's personally added yellow pinstriping down the sides, in addition to sticking up miniature, square, black and white checkered racing flags on the corners of the front bumper. He's also sawed off the muffler to give the car that extra macho touch. Apparently, here in Mexico, you can get away with doing such a thing. Yes, the redone *body* of the Beetle's a striking sight, for sure; but the *engine* remains a true original.

After half a minute or so of this racket, the baby took off, and the Beetle tore noisily down the block and off on down the hill. I breathed a sigh of relief. "Oh, that baby!" I could still faintly hear the rattling bug as it rounded the base of the foothill; but soon the great silence of Lomas completely reasserted itself.

The kitchen door opened and here was Evelyn in her nightgown. She closed the door behind her and, coming up to within a few feet of me, asked me, rather irritably, "Was that Diego?"

"Sí," I concurred, "that was Baby Diego."

"*Baby* Diego!" She exclaimed. "He waked me up! You too?"

"No," I replied, "I've been out here awhile. I couldn't sleep." I could've said more.

There was a hard edge to her voice as she almost shouted, "Where in the world's he going at this hour?"

I actually let out a laugh. "Who knows? Who cares?"

I might mention that the light-shine from the brilliant on brilliant, but distant metropolis, as always, only minimally penetrated the darkness enveloping the colony, so that, as we stood there talking, neither of us could really make out the other's face in the dark yard; and it was our words, themselves—their tone—not any facial expressions or exchange of glances—that conveyed our feelings. (Either Evelyn or I could've simply switched on the outdoor light, but didn't.)

Our conversation continued as Evelyn asked me coldly, "Why'd you close my door?"

"Guess."

"I wasn't snoring!" she exclaimed emphatically.

I didn't say anything.

"You know very well I have to keep the door open at night so that Gigi can go to her box," she said, in her best schoolteacher manner. (Gigi sleeps with Evelyn, even if I don't.)

"I know that. Lo siento (I'm sorry). It slipped my mind."

She acted as if she didn't hear me by saying, after a moment, curtly and reproachfully, "You've never liked Gigi."

"I wouldn't say that."

"I would."

Sticking my hands in my pockets, I said, perhaps a bit sarcastically, "Well, Gigi's sweet and affectionate, at times (—I was tempted to add, "like most women," but checked myself—) but she's still the cat that she is. Cats! They ain't dogs. They're so aloof! They're always so coolly watching you. I think Greta Garbo was a cat. Anyway, there's an expression, 'Independent as a cat.' That's an understatement. I don't care what they say on the internet, you can't correct them. They never come when you call. Gigi never does. You can't teach them anything, take them for a walk, or keep them off the furniture."

Evelyn's voice rose, with an edge, "Are you through?" There was no mistaking her feelings as she slowly said, more to herself than to me, "You can say what you want . . . I love my Gigi . . . She's all I've got since Didi died."

I started to say something (sarcastic), but held my tongue. I took my hands out of my pockets. Evelyn stood there on my right like a statue. There was a silence between us for some moments, during which a dog barked briefly off somewhere, its barking sounding very clear in the hushed, still atmosphere. Then, letting out a sigh, Evelyn spoke up—quietly—sadly, "I didn't tell you, I had another dream about Didi last night, Chrisito . . . poor little Didi! . . . You remember Didi?" Though she asked me this matter-of-factly, it was asked not so much as a question, but as a woman might ask her lover, "Do you love me?" seeking emotional affirmation.

"Of course I do," I replied. "They'll never be another Didi."

She said reflectively, "I don't remember very much about the dream, except that Did was so real, just like she used to be. I could've reached out and touched her—petted her."

I really didn't know what to say; and I don't think Evelyn wanted to say anymore. OK, we're only talking about a *dog*; but precious little Didi was more than a dog to us—to a childless couple like us, she was a cherished member of the family (of two), and her death hit very hard, leaving such a void. Didi, who was then in her ninth year, bolted out the front door of our house in Fort Worth while Evelyn was standing there talking to the mailman, and was hit by a car. I was in the back of the house when it happened, and was so upset and so mad at Evelyn that I remember I exclaimed, "I wish I could leave the door open and *you'd* run away!" which was very unfair to her since she was devastated.

We'd bought Didi as a puppy (for $300) from a breeder in Midlothian, Texas, in the seventh year of our marriage. A new neighbor on the block had a Shih Tzu (—neither of us had ever seen one before—) and we were both captivated by the delightful creature and decided to get one for ourselves.

A pint-sized, bouncing, black and white Shih Tzu with beautiful, expressive, deep blue eyes, (whose hair I kept cut short in what they call a "puppy clip,") Didi was quite a character. She loved to fetch 'n come; and she loved to smother you with kisses. I'll never forget the way she used to beg for table scraps. She'd prop herself up on her bottom, in a vertical sitting position, and rapidly—even frantically—shake her little front legs up and down in mid-air, all the while looking at you with imploring—even desperate—wide-open eyes. Oftentimes, if you didn't promptly respond to her pleadings, she'd let out an impatient and imperious bark or two. It was the cutest and funniest thing you ever saw. There has to be a happy, laughing God somewhere who could create such an exuberant, utterly adorable creature. Yes, Didi had such a vibrant and perpetually cheerful personality that once she was gone it was like a bright light had been switched off in our lives.

About two years after we lost Didi we got Gigi. Evelyn said, after Didi's death, that she never wanted another pet, which, of course, spoke of how deeply she remembered Didi; but when the opportunity came along to acquire a calico kitten (for free, from a friend of ours,) Evelyn unexpectedly took a shine to the idea, and so we got the cat. Evelyn's grown very fond of Gigi. I haven't. The feeling's mutual. Gigi and I merely tolerate each other, for the most part. Gigi's no Didi. Then, I'm not a "cat person," and never will be. (I'm not a "bird person," either. Back in my single days, in the 80s, I had, for awhile, two green and yellow parakeets, Basil and Sybil, in one of those standing birdcages in the corner of the living room of my apartment. I eventually gave them away to a single, garbage man neighbor, not being able to deal with their off and on screeching squabbling, their obvious disdain for me, and their messiness anymore.)

Evelyn, with her effervescent Latin temperament—and to her credit—never stays in any kind of melancholy mood for very long, (unlike her "colder" gringo esposo.) Without saying anything, she suddenly stepped over to me, put her arm around my waist, and drew close to me as I stood there, at the same time, gently resting her head on my shoulder. With her long, thick, silky hair it was like a somewhat heavy pillow had been set on my shoulder. After a few moments, she sweetly murmured, "Would you just look at that view! Isn't that beautiful!"

"It really is," I murmured myself. She shifted her head slightly—snugger—on my shoulder. I continued, "It's not only beautiful, it's unbelievable—to me. I mean, here we have all this, a three bedroom/two bath solid cement house up on this hill, with this big yard and big pines, and this 'million dollar view'—and all for $30,000!" Evelyn relaxed her embrace a bit. "I still can hardly believe it. $30,000!! Why, that might *just* buy a one-bedroom clapboard *shack* next to the railroad tracks on Fort Worth's seedy south side, maybe with 'a view,' across the tracks, of a junkyard."

Evelyn let out a little laugh as she lifted her head off my

shoulder. After a second, she commented, "You don't have to tell me."

"Yes—well—we're very lucky."

"We are," she agreed. "Just remember all this the next time you start complaining about Mexico."

I let out a sort of snort, then said, "You're right. I shouldn't complain at all, all things considered. At our ages, and our income level—as such—and after what happened in Texas, this is the best—way *beyond* the best, really—that we can do, unless you want to go back to Fort Worth and live in a cracker box apartment, or do the same in Monterrey." Evelyn said nothing, but I knew she hardly wanted to do, or be forced to do, that. "Still," I concluded, "it's hard having to make the adjustment here, which is probably *because* of my age."

Evelyn broke her embrace, but remained standing where she was, practically touching me. She sort of sadly-humorously said, "Oh, Chrisito . . ." then said, more directly, "Don't worry. I know it's hard for you here in Mexico, but you'll make the adjustment in time. Just take each day as it comes."

I rolled my eyes, and merely responded with a "Yea." We were silent for a bit, gazing out at the light feast in the distance. You couldn't help but feel happy, and even peaceful, in a way, taking in the bedazzling view. It seemed like the whole city was smiling at us. In the extreme distance an airplane was gradually descending like a slowly falling shooting star, silhouetted against the dark mountains, towards the Saltillo airport.

After a minute or so, as the plane was about to be lost from view—swallowed up—in the acres of bright lights below it, Evelyn audibly yawned, and said, "Well, Chrisito, I guess I'll go back to bed now. I have to get my beauty sleep, you know!" As I lit up a cigarette, she asked me, "You're gonna stay out here awhile?"

I nodded.

"OK, I'll see you then in the morning." She added, slyly, "Maybe I'll come visit you in the morning." She gave me a light kiss on my cheek, and a little tug on my moustache, then turned and went on inside.

    P.S. "... and our income level—as such—..." In Mexico, we get by, just. Our whole income consists of my early (and pitiful) $563 monthly social security (—more like anti-social insecurity—) check, $500 a month rent from Evelyn's old apartment in Monterrey, some money in the bank here in Saltillo remaining from the sale of our house in Texas, and whatever pesos we can pick up teaching English part part-time to the inhabitants of our colony, which is very erratic. Thankfully, our "three bedroom/two bath solid cement house" is paid for, and the monthly utility bills are almost laughably cheap. The annual property taxes on the 1340 square foot house run around $25. We drive a white, 2005 Nissan Sentra with high mileage—"the ghost"—paid off five years ago. Still, there's food, gas, phone and internet, credit cards, recreation, and there's always the unexpected. In any event, nobody knows better 'n me that "our income level—as such—" would, indeed, only allow us to "live in a cracker box apartment" in Texas, and a downright shabby 'n shoddy one, I'm sure. "No thank-you, Ma'am!" I'd rather live in genteel poverty in Mexico than in *real* poverty in Texas, not to mention having, in Mexico, practically free healthcare. American economic policy today (which, for the average American, has been headin' down the Highway to Hell since the 1970s,) is cynically and selfishly rigged for the exclusive benefit and comfort of those at the very top; and it's only gonna get worse in the future. Democracy? Please, don't make me laugh. The "people"? Don't make me laugh even harder. "... and that government of the wealthy, by the wealthy, for the wealthy, shall not perish from this Earth"— not anytime soon. Yes, indeed, Mexico's for me—or, rather, Saltillo is—definitely at this stage of my life.

    P.P.S. I mentioned that little house on Nicholson Drive where I grew up with my mother and sister. That house, by the way, was only a couple of miles from the Texas Theater, where Oswald was apprehended; and I often spent long, "coke and candy" Saturday afternoons watching the cowboy, epic, and adventure flicks there with my best friend Ned. I'll never forget the gripping excitement I felt watching the fast-paced, dangerous, and thundering chariot race in *Ben Hur* there, for the first time, up on the big screen, in 1959. Well, *today*, that house no longer exists. How I first came to know this makes for an interesting anecdote, I think. It was only about a month after Evelyn and I were married and living in our first house in Fort Worth. I suddenly decided, one sunny summer Sunday afternoon, right after church, to take a trip—to drive the thirty miles—to Dallas and show Evelyn "the old neighborhood" in Oak Cliff where I'd grown up, telling her that we could grab a bite to eat for lunch somewhere in Dallas. We left directly from All Saints still dressed in our Sunday best, me in a light, white suit, and Evelyn in a short-sleeved yellow dress with white pinstriping. (Back in those days, we went to church much more frequently than we do nowadays.) Back then, we had a white 1984 Chevy Chevette, (more like a Chevy Regret) which spent about as much time in Fred's Garage as it did in our driveway; but, on this occasion, it made it there and back without any problems. It'd been a long time since I'd been back—years, really—and it was Evelyn's first trip to Dallas. I decided, on the way over, that our first stop would be at the house on Nicholson Drive. I was curious and rather impatient to see it again. After that, I told Evelyn, we'd find some place to have lunch. I pulled up alongside the curb (against the traffic) and stared in disbelief, the house on Nicholson Drive was GONE! So was the one and only tree that had stood in the middle of the backyard, a large, shady pecan. All that greeted the eyes was an empty, neglected, grassy lot with tall, ugly, deep green weeds sticking up here and there, looking far more healthy and vigorous than the yellowish-green, overgrown grass around them. Of all the older homes on the block, "my home" was the only one to have met the bulldozer. It even made me mad. "Can you believe that?" I exclaimed to Evelyn. "Totally gone, without a trace!" That expression, "You can't go home again" was, in this case, literally true.

"That's sad," Evelyn commiserated.

"Why d'you think they teared it down?"

I gave her look. "*Tore* it down." Looking back at that vacant lot, I could "see" that event happening as I slowly answered her, "I don't know . . . It always was just a cheap, 1940s frame house, often requiring two blankets-a-bed in the winter, and window air-conditioners kept at full blast in the summer, and it finally deteriorated, no doubt, to the point of demolition. You've no idea . . . I was so happy there, for so many years!"

After a moment, Evelyn said, almost nonchalantly, "It's just a house . . . The past is gone."

Staring at that piece of nothingness, my eyes hardened as I exclaimed, just as hard, "I know the past is gone! I don't need you to remind me of that!"

"I'm sorry," she said softly.

It was quite a shock. Staring at that sad space, the tall, unsightly weeds seemingly mocking me, my heart sank like a rock. It was as if, in a sense, my childhood and adolescence had been only a dream, or, in fact, had never happened.

CHAPTER 4

Some Definitions

Dissatisfaction, The quality or state of being dissatisfied, DISCONTENT.

Dissatisfied, Expressing or showing lack of satisfaction, not pleased or satisfied.

Discontent, Lack of contentment.

Satisfaction, The quality or state of being satisfied, CONTENTMENT.

Contentment, The quality or state of being contented.

Contented, Feeling or manifesting satisfaction with one's possessions, status, or situation.

(Webster's Ninth New Collegiate Dictionary).

Mid-life crisis, A term coined by Eliot Jacques stating a time where adults come to realize their own mortality and how much time is left in their life.

(Wikipedia).

CHAPTER 5

A Little Background Information

Well, I "stopped the story" to give some relevant definitions, and am now going to digress some more because I feel it's necessary to give a little background information in order for what will follow to make any sense. Why are we in Mexico? Who are we—the two people, Chris Steer and Evelyn González—anyway?

We married late in our lives after living the single life for many years, I as a college student, telephone solicitor, clerk, teller, and finally English teacher in Fort Worth, and Evelyn as a college student, jewelry store employee, and finally real estate agent in Monterrey. We "tied the knot" (—what a grim expression!—) when Evelyn was thirty-six and I was forty. So, though I guess you could say that we married on the threshold of our middle age, we didn't recognize it. Like a younger couple—almost (happily) like teenagers—those initial years of our married life in Fort Worth were full of so much excitement, (sexual and otherwise,) variety, and activity that we didn't have the time, or any reason to take an especially critical look at where we actually were (or were heading) in our lives and careers. We were busy, healthy, and very contented. Life was good. The times were good. Bubbly Bill was in the White House and all was well. We both had steady and rewarding jobs as teachers in the Fort Worth ISD, she in Bilingual Pre-K, and I in Adult Education (—talk about opposite ends of the same spectrum!—) we had no money worries to speak of, and, as a result of this, we could thoroughly indulge our shared passion for traveling, antiques, and beautifying our house and garden.

But (—and I'm only speaking for myself, not Evelyn—) as I passed into my fifties, when my marriage with Evelyn had become, in many respects, like a series of old reruns; when my few remaining family members began dying off; when I, who had always been the picture of health, began suffering from bouts of sickness from recurring migraines and stomach problems; and significantly when, in 2006, I lost my long-standing job in Adult Education due to budget cuts in a tough and mean Bush-baby economy, my mental attitude, at least, began to change—to darken.

It was this last "when" that proved the turning point. Evelyn still had her teaching position; but with our income halved, and finding myself unable to land any position except part-time subbing—and that iffy—(I suddenly discovered that I *was* over fifty—) it became increasingly more difficult to make ends meet and maintain a home, not to mention my dignity, in Texas. The resulting burden and struggle made me feel, as they say, like I had an albatross around my neck. Then, the Great Recession hit. Even the subbing pretty much dried up. That was it. We put our house in Fort Worth up for sale, hung around until it *finally* sold (after over a year, and not nearly at what we asked for it,) then moved permanently to Lomas. The good thing was that we at least we paid off the mortgage.

Our house in Lomas was originally bought with savings to serve as a summer home only, a place up in the cool foothills of Saltillo where we could gratefully escape the brutally hot, scorching Texas summers, (where going outside can be like stepping into a blast furnace,) since we both, being schoolteachers, had the summers off. Now, our Lomas home, instead of being simply a sort of summer resort, became our *last* resort.

All this, though, has taken its toll—on me, anyway. Though I'm very thankful and relieved to have our house in Lomas (—to have *any* house—) all paid for, with its very cheap utilities, its fantastic view, and its surrounding, enchanting climate, I'm still resentful, when I think about it, of having to be in Mexico, as having no other alternative (that I care to consider.) Things—life—my life—shouldn't be—shouldn't have turned out—this way. Call it a "crisis" or not, a cloud has come down; and the undisturbed peace and quiet, not to mention seclusion of Lomas only affords me that much more of an "opportunity" to reflect upon my whole situation, which, no doubt, ain't that good for me.

Reflect, indeed. Though it's hard to talk about yourself, in a personal way, without sounding conceited, (unless you're Paul McCartney,) I will say that it seems I've got enough baggage to sink a small battleship, loss of family, loss of friends, loss of career, loss of income from it, loss of home, loss of country (—for Evelyn, Mexico *is* her country, as she grew up—was raised by her grandmother—in Linares, Nuevo León—) and loss of familiar surroundings and routine. Then, of course, above and beyond all this, there's the chilling and nothing-you-can-do-about-it-anyway prospect of growing old, without any children. In fact, forget the children, there're just the questions associated with diminishing time, and perhaps diminishing body and mind, themselves.

Grow old along with me!
The best is yet to be . . .
Is that so? I'd like to see one example of that. There's the continuing anxiety of trying to adjust, at my age, to life in a foreign country where I have no connections and can barely speak the language (—through my own lazy fault, even after all these years—) where I can barely communicate with anybody. It's both isolating and confining. All of these things weigh/prey on my mind, and, I suppose, could be summed up in one word, depression. (I sometimes feel, in my darkest moments, that the only thing worse than death is life.) It's a funny thing, though—well, not *funny* funny, but odd, for I don't see myself, nor do I think others see me, as a depressing person. I still function capably enough, and still go about my daily life enjoying my little daily joys like anybody else; and, of course, it's the little ones, not the big ones, that count. At

the same time, though, I have to admit that, on a deeper level, in my heart of hearts—at the core of the apple, so-to-speak—I'm not the man—the happy, social man—I used to be.

"The problem with you is you think too much," Evelyn's told me more than once. Though I take that as an indirect compliment, I don't deny that I'd be better off if I was more like her. Evelyn doesn't dwell on the past, or worry unduly about the future, or let other people or events get her down, but tries to enjoy the present as fully as possible. "Totally Today" could serve as her motto. I'm lucky to have her. Evelyn also has no vices, and her healthy habits of body and mind are reflected in her appearance. It's kinda amazing, she looks twenty years younger than her age. This extends, by the way, to what's under her clothes.

Yes, Evelyn's a strong person (—perhaps, sometimes, too strong—she's not your passive little Mexican woman—) which stems partly from her realistic outlook on life, and partly, I think, from her upbringing—perhaps these being two sides of the same coin. Born in New York City in 1957, her mother, Mireya, originally from Santo Domingo, died only three years later, at thirty-one, from complications of diabetes. Evelyn was her only child. This left Evelyn's ne'er-do-well, wandering father, Enrique, who was in no shape to raise a little girl, having already descended into the alcoholism which would eventually kill him at forty-six, when Evelyn was thirteen. Eliminating Enrique, this only left her grandmother (Enrique's mother), María del Consuelo de Barrientos de González, already in her late fifties, and a widow, to raise little Evelyn—in Linares, a small, dusty, old colonial town about sixty miles south of Monterrey. On an interesting note, María del Consuelo was a second cousin of the celebrated Mexican muralist, Diego Rivera. I've seen a number of photos of Evelyn's grandmother. A stout, bespectacled woman with short, iron gray hair, in all of her photos she stares unsmilingly into the camera like General Patton—like someone you wouldn't want to mess with. Evelyn says she was like "a rock." She raised Evelyn all by herself in the big, balconied, red brick house in Linares, a few blocks from The Cathedral, the same house where she had come as a young bride in 1920. Here Evelyn lived until she went off to college when she was nineteen. Evelyn's told me that though her grandmother was good company, and very loving towards her, she was also a pretty cynical woman, telling her, among other things, that most of the people who go to church are total hypocrites, and that she'd be better off if she never got married; but, if she did, to never have any children, telling her that children only bring you grief in the end. Funny thing is, this grandmotherly advice has borne (or not borne) fruit in Evelyn's life.

Then, Evelyn's said, her grandmother had led some life, coming of age during the violent Mexican Revolution; marrying a man she didn't even know in an arranged marriage, then losing him to suicide when he was thirty-three; and having four children—all boys—one of whom died in infancy, two of whom, once they came of age, left "sleepy old Linares" for good, and only on rare occasions ever wrote to, called, or came back to visit their mother; and then there was Enrique, the youngest child and his mother's favorite, who became a hopeless alcoholic, and who, according to Evelyn, caused her grandmother never-ending concern.

I've seen the few photos Evelyn has of her father. Dark-haired and handsome, with a neatly-trimmed moustache, he kinda looks like a Mexican Johnny Depp; but, though he has a pleasant enough smile, he has the saddest eyes I've ever seen, with a sort of faraway look.

In any event, Evelyn's said her grandmother was a very strong woman, (which isn't surprising,) who was very realistic about life and about other people; and she obviously left her imprint on Evelyn, who's the strongest and most realistic (and least neurotic) woman I've ever known.

Pancho Villa

I hate to waste a good anecdote. Here are two, as told

to me by Evelyn as told to her by her grandmother. The following two incidents occurred during The Mexican Revolution, when Evelyn's grandmother was a young, attractive, dark-haired señorita of eighteen, unmarried, and still living at home in the same house in Linares that she'd grown up in. In 1916, the notorious Revolutionary leader General Francisco "Pancho" Villa and his Division del Norte briefly took control of Linares. I've read about Villa. For all his savagery, he could have stayed at the YMCA, for he neither smoked nor drank nor did drugs, and he had a certain nobility about him, except, he had one major vice, women—lots of 'em—married, unmarried—it didn't matter. Indeed, he was as famous (or infamous) for his "terrible reputation" with women as he was for his military exploits. He also, I've read, wasn't above, on occasion, getting his way with women at gunpoint. Apparently, his subordinates were in on the game. María del Consuelo was in the habit of going to the fruit and vegetable market every Saturday morning to get fresh pickings for the family table. That time had come around again. The fact that Villa had just taken over the town didn't stop her. (Evelyn said her grandmother admitted that she was very headstrong back in those days, and that she laughed and said, "I just put on my old brown dress with the deep pockets—my 'goin'-to-market' dress—picked up my basket—and I was off.") As she walked down the street to the market, suddenly, from around a corner, a little distance ahead of her, a skinny soldier stepped into view. Her grandmother remembered his arresting appearance – his long black moustache, a huge black sombrero (hat), crossed carbines over a red shirt, pistols on each hip, and black pants and rattlesnake boots with silver spurs. A formidable figure! He calmly eyed María del Consuelo as she approached; then, as she drew near, he removed his sombrero with a left hand she noticed was missing the middle finger, made a wide flourish with it, bowed slightly, and said, in the most flattering manner, "¡Señorita! ¡Buenos días! ¿Cómo está usted en este buen día? ¡El general Francisco Villa, al mando de la División del Norte glorioso y victorioso, desea verla! Por favor, deje que la lleve a él." ("Señorita! Good morning! How are you on this fine day! [She made no reply.] General Francisco Villa, commanding the glorious and victorious Division of the North, wishes to see you! Please let me take you to him.") He actually rested his right hand on his pistol. Naturally taken aback, María del Consuelo soon recovered and replied, "¡Tú a mí no me llevas a ningún lugar!" ("You're not taking me anywhere!"), brushed past him, and continued walking down the street. The Villista just laughed. In the other incident, which happened on the same afternoon, two soldiers in khaki uniforms broke into a loud and heated argument in the street right outside the Barrientos' house, which María del Consuelo, in the house alone at the time, witnessed furtively and nervously from behind the living room window curtains. (Evelyn said her grandmother only vaguely remembered the argument as being over some woman named Juana.) Angrier and angrier words led to gunplay, with the result that one of them (the loser) dropped dead right on her doorstep.

The Linares Cemetery

I've been with Evelyn, a couple of times, to Linares, and have seen the stately, two-story, red brick house where she grew up that takes up a third of the block, and is now inhabited by other people/strangers. We've visited the Cathedral Plaza and have gone to the Linares Cemetery on the southern edge of town, which is as peaceful as a pond. The cemetery's a quaint old place of dappled sunshine and shadow, whose walkways are bordered with towering pines and equally tall, column-like, deep green cypresses; and where a number of graves are honored with beautifully-carved (if moss-encrusted) white marble saints or angels standing on pedestals. (Well, it *is* a Catholic country. Also, I have to admit that I always feel a great contentment spending time in cemeteries, where I always feel, oddly, very much alive. There's something strangely comforting about "seeing" all of these people at rest at last, their struggles, troubles, and problems gone for good, like they never even occurred.) Here's where Evelyn's grandmother, grandfather, and father lie buried in a simple family plot bordered by a low, brown brick wall (that's very low, being only three bricks high.) They're no saints or angels, just three identical, flat, gray granite headstones inscribed with names and dates only. The left headstone, marking Evelyn's grandmother's grave, reads, "María del Consuelo Barrientos de González/1898-1979"; the middle headstone, marking her grandfather's grave, reads, "Alejandro Guzmán González/1899-1932"; and the right headstone, marking her father's grave, reads, "Enrique Barrientos González/1924-1970"—poor Enrique, who finally succeeded in drinking himself to death. The story is that he collapsed in some dive in Mexico City and was rushed to the hospital; but he'd slipped into an alcoholic coma and couldn't be saved. His mother paid for his body to be brought back to Linares, by train, in a pine box.

Two Fathers

It seems this "little background information" is getting longer and longer. Nevertheless, I want to touch a bit more on Evelyn's father and say something about mine, as well as something about my mother and sister. I feel that only by doing so can this "little background information" cover all the bases.

I've already touched on my upbringing in Dallas, and have just touched on Evelyn's upbringing in Linares. In both cases, the "father figure" is missing; and in both cases he pretty much *was*. Evelyn told me once, concerning her father, "He'd show up, unannounced, now and then, at the front door of our house in Linares, having taken the train up from Mexico City where he'd moved to after my mother's death. He'd always show up in the same navy blue suit carrying this old black satchel bag, like the doctor come calling; only *he* was the one who could've used a doctor. He'd stay with us a few days, always remembering, while he was there, to get some more money from his mother who supported him mainly. Then he'd go back. My poor father! He was really a very intelligent and cultured person, who loved to read; and he could tell the most wonderful stories about his travels. He always carried a copy of *Don Quixote* with him in his bag. But his damn drinking, it turned him into such a weak and irresponsible man, and such a lonely man. I must say, though, he was always, for the most part, tender and caring to me, never criticizing me about anything; and he said to me once, "Whatever you do with your life, don't be like me. Have a *purpose*, and stick to it always."

My father was a mostly missing person, too, but on a darker level, a person who, you could say, went to the devil long before the devil came for him. Like Enrique, he liked to "pop a cork," and was a dedicated smoker as well, but he never let the booze get the better of him. I guess you could say he was a heavy drinker; but he wasn't an out-and-out alcoholic like Enrique. Still, his heavy drinking definitely colored (or discolored) his personality, (as will be seen.) Yes, sarcastic, hard-drinkin' Dad, dead now twenty-five years. Whenever I watch old Humphrey Bogart movies—*that's* Dad—especially in *Casablanca*. The master of the put down. My mother once told me someone once told Dad that he looked like Bogart, (he rather did,) which, she said, he never forgot, and wasn't against mentioning around other people on odd occasions.

My mother and father, both born in Fairfax, Virginia, in the same year, 1929, grew up together as literally the boy and girl next door. They were childhood playmates, clinging teenage sweethearts, and fiancés all under neighboring roofs, so-to-speak. My mother once told me, when I was in my twenties, "I can't remember a time in my life when I didn't know your father—until we moved to Texas." They got married in 1947 and moved into a house in the same Fairfax neighborhood where they'd always lived, which was the house where, back from the local hospital, my sister Carol set sail in life in 1949 and I in 1953. Unfortunately, this "whole history of togetherness" didn't ensure that their marriage would work—would last—and it didn't. They divorced in 1957. My mother gathered up Carol and me and we moved to Dallas where Grandma (mother's mother) lived with her second husband, Mort. Years later, my mother told me that she moved to Dallas so that we could be close to Grandma and Mort, but also because she wanted to distance herself from Dad, who, she said, would've never left her alone had she stayed in Virginia. She said that Dad never accepted the divorce, (which she instigated—she said she "finally had it"—) even though he caused it with his drinking and playing around. She also said that Dad's problems, since his adolescence—his drinking, his anger, and his womanizing—were mostly, in her opinion, a reaction against his relationship with his strict, puritanical, and critical father, my Grandfather Steer, who, she said, never gave Dad the love and acceptance he needed. I have no memories of my Grandfather Henry Bake Steer, who was a dentist. He died, of a heart attack, back in Virginia, only a few months after we moved to Dallas, when I was barely four; but I have three black and white photos of him handed down to me through the family, in that same old photo album I mentioned earlier. All three photos were taken late in his life; and they show him looking, for all the world, like a gray and aging (and grim) 28th U.S. President Woodrow Wilson, complete with wire-rimmed spectacles. Of the three photos, my favorite one is the one that shows him, fairly close-up, wearing an open-necked, white, long-sleeved shirt, dark suspenders, and dark pants, sitting in a rocking chair on the front porch of his house. He's holding me as a baby (wrapped up in a little white blanket) in his arms. He's holding me and looking down at me not that "grandfatherly"—more like I'm simply a stage prop—like he's mainly holding me for the benefit of the camera—and he's looking sternly down at me as if he doesn't know quite what to make of me. (Such is how, I'm afraid, the world's been looking at me ever since.) Though it's not exactly a "loving portrait," and is hardly a good picture of me (—I'm not even visible except for the left side of my chubby face—) still, it's the only picture I have of the two of us together—connected—and for that reason it's special to me . . . Well, to get back to what I was talking about, We moved to Dallas and into the little house on Nicholson Drive, and life went on, with only a yearly, two-week interruption, Dad's custody.

My mother never remarried (or even dated), but Dad remarried within a year of the divorce; and within five years he'd fathered two more sons by his second wife, Pat. Good-looking, platinum-blonde Pat, who bore a striking resemblance to the actress Kim Novak, and who could match Dad drink for drink. She couldn't have been a greater contrast to my brown-haired, ordinary-looking, firm, and tea-totaling mother. (Dad eventually divorced Pat, too—his last wife, but not his last girlfriend. I wonder whatever happened to her?) My mother told me, later in my life, she always suspected that Pat was *one* of the women Dad was seeing while they were still married. Anyway, every summer he'd fly down to Texas, pick up Carol and me, and we'd fly back with him to Virginia. When the visit was over, (and when we were still small,) he'd fly back with us to Texas and return alone to Virginia. When we got older, though, Carol and I would fly both ways by ourselves. This was cheaper, of course, for Dad—not that he wanted for money. He had a solid and well-paying job (for thirty-three years, until he retired from it at fifty-five,) as a hard working traveling salesman for RCA, back when RCA was *the* manufacturer of high-quality, exclusively MIA products, Made In America (—not anymore!) Incidentally, though Dad detested rock 'n roll, he never had a bad word to say about Elvis Presley, since Elvis recorded for RCA. Also, Dad consistently ranked as one of RCA's top salesmen, which resulted in him receiving awards and perks from the company, such as all-expense-paid trips to Las Vegas and front row seats at Washington Redskins games. In Dad's white, two-story, colonial style brick house in Fairfax, whose windows were bordered with black shutters, Carol and I would always bunk together in the upper floor spare bedroom.

Even though Dad had his moods, and his ever-present Canadian Club, and would occasionally get mad about something or other, he generally was on his best behavior during the two weeks Carol and I stayed with him and his second family; and he generally showed us a good time—though I will say this, I began to sense a certain distance—a certain aloofness—even a certain disapproval on Dad's part towards me as I progressed through my adolescence and went from being a "charming child" to an independent, budding adult with opinions and a lifestyle of my own. Sporting long hair and listening to Janis Joplin and Jimi Hendrix on my transistor radio didn't help matters. Once, Dad passed by the spare room one Sunday morning while I was lying in bed listening to Bob Dylan belting out "Like A Rolling Stone" on the same radio. Looking rather ominous in a black silk lounging robe, he stopped, pulled himself up in the doorway, and made the biting comment, "He sounds like a hardened convict with his jock strap on too tight." Carol never experienced any "turned up nose" as she grew up, as far as I could ever see. No, my pretty, raven-haired sister was always "Daddy's little girl," and she played the part, for the most part. With me, though, as a teenager, the camaraderie just wasn't there like it used to be when I was Dad's worshipful little "Christyfofer."

I said I wanted to "say something" about my father, mother, and sister. This (perhaps long-winded) account has only been given to "set the scene" for what was one of the most awful incidents of my life, an incident which shows my father, Joseph Henry "Joe" Steer, as the type of person he could be.

Dad's custodial rights completely ended with my eighteenth birthday. They'd ended with Carol four years previously when she'd turned eighteen; but she continued going along with me each summer during the four year "extension." Rights or no rights, Dad invited us up during my nineteenth year. We went. It was during this visit that it happened at dinnertime one night. We were all seated around the long dining room table, Dad at the head of the table, Pat opposite him, I on his right opposite Carol, and my two half-brothers, Danny and Ricky, (then, thirteen and eleven, respectively,) seated, Danny on Carol's right, and Ricky on her left. Interestingly, at this stage of their lives, dark-haired Danny was the spittin' image of his father—like a miniature Dad, really—while tow-headed, almost feminine-looking Ricky was a sure chip off his mother's block. Since this memory's seared in my mind, I remember its little details, It being summertime, Dad, Danny, Ricky, and I were all dressed casually in light-colored, short-sleeved shirts and blue jeans, and Carol was dressed as casually in a short-sleeved, checkered dress of little red and white squares, looking like the farmer's daughter. Only Pat was dressed rather formally in a tight-fitting, dark green, short-sleeved dress buttoned up to its black lace collar. If Carol's long raven hair was simply loosely swept back from her forehead, Pat's platinum-blonde beehive was teased up and sprayed into rigid perfection, looking like you could drop a brick on her head and it'd just bounce off. Anyway, Dad had had three or four stiff whiskey and sodas before coming to the table; and, at one point during the meal, as Carol was going on and on about all the fun activities she was enjoying with her boyfriend back in Dallas, Dad abruptly/rudely interrupted her and demanded of me, "And you, young man—what about *you*? When I was your age, I was already married—to your mother. And before that, I'd had *dozens* of girlfriends . . ." Pat frowned. He went on, "You haven't got *one*—never *have* had, so your sister tells me." Carol gave Dad a severe look. He paused and gave us all a thin smile. Then, looking straight ahead, as if Pat were invisible, he evenly said, "I'm afraid the only hope for you is masturbation." After a stunned silence for some seconds, during which you could've heard the proverbial pin drop, Carol pushed her chair back hard, stood up, threw her napkin down on the table, and, without a word, marched off to the kitchen; Pat just stared down at her plate; Danny and Ricky, unappreciative of Dad's remark, but obviously sensing that some sort of bomb had been dropped, sat very still, their eyes open wide; while I sat there speechless, as well, feeling like a person might feel sitting strapped in the electric chair, waiting for the man to flip the switch—in other words, helpless. Dad had *never* talked to me like this before. He paid us no mind; but, still retaining his slight smile, and seemingly satisfied with himself, he went back to his meal, saying nothing more for the time being.

When we got back to Dallas, I, naturally, didn't mention this embarrassing and humiliating incident, but Carol did, over dinner, our second night back. Mother heard her out, and was she furious! The first words out of her mouth were, "That bastard!" which was the first time in my life I'd ever heard my mother swear. After dinner was over, and she'd done the dishes, she went and grabbed the phone in the hall alcove, called up Dad long-distance, and let him have it, in so many words. Needless to say, this was our last annual visit to Virginia.

One other thing. I don't know whether it's a fallout from my "relationship" with my father or not—whether, in other words, it's a psychological thing or not—but never, in my whole adult life, have I ever been able to achieve any kind of close and meaningful companionship with another man, (which, of course, works both ways.) Oh, I've had drinking buddies, sports buddies, and maybe work buddies—friends after a fashion (—a superficial fashion—) but I've never been able to foster and enjoy any kind of deep and satisfying friendship with another man. I might add that I've always found most men, with their self-absorbed, colossal egos, and at whatever social level, to be difficult, if not impossible, to get to really know, which is a trait I may be more guilty of myself than I care to admit. Women are much more "accessible."

CHAPTER 6

The End Of The Middle Of The Night

I did stay outside maybe twenty minutes longer, (during which, to my delight, a bright shooting star tore across the sky for a few seconds,) before heading back inside myself. I stopped off in the kitchen for a minute to pour myself a small glass of wine. No sooner had I done so than Gigi appeared in the doorway from down the hall, ostensibly to go to her litter box under the counter; but, shooting me a sharp glance—as if to say, "What are you doing here?"—she stalked off towards the living room, instead. I downed the wine in one gulp, switched off the light, and went to my room. Doffing my robe and slippers, I got into bed once more, and once more switched off the lamp, pulled up the covers, stretched out, and rested my head on the pillow. Evelyn was apparently fast asleep (with her door open), and there were no sounds of snoring coming from her room. I didn't hear so much as a peep, indoors or out. There wasn't "a mouse stirring," especially with a cat prowling around. The whole house was dark, silent, and still, silent and still in the sort of "pressurized" way that's characteristic of Lomas at such an hour. In a matter of minutes I dropped off to sleep; but just before doing so I did hear something, Gigi scratching around in her litter box.

CHAPTER 7

Next Morning

I woke up "gradually, and then suddenly," to quote Hemingway, in another context. That is, at first, and for some moments, I was drowsily aware of birds singing outside. Then, more strongly, I heard a voice close to my bed distinctly say, almost like a command, "Chris!" My eyes shot open.

Standing on my left was an all-too-real vision of desire. Evelyn looked down at me with a proud smile on her face, dressed in nothing but a short black negligee. Her silky, dark brown hair, that's a little fringed with gray on her forehead, hung down to her shoulders—voluminously—like she'd just brushed it out. She wore no make-up (—which I prefer—) but somehow still looked radiant. Her dark eyes looked deeply into mine; but I still managed, anyway, (How could I not?) to notice that her negligee was only one piece. In other words, she was "bottomless," as they say. Without another word, she bent down and planted a deep-tongued kiss on my lips while, at the same time, she took my right hand in her left one. I thought, at first, that this was a sort of romantic accompaniment to the kiss—nothing more. As we continued kissing, though, she slowly raised my hand upwards until it came to rest on her voluptuous, smooth derriere. "Massage me there," she broke our kiss long enough to half-whisper to me from deep inside herself. I did—and I did more than that.

Afterwards, having enjoyed our lovely lovemaking, (which, by its very infrequency anymore, is all that much better an event,) we lay there, hip to hip, Evelyn being on my right, and engaged in small talk, as if such idle chit-chat was the most pleasant and satisfying thing in the world. We talked of different things. I'll only mention two of these things. At one point, I asked her, "What d'you think about Baby Diego? Two o'clock in the morning!"

"I try not to think about Baby Diego," she said half-seriously.

"Well," I declared, "the man's more or less a moron, but he's friendly enough. He always waves or says hello when he sees me."

"So what?" she exclaimed. "He can wave all he wants. Always in those green overalls . . . He's a fate ape—a grown man, in his forties, who acts like he's fifteen. And that wife of his—*Berta*—in her skin-tight blue jeans showing her huge bottom, I think *she's* missing some connections as well."

I laughed. "At least they're quiet neighbors most the time, thank God!"

"Thank God!" she seconded.

At one point, I also brought up the movie we'd seen a few nights before on TV, oddly enough, for the first time (with Spanish subtitles), *JFK*, "Remember the movie, *JFK*, we saw the other night?" Without waiting for her to reply, I went on, "I was living right there in Dallas, you know, when Kennedy was assassinated. You remember that time, after we were first married, when we took that trip to Dallas to see my old neighborhood?"

"Yes," she answered, after a moment.

"Well," I continued, "you'll also remember I showed you my old elementary school—that red brick, fortress-like building where I went from first to sixth grade, Margaret B. Henderson. It was there where I first heard the horrible news." I changed course, momentarily, "What about you—let's see—1963—you would've been six years old. Was it on all the TV stations down in Mexico, too? You remember that?"

"We didn't have TV service yet in Linares in 1963," she replied, "but I think I remember hearing something about it on our radio."

I was both surprised and rather miffed by her answer. "Well, in *Dallas*, that *long* afternoon, you'd have thought the world'd come to an end. Businesses closed, schools shut down, and people gathered in the streets. All TV programming stopped except for coverage of the tragedy. I'll never forget it. You see, in that year, 1963, I was in the fifth grade at Margaret B. My class schedule was such that every Friday, right after lunch in the cafeteria, I had an auditorium class in the school's big auditorium. Though the class of twenty-five or so students looked kinda ridiculous taking up seats in only the first couple of rows of the great room, we, nevertheless, would sit there for fifty minutes listening to an invited guest speaker up on stage talk (often with the aid of big charts) on some topic which was supposed to be of vital interest to us kids, personal hygiene, proper nutrition, Jesus on the football field, etc . . . Anyway, on that Friday afternoon, November 22nd, as I sat in the middle of the second row half-listening to some overdressed woman droning on and on—about *what*, I don't recall—suddenly, Mr. Boley, our bald and no nonsense Principal, interrupted the speaker—and all classes—by coming on the school intercom and announcing, in his gravelly voice, "Students and teachers, may I have your attention, please! This is your Principal speaking. Our President, John F. Kennedy, was shot by an assassin in downtown Dallas this afternoon, about forty-five minutes ago. He was rushed to Parkland Hospital, along with Governor Connally, who was wounded as well, but will recover. I've just received word that the President's life couldn't be saved; and he was pronounced dead a few minutes ago . . . There's no cause for alarm. The situation's well under control. Vice-President Johnson's set to be sworn in as our new President later this afternoon here in Dallas. I repeat, everything's under control. I'll keep you informed of any further developments. Thank-you, and please continue with your classes."

"Wow!" Evelyn exclaimed. "That must have been some shock! . . . I don't see how you can remember that word for word after—what?—over fifty years!—and only hearing it once."

"If you'd been there, you'd remember it, too . . . Some students started crying. Down on my right, one girl, Lesley Lindsey, for some reason, stood up and started crying. Lovely, blonde-haired, blue-eyed Lesley Lindsey—standing there in her white skirt and sky blue sweater—she looked like the very picture of a sorrowful angel." Evelyn raised herself up on her elbow to look at me. I concluded, "And my reaction? I remember I involuntarily pulled my black jacket tighter around me as I sat there stunned, everything else gone clear out of my mind except for that unbelievable announcement, about the last thing on Earth I expected to hear. What stuck out in red were the words, 'was shot by an assassin,' meaning it wasn't an accident or a heart attack or something, but *murder*. This wasn't some John Wayne movie—this was *real life*—our President!"

"Then what happened?" Evelyn asked me, somewhat hesitantly.

"Probably not," I replied, "what Mr. Boley could've foreseen. There was a general consternation throughout the school. Students, teachers—janitors—everybody was upset and confused, and more than a few, frightened. Mr. Boley's words reassured nobody. As a result of this, about thirty minutes after the terrible announcement, all classes were dismissed early."

Actually, there was one other little exchange that's worth mentioning. It occurred shortly after we'd made love. Evelyn was half-leaning over me, running the fingers of her right hand idly through my hair. Suddenly, she stopped, and—still keeping her hand in my hair—looked me in the eyes and said, "Always remember one thing."

"What's that?"

"Always remember you're mine, and I'm yours—only—forever."

I was rather taken aback by such a sweeping statement. "Forever?"

"Forever."

"That's a long time."

There was a twinkle in her eyes. "Yes, it is . . . and don't ever forget it."

After some forty-five minutes, as the birds' beautiful singing outside was tapering off, our free and easy tête-à-tête came to an end as Evelyn sat up and announced that she needed to go fix my breakfast. She climbed over me out of bed and went across the hall to her bedroom. Presently, she reappeared wearing her gray night robe and white slippers—paused, for a moment, to tell me, "Give me ten minutes or so"—then went down the hall to the kitchen. I remained in bed, figuring on getting up when breakfast was ready.

CHAPTER 8

Breakfast

Evelyn had fixed me a big, delicious breakfast of scrambled eggs, Mexican-style, with lots of chorizo, cheese, and broken-up pieces of fried corn tortilla mixed in, plus a bowl of melon slices and strawberries all swimming in cream. Even a glass of freshly-squeezed orange juice. Evelyn always assumes, after making love, that I'm ravenously hungry. Usually, just the opposite is the case, as it was on this morning.

My breakfast was waiting for me on the dining room table when I came down the hall, having slipped into my slippers and robe after Evelyn had called out to me from down the hall, "¡Tu desayuno está listo!" ("Your breakfast is ready!"). Before I sat down, though, I went over and looked out the dining room window. The sliding window was partially open, and a fresh, delicate breeze lightly danced into the room. It was a clear, sunny morning, and the view was magnificent. I noticed some puddles of water on the cement walkway under the window. It must have rained for a while after we'd gone back to bed, I figured. It hadn't woken me up; but that wasn't unusual up in Lomas where the rain, most of the time, consists of gentle showers, merely—rarely in loud, crashing thunderstorms (like in Texas.) In any event, the rain had had the effect of clearing the air, so that everything, both near and far, looked very distinct and bold in the bright morning sun under a brilliantly blue, cloudless sky, like a very sharp and colorful picture postcard. Yes, the distant, sprawling metropolis was color itself, and looked as "new" as if it had just been built yesterday.

Even portions of the second and third rings of mountains could be seen in the extreme extreme distance. Though, as viewed from the heights of Lomas the city of Saltillo sits at the bottom of great enclosing bowl, this isn't the whole picture—not always. If you were looking down at the city from a very high altitude—say, from an orbiting space shuttle—it'd look, I'd imagine, like the center of a gigantic rose blossom, whose bands of petals, radiating out from it, would be, in fact, the multiple rings of mountains surrounding the city. These outer rings are normally only imperfectly seen, at best, from up in Lomas. This is due, of course, to weather and man-made conditions. Occasionally, when the city's blanketed in thick and high white fog, you can't even make out the inner ring—or only its undulating, upper blue edge. On most days, though, this inner ring is plainly visible, but little beyond it, due to mist, haze, and, in varying degrees, to smog. After a good rain shower, though, the "veil is lifted" and you're afforded, from up in Lomas, a truly stupendous, far-reaching, even epic view. This was the vista maravillosa (marvelous view) that was given to me, like a gift, on this morning.

I turned and sat down at the round, pine table, facing the window. I looked down at the desayuno generoso (big breakfast) before me. Brother! When you're not really hungry, but, at the same time, are presented with a heapin' helpin' of food, and, moreover, feel obliged to get it all down "to be nice," it can be an intimidating thing. You stare down skeptically at all this stuff, and it stares back up rather defiantly at you —and you wish you were somewhere else.

Evelyn entered the dining room carrying a half-full fruit bowl and a glass of o j. *She* obviously wasn't ravenously hungry. She sat down on my right.

"How is it?" she inquired.

"¡Muy delicioso!" ("Very delicious!") I replied, practicing my Spanish.

"There's more if you want it," she informed me.

I smiled a small smile. "Well, we'll see."

Evelyn, contented, started in on her fruit bowl while

gazing out the window at nothing in particular, taking in the razor-sharp, colorful panorama. After some seconds, she commented, "How clear everything is this morning!"

"That's because," I explained, "it rained last night for awhile after we went back to bed. They're puddles on the front walkway."

She said earnestly, "I don't think, in all the time we've lived up here in this house, I've ever"—the phone rang.

CHAPTER 9

A Phone Call

Between our kitchen and dining room is a window that—well—isn't a (glass) window, but a large square cut out of the wall through which you can see into either room. The base of this "window" forms a waist-high pinewood counter; and below the counter, on the dining room side, are two black metal, backless barstools with black cushions. Since I could've easily gotten up and grabbed the phone on this counter, just behind me, I made to do so; but Evelyn, though she sat farther away, beat me to it. This didn't surprise me. A ringing telephone has about the same effect on Evelyn as would a fire alarm. Well, maybe that's stretching it; still, when it's a question of who gets to the phone first in my own home, I usually lose. Like most females, Evelyn has a quenchless passion for talking on Mr. Bell's instrument; and she can gab away for hours on end, as fresh at the end as at the beginning. I've promised her (to her amusement) that if she goes before me, I'm gonna place a phone (plus a mop) beside her in her coffin.

"¡Bueno! ¿Belinda? . . . Muy bien, gracias—¿y tú? . . . Que bueno . . . Oh, él está bien, también. ¿Cómo está Bertie? . . . Que bueno. ¿Qué pasa? . . ." ("Hello! Belinda! . . . Fine thanks—and you? . . . That's good . . . Oh, he's fine, too. And how's Bertie? . . . That's good. What's up? . . .") Evelyn propped herself up on the right barstool, crossed her legs, and the conversation was off and running, en español (in Spanish). I shifted my chair around to face her. (Yes, she crossed her legs; and, in doing so, her night robe naturally parted, or fell back, revealing most of her long lower legs—a showgirl's long lower legs—even at her age. Of course, she was utterly unaware that she was showing me anything, as she chatted away; but what was there was there, and I couldn't help but feel a sort of possessive satisfaction in the view.) Belinda's fluent in English and Spanish, while Evelyn still has trouble with English sometimes; but, more than that, it's just more natural for her to speak in her native tongue. When it's just the two of them talking, or when neither Bertie nor I are included in the conversation, such is how they converse.

My command of Spanish makes Evelyn's command of English look like total fluency. Though I caught a few (simple) words and phrases of Evelyn's rapid-fire Spanish, I couldn't tell what in the world they were talking about. In any event, not wanting to appear as intruding on a private (and likely, long) conversation, I was about to get up and head outside when, to my surprise, the conversation came to a close.

Evelyn hung up the receiver with a kind of flourish, signifying, I figured, some happy something. She turned to me on the barstool and brightly said, "Chrisito, that was Belinda! She was calling from work and had time only to say she wants us to come to dinner tonight. She and Bertie are giving a garden party. It'll start around eight o'clock, she said"—

"and'll continue, no doubt, till eight o'clock the next morning. Yes, parties are the one thing which Mexicans take dead seriously."

She brushed this sarcasm aside—even good-humoredly—exclaiming, "Well, you know Mexican parties!" After a moment or two, she added, "So, what if it does? We can leave anytime we want."

I avoided her eyes. "Let's hope so."

Now she flared up, "Listen, Mr. Grumpy, not only are we *going*, I'm not gonna start worrying *now* about when we're *leaving*! She let out a laugh, in spite of herself, at my attitude. "You're such a neurotic! How do you know . . . Maybe you'll have such a great time you'll *want* to stay 'till eight o'clock the next morning.'"

Picturing Bertie's smug mug in my mind, I started to say, "Do pigs fly?"—but let it slide. Instead, I asked, indifferently, "I wonder who all's gonna be there?"

"Mike and Wanda she said are coming."

I was surprised. "Really? I didn't know Mike was back."

"See—there's four people right there you can talk to in English." She said this like this clinched the deal.

"Yea." I was hardly overjoyed. "Bertie's the most obnoxious man on Earth."

"Oh—really—Chrisito—he's not that bad." She said this in a motherly manner, as if trying to reason with a spiteful child.

I looked at her in wonder. "How can you say that? Bertie's a little man with a big inferiority complex which he tries to compensate for by acting like a strutting, boasting Napoleon. I can't stand him."

I think she suppressed a laugh. "Well, just for tonight, please try."

"Do we have to go?"

She gave me a hard look. "You never want to go *anywhere*! You don't have to spend the whole time with Bertie. I'm sure others'll be there. You know Belinda, she knows everybody! You like Mike and Wanda." She said this like a statement of fact. I didn't say anything. Then, looking at me like the local county prosecutor, she let out, "¡Sólo vas a tener que comer tus verduras!" ("You're just going to have to eat your vegetables!"—a Mexican, and one of her favorite expressions.) She paused, then added, in a steady voice, "I want to go and we're going!"

After a few moments, she got up off the barstool. Without a word, or so much as a glance at me, she went over to the window. She crossed her arms, straightened her back, and stood there like a stone statue (and as silent), her back facing me like a wall, apparently staring out at the city.

P.S. Speaking of "Evelyn's command of English," I must say, that her speaking ability, and her reading and listening comprehension have vastly improved since we were first married. Back then, one morning, I was cleaning the baseboards in the dining room of our rental (first) house in Fort Worth, with soap 'n water. When Evelyn came in to check on my progress, wanting something stronger, I asked her, "Could you please bring me the 409?" which is one of many cleaning fluids available in the U.S. She returned, presently, holding, in either hand, a fork 'n knife. I was so surprised that, for five seconds or so, I couldn't even laugh; but then, I'm afraid, I really did.

CHAPTER 10

"What are you smiling at?"

I suddenly felt guilty—only thinking of myself—never of Evelyn—being so negative—putting such a damper on her obvious enthusiasm. It wouldn't kill me to go. "Mr. Grumpy." Is that what I really had become?

I considered the situation. If I was becoming, up in my house on the hill, like Heathcliff—like a moody recluse—Evelyn was, by contrast, still (bless her!) very much an outgoing, social animal, even if she was hard-pressed to find much of a social life in humdrum Lomas de Lourdes, except among the dowdy, gossipin', tortilla-rollin' housewives (amas de casa) on our block. This uptown garden party'd be a real treat for her. She and Belinda got on especially well together. Yes, I needed to consider my wife for a change. In spite of our differences, and in spite of the inevitable tensions arising from living with a member of the opposite—*opposite*—sex day after day, week after week, month after month, year after year, and decade after decade; still, I had to admit, Evelyn was the only person on the whole planet who gave a damn about me, (and who ever had, except for my poor, misguided mother—and this was in spite of the fact that Evelyn had spent years living and putting up with a multiple personality like myself. If it hadn't effected her physically, it had emotionally. She was no longer the "laughing girl" I once knew—that girl coming to the fore only now and then anymore. Nor was our marriage like it used to be as regards to our love life, which was like an hourglass in which the sand was once mostly at the top, but was now mostly at the bottom. Still, there's a lot more to a good marriage than just that, regardless of what many people would have you believe.) Yes, Evelyn was the only person I had—left—without whom I'd be absolutely alone, on a moon of my own. There couldn't be any better comment, I thought, on my life than that. She deserved better from me. I was about to tell her I'd be glad to go when she spoke up first. Turning around to face me, with her arms still crossed, she initiated the following exchange, in a monotone voice,

"I don't understand you, Chrisito."

"That's OK."

"Don't get cute. I'm serious."

"What don't you understand?"

She dropped her arms, resting her hands on the window ledge. "Your attitude. Your bad attitude. Here we have the chance, for a change, to get out of this house for awhile for a evening and be around other people (—she stressed the word "house" like the word had been "prison"—) and look how you're acting! What's your problem? I'm starting to worry about you. You're losing weight. You're becoming more and more—I don't know what the word is—*strange*. You make no efforts to make any friends here. I think sometimes you *enjoy* being lonely. Thank God you haven't turned to drink—yet—like your father, or my father." She sighed, then said resignedly, "Other people mean nothing to you, really. I wonder sometimes about myself."

I smiled.

"What are you smiling at?"

I ignored her question, and dropped my smile. "Evelina, you're right! It's wrong and selfish of me to act, as you say, like 'Mr. Grumpy' about it. This shindig's just for one night." I paused, then added, as sincerely as possible, "What I'm trying to say is, I'll be glad to go."

Surprised, Evelyn was speechless for some seconds as her eyes widened and a smile formed on her face. She looked at me curiously, as if seeing me for the first time. "Well, I'm—I'm happy to hear it! And I'm sorry I called you 'Mr. Grumpy.' I didn't mean it . . . Poor Chrisito, having to live with this crazy

Mexican woman—a woman you met in a magazine!" I took a sip of my OJ. "You'll see, Chrisito, we'll have a good time!" It's amazing how little it takes to make a person happy. Just substitute a "yes" for a "no"—a positive for a negative. "It'll be nice," I said, "to talk to Mike. I can ask him about Texas." I smiled to myself. "Like I don't already know."

Evelyn asked me, "You think Mike, for once, 'll actually get dressed up?"

I looked out the window. "Hmmm . . . I think getting *dressed up* for Mike means putting on some clean old clothes in place of the old clothes he's been wearing for days."

Evelyn smiled broadly at my turn of expression. "Mike's odd. You say he comes from a rich family in Boston. He dresses like he comes from some pueblo pobre (poor village) in Chiapas—like a campesino (peasant). You know he knows better than that."

"Sure he does," I agreed, "but he doesn't care. Mike's your classic, eccentric old gringo, fully retired, who figures he's paid his debt to society, and is now free to do whatever he likes, which includes wearing whatever he wants or *doesn't* want to wear." Evelyn grinned. I leaned back in my chair, crossed my arms, and let out a sigh. "Well, Evelina, what time do you want to leave? Around seven-thirty? Or maybe we should do like the natives do and show up around eleven?"

Evelyn saw no humor in my remark, and tersely said, "Very funny. All Mexicans aren't like that and you know it. Seven-thirty'll be fine." She sort of "shoved-off" the window ledge into the room and came over to the table. After a moment, she said, "I've got things to do around the house. You want anymore breakfast?"

Looking up at her, standing there like a no-nonsense waitress, I replied, "No, thank-you. I'll just finish up what's left here."

She rather pointedly picked up her glass and fruit bowl and headed for the kitchen.

P.S. I might add that old bachelor Mike, pushing seventy—

little Mike—him with the salt 'n pepper hair, the completely gray walrus moustache, and the thick horn-rimmed glasses through which he observes the world with a sort of ornery amusement, he's now relaxingly retired, after having spent years working as a computer technician in Austin. Back in his working days, so he's told me, he became friends with a single co-worker from Saltillo, one Rodolfo Ríos, who invited him one year to spend the Christmas holidays with him at his parents' house in Lomas. I recall Mike's very words, "It was during this visit, which was my first one south of the border, that I fell in love with Lomas and decided to buy some pleasant place in it somewhere as a second home." His small, white, adobe, box-like house, containing only one bedroom, (which Evelyn calls "his mouse house"—also alluding to his small stature—) sits by itself out in a field about half a mile from our house. Mike's at home in Lomas on and off throughout the year, as he spends his time shuttling back and forth between Saltillo and Austin, where he keeps an apartment.

CHAPTER 11

A Feeling And A Circling

Actually, the only thing left to "finish up" was the fruit bowl, as the eggs were long gone; but I lingered over the creamy, fruity mixture, which was almost too rich for my taste. Anyhow, as I picked at the fruit bowl with my fork, I gazed out the window at the widespread, distant city, so wonderfully and richly detailed, of which—jurisdictionally, at least—our house was still a part. I experienced that curious feeling that I've experienced on more than one occasion in looking out at the distant, sprawling metropolis—namely, that there's a certain unreality to it as seen from up in Lomas. Perhaps "impersonality" would be a better word. I mean, in spite of the "spectacularity" (to coin a word) of the view, it just comprises a vast conglomeration of silent buildings, houses, and plazas, no more "alive" than a photo or a painting of it would be. In fact, it's like a view of a vast ghost town, (and a vast lit-up ghost town at night.) It's easy to forget that there's close to a million people down there living and loving, working and playing, going to school, shopping, buying groceries, eating out, socializing and partying, attending concerts and sporting events, walking to and fro, and driving or riding here and there. I remember once seeing a documentary on TV about WW2 submarine warfare. In it, at one point, a veteran American seaman recalled, "Submarine warfare's the most impersonal thing in the world. Across the water you see a ship in your sights. You torpedo it. That's it. You never consider that there are actually human beings inside it." Minus the cold-blooded, lethal attitude, I experience a similar feeling (or lack of feeling) sometimes when looking out at the distant city, as I did now.

I noticed a large black hawk circling over the foothill, low enough down so that the serrated feathers on the tips of its wings were visible. As I watched it slowly and effortlessly circling—occasionally flapping its wings—and seemingly unconcerned about anything—I said to myself, "Now, there is freedom!" It was a pleasure to behold.

As I took the last bites of my fruit bowl, it occurred to me that maybe Evelyn was right, maybe I would have a "great time"—or, at least, a good time—at the garden party. It would be nice to get out of the house and "be back in society" for awhile, even if it meant having to be around little big man Bertie. In any event, I figured that I might as well look on the bright side since we were clearly going.

P.S. In talking about the "impersonality" of the view, this takes in the mountains as well, to a degree. In looking at them, you're looking at formations which are millions of years old, and yet are still "living" things in the sense that they're covered in trees and/or vegetation, and inhabited by all kinds of creeping, crawling, and walking creatures, as well as those with wings. Well, this is "up close and personal." From a distance—from up in Lomas—they surround the city like a great, silent, blue wall, (though, of course, those slopes rising up behind and in the vicinity of our foothill are quite green.) Though they are, indeed, to the view, about as impersonal as a wall, I do take a kind of comfort in them. The fact that they've been there, relatively pristine and unchanged, for many millions of years—since the age of the dinosaurs, or even before—and will be there, just the same, long, long, long after I'm gone, in spite of what Man, in all his petty, passing vanity does down below, makes me feel very contented, somehow, whenever I gaze at them.

P.P.S. Coahuila state, by the way, of which Saltillo is the capital city, is renowned as "Tierra de Dinosaurios" ("Land of the Dinosaurs"). There's a fairly new museum—a large, long, blood red building perched picturesquely up on a wide hill overlooking the city, El Museo del Desierto (The Desert Museum)—in eastern Saltillo, which displays many of the dinosaur finds found throughout the state, including a brownish, enormous and complete, standing T-Rex skeleton with a ferocious-looking, gaping mouth full of oversized, ripping teeth.

CHAPTER 12

Widely Separated Areas

Lomas de Lourdes is a real cross-section of Mexican society. In widely separated areas, you have the well-to-do living in stately neighborhoods in their two-story, balconied, white or beige, cement mansions; you have the middle class (like us) living in nice 'n neat neighborhoods in much more modest one or two-story cement row houses of different light colors—white predominating—and you have the poor living in rundown neighborhoods in much smaller, one-story cement row houses—almost huts (—virtually all of them 1970s and 80s cheap government housing—) which are invariably white, or what was once all white. These decaying neighborhoods—"decorated" with multi-colored graffiti on walls, and with streets with trash strewn about everywhere—are little more than slums. Finally, you have the extremely poor living in *real* huts out in fields, here and there, across the colony. These are "squatters' huts," whose walls consist of vertical tree limbs and old wooden pallets, and whose roofs consist of more tree limbs supporting rusting pieces of scrap metal held in place with big rocks. We're talkin' stone age, here, these dirt floor "dwellings" have no electricity, gas, or plumbing, meaning their residents have to go off in the field somewhere to go to the bathroom. Welcome to Mexico. They're a depressing sight, for sure; and it saddens (and maddens) me that human beings have to live in such miserable, shocking hovels on a daily basis, but they do. On the other hand, I suppose you could say it's better than living in a cardboard box, along with your possessions in a few plastic bags, like the homeless people do on the streets of New York City; though this is like saying it's better to live like a pig in a pigpen than like a rat in a garbage can. In any case, there's only a handful of these "homes" scattered about the colony, all of them away from the residential areas.

The northside of town, where Belinda and Bertie live, is another story. This affluent area is crisscrossed with spacious avenues lined with millionaires' mansions, sparkling shopping centers, fancy restaurants, glass office buildings, luxury car dealers, and exclusive shops offering the latest in women's fashions. They're no slums or tree limb dwellings here.

The city folk—and particularly those on the tony northside—tend to look on Lomas de Lourdes with a squinting eye, regarding it as a lonely and boring locality, too backward and isolated to tolerate—to actually *live* in. Belinda and Bertie certainly think so. We once had them up to our house for a late afternoon barbecue. They both spoke admiringly of the view. Later, though, after dinner, and after night had fallen, their horns peeped out. As we all stood in the silent, dark backyard, as silently taking in the splendid light show in the distance, (lined up in a row, from left to right, Bertie, Belinda, Evelyn, and me,) Bertie spoke up, saying, matter-of-factly, to either Evelyn or me or us both, "It may be nice—you've got a beautiful spot with a beautiful view—but I couldn't stand it living up here for more than two weeks!" After a moment, Belinda chimed in with, "Maybe a month." The fact that they said this in front of Evelyn and me didn't perturb them in the slightest. Then, that's Belinda and Bertie for you.

Belinda and Bertie's two-story, cream-colored house is located in an upscale northside neighborhood. Though the $100,000+ cement homes in this neighborhood are still essentially row houses, they're "big and fat," with two (or three) stories, chimneys, bay windows, and built-in, two-car garages. Though this neighborhood isn't new (like those springing up farther north,) it isn't that old, either, with most of the homes in it dating back to the 1990s.

The B&B house, like ours, has an atypical backyard,

instead of the usual small back patio; and, like our yard, it's technically a *side*yard. The house being on a corner, this rectangular yard, inside a bare pine fence, faces both the street in front of the house, and the street running along its length. It would be here, in this yard, where the dinner/garden party would be held.

CHAPTER 13

Ready To Go

I sat down on one of the barstools in the dining room, all dressed, hair combed, ready to go, and lit up a cigarette. Being a man, it'd only taken me a few minutes to "finish" myself. My woman-wife, as usual, was taking longer. She always tells me to "hurry up now and get ready!" then l'm the one—all ready—who ends up waiting.

"Meow!" "Meow!" I looked down. Gigi had put in an appearance from somewhere off in the house. She slowly circled my barstool, then suddenly leapt up into my lap. Sitting upright, she looked about the room, but not at me. I put out my left hand to pet her; but no sooner had my hand touched her back than she just as suddenly leapt back down and nonchalantly wandered off.

"Well, hello and good-bye to you, too!" I said, under my breath. As I stubbed out my cigarette in the ashtray on the counter, I heard Evelyn coming down the hall lightly humming some tune. I got off the barstool. Presently, she stood before me, and, smiling sweetly, asked me, "How do I look?" She was finished to a fault, wearing one of my favorite dresses of hers, a snug-fitting, navy blue, short-sleeved dress with a triple band of tiny white flowers around the neck; and she had on black patent, slightly high-heeled shoes.

"You look very nice!" I complimented her. "l'm glad you selected that dress. lt's one of my favorites of yours."

"Yes, I don't have the chance to wear it much anymore."

Whether or not I detected a touch of resentment in this remark, she followed it up by cheerfully saying, after giving

me a quick once-over, "You look very nice, too!"
I smiled. "Thanks!" I was dressed in a long-sleeved, tan shirt, black slacks, and brown "cowboy" boots.
Evelyn picked up her black handbag off the counter, and, tossing me a smile, said, "I guess we're ready. Let's go!"

CHAPTER 14

Heading Out

Twilight had fallen by the time we headed down (literally) the long and winding, gradually descending blacktop road towards Los Arcos and out of the colony. Evelyn was driving. Usually, whenever we go into town, she does, since, being a "wily Mexican" herself, she's more adroit and alert than I am to the unpredictable and frequently hair-raising ("Oh my God!"), carefree way that the locals love to drive. When driving in Mexico you need eight eyes, two in front of your head, two in back of your head, and two in each side. Even as just a passenger, it makes me tense and nervous.

As we gradually descended, I gazed out at the brilliant city lights in the distance, some of them coming, or popping on even as I looked. The twilight seemed to be fading—or, rather, darkening—by the second, so that the legions of lights were increasing in intensity even as the everyday city itself was disappearing.

At length, the somber-looking, box-like Los Arcos appeared up ahead. Los Arcos (The Arches) is a big, brown brick, double archway serving, alternately, as the entrance into and exit out of the colony. The arches themselves are about halfway down "the box," leaving a flat upper square on both sides. Los Arcos is nothing to write home about, being dark and utterly plain, but it's still an impressive structure. We soon passed under it and left Lomas behind.

CHAPTER 15

On Our Way

Once we were on Luis Echeverría, the thoroughfare that would take us to the northside, I turned to Evelyn and said (for no apparent reason), "I've heard that the one quality women like most in a man is a sense of humor, the ability to make them laugh a lot. I guess you lucked out there."

Without taking her eyes off the road, she replied, "Oh, you make me laugh sometimes."

"Like when?"

"Like when you think you can play the piano."

She said this completely deadpan. *I* let out a laugh, in spite of myself. We have an upright piano in our backroom which Evelyn plays like a pro, being especially fond of Beethoven and the Mexican composer, Augustín Lara. I like to strike the keys myself, now and then, in my clumsy, amateurish way. Speaking for myself, when it comes to "serious" music the composer I like to listen to the most is Charles Ives, which Evelyn doesn't understand at all, "That isn't music—it's just *noise*." I also like Scott Joplin a lot—if that can be called "serious" music.

I changed the subject, "You know, I think Bertie's basically a gigolo."

Evelyn gave me a glance, and asked, "OK, why do you say that?"

"Why? Just look at the facts. The house is Belinda's. All the furnishings in it are Belinda's. Both cars are Belinda's. I wouldn't be surprised if Belinda pays all the bills. Even Bertie's part-time job as an English teacher is Belinda's doing, thanks to her connections with the local school districts.

All that Bertie brought into their marriage was the shirt on his back, as they say—and something up front, no doubt. Belinda clearly *wears the pants*. You know what I think? I think Belinda essentially *adopted* Bertie, like a woman would a stray dog, as a creature to keep her from feeling less lonely."

I don't think Evelyn was really listening. She merely said, "Well, maybe so; but they seem happy together. They've been married for seven years." I didn't even bother to say anything to *that*. Then Evelyn added, casually, "I think maybe you're a little jealous of Bertie. You'd like to have it so easy."

I couldn't believe my ears. "I would not. Seven years! After twenty-three years you don't understand me at all! Imagine you saying such a thing to me."

"I'm sorry," she said contritely. "Look—I'm trying to drive this car through all this traffic. I can't do that and debate things with you at the same time! I know you don't like Bertie—OK?—but we're *here*—and'll soon be *there*—so just forget about him!"

I said no more, but didn't forget about him.

CHAPTER 16

Arrived

Belinda's big, two-story house, which is practically a mansion. . . She moved into the newly-built house twenty-five years ago when she married a Mexican man from the city (a car salesman) by whom she had a girl and a boy. Belinda's originally from Florida; and she was, by her own admission, pregnant with the girl when she got married. Eventually, the marriage to this "cabrón mexicano" ("Mexican bastard"), as Belinda puts it, went down the drain, though she managed to hang on to the house. Then, seven years ago, she found her Bertie online—divorced, with no children. He soon flew down from Peterborough, Ontario to Saltillo, married Belinda in a civil ceremony, and took up permanent residence in the big house. Though, at that time, Belinda's two children (who, of course, she'd retained custody of,) were still living at home; now, seven years later, they've both left the nest, both of them having married—the son, two years ago/the daughter, three—and Belinda and Bertie have had, since the son's marriage, the house all to themselves. They're now, both of them, in their mid-fifties.

I rang the doorbell. Belinda answered the door with a welcoming, toothy smile, (which made her look, I thought, with her long face and high cheekbones, unfortunately, like a happy horse.) After we exchanged greetings with her, we followed her down the central hallway, lined with family photos on both sides, to the rear kitchen. Belinda was wearing a short-sleeved, native Mexican "peasant" dress, and a very colorful one, its black background almost invisible behind a rich fantasy of crowded bright flower blossoms of red, purple, yellow, orange, and white. Only her shoes were plain, simple black loafers. Her flower show of a dress made Evelyn's navy blue dress look positively formal and conservative, by comparison, and produced a curious effect. Such a vividly colorful dress would've looked normal and attractive, and even sexy, on a brown-skinned, dark-haired Mexican woman—the browner the better. Against Belinda's white skin and (dyed) strawberry blonde hair, though, it looked artificial, as if she was merely play-acting, in an overdramatic fashion. Of course, such a striking dress couldn't go without comment; and as we walked down the hallway—Evelyn on Belinda's right, and I behind them—Evelyn exclaimed, "That's a really beautiful Mexican dress!" to which Belinda soothingly responded with, "Thank-you, my dear. And isn't yours just lovely, too!" I smiled to myself.

Belinda motioned for us to sit down at the kitchen table in the middle of the room. More Mexicana. The rectangular wooden table was painted a corn stalk green, with matching green, slat-backed chairs with basket weave seats. There were two chairs on each side, and one on each end, and the slats of the chairs were painted a bright yellow. Evelyn exclaimed, "What a pretty table and chairs!—this is new?" to which Belinda answered, obviously pleased, "Yes, I just bought the set a week ago." In the center of the table there were two uncorked bottles of red wine and some wine glasses. Evelyn and I sat down at the table (Evelyn on my right) facing the kitchen window over the sink, through which I noticed a portion of the bare pine fence.

We'd arrived nearly on time, at around eight-ten, but nobody else had, which didn't surprise me. Still, it made me feel uncomfortable and foolish, like we'd committed some social gaffe. It made me recall cynically what I'd said earlier jokingly about eleven o'clock. There were no signs, in looking about the kitchen, that any dinner was in any state of preparation; and I, for once, was pretty hungry. Why had Belinda said "eight-o'clock" (—though any stated time would've probably produced the same result—) and why had

Evelyn been so concerned about being *on time*? Not even Bertie was there. It made me feel quite dissatisfied with both Belinda and Evelyn.

Belinda came over to the table and sat down opposite us with a corkscrew in her right hand. Giving us a smile, she said, good-humoredly, "Let's have a little wine." She uncorked one of the bottles, poured out the wine into three of the glasses, and passed us our two glasses. She raised her glass and said, "How about a toast?"

"Allow me," I offered. Evelyn and I raised our glasses. "Be it ever so humble, there's no place like somebody else's home. Cheers!" Belinda and Evelyn gave me a puzzled look for a mornent. We clicked our glasses together—they repeated "Cheers!"—and we all took a sip of wine.

"A very nice wine," I said.

"Yes," Evelyn seconded.

"Thanks. lt's Italian." Then, as if reading my mind, Belinda said, "l don't know how much of a garden party this'll be. One couple has already called to cancel. So has Wanda. She says she's feeling sick to her stomach. Hopefully, the other people I invited'll show up. I'm sorry about this."

"Don't let it bother you," I said magnanimously, adding, knowingly, "This is Mexico. They'll come."

Belinda made no comment to this, but took a deep gulp of wine. She then said, "The dinner's in the refrigerator. Bertie ran down to the store to get some more charcoal. I told him what he's got going should be fine; but he thinks he needs more. He should be back any minute. We can put the meat on at any time." No sooner had she said this than we heard a door slam shut outside, followed, shortly, by the sound of the front door closing.

CHAPTER 17

Enter Bertie

Presently, Bertie entered the room toting a bag of charcoal in his right hand. He was dressed in a grass green, short-sleeved, Mexican guayabera shirt and black jeans, and was wearing white tennis shoes that looked brand new. He had a serious expression on his face. I say he "entered the room," but he did so in a continuous motion as he walked right past us—managing a grudging "Hi there" to Evelyn and me—and out the kitchen door into the backyard before anybody had a chance to say anything, though Evelyn said "Hi" in reply—not that he seemed to hear her.

Belinda looked embarrassed; and she tried to make light of Bertie's "greeting" by saying, "You must forgive Bertie. He takes doin' his barbecuin' so seriously!" She took another sip of wine. Then, smiling charmingly at me, she said, "Why don't you, Chris, go outside with Bertie and keep him company." I would've much preferred to stay where I was. Nevertheless, I got up from the table and, with my glass of wine cupped in my right hand, went outside. Along the side of the house three strong light bulbs projecting out, some ten feet apart, under the eave, lit up the backyard like a facsimile of the day. Bertie was standing beside a round, black, portable barbecue grill, a few yards down from the door. The round grill grate and cover were lying on top of a square, white, metal table in front of and to the right of the grill. Bertie was standing facing me, on the other side of the grill, staring down at the burning coals which he was poking at with a stick in his left hand. He looked very different from when I'd seen him last, nearly a year ago. Then, he had longish hair and a beard and a moustache, which were all somewhat gray. Now, his brown hair—grayer—was close-cropped—almost like a burr—and he was clean-shaven except for a trim, military-style moustache, also grayer than previously.

"How's it going, Bertie?"

Without looking up from the grill, he replied, "I don't think I'll need another bag, after-all, seeing as to who's only arrived."

"Don't you think others'll be arriving later?"

"Who knows?" which he said more like a statement than a question.

He continued poking about with the stick. I moved closer to the grill. "Looks like you've got a good fire going there."

"It'll do." After a few more seconds, he looked at me for the first time (with the same serious expression) and said, "I remember you have a built-in barbecue at your house."

"Yes."

He looked back down at the smoldering coals. " *We* aren't so lucky."

Just then, Belinda and Evelyn came outside, lightly laughing about something. They came up to the grill—Belinda on my left/Evelyn on my right—and looked down at the glowing coals as if they were of deep interest to them. I noticed that they'd apparently left their wine glasses back on the kitchen table. Then, Evelyn looked over at Bertie and rather playfully and teasingly said, "Bertie, you're looking fine—with your new look—just like a soldier!" Bertie perked up at this. His serious expression quickly dissolved into a smile, and he said to Evelyn in reply, "Thanks. I was getting tired of that rugged look. I think this suits me better."

"Oh, it does," Evelyn agreed.

Belinda, not to be outdone, stepped around to Bertie and gave him a momentary light pinch/tug on his right cheek, exclaiming, "My little soldier!" She followed this up by giving him a kiss on the same cheek. Bertie tried to appear embarrassed, but to me he looked quite satisfied.

CHAPTER 18

Enter Mike

Belinda glanced down at the grill. "What d'you think, Bertie? We should go ahead and put the meat on?"

"What time is it?" he asked.

Since Evelyn was the only one wearing a watch, she answered, "It's about nine o'clock."

Bertie considered this for a moment. "Well, why don't we give it another twenty minutes or so."

"That sounds good," Belinda concurred, "we can't wait forever." After a moment, she said, "Evelyn, why don't you come inside and help me with the preparations."

"Sure." I handed Evelyn my virtually empty wine glass. Belinda noticed this and asked me obligingly, "Would you like some more wine? You don't need to bother—Evelyn can bring it out to you." I smiled and replied, "No, thank-you—maybe later, with the meal." They went back inside and I was left alone again with Mr. Bertie to carry on my pretty much one-sided conversation with him.

In addition to the grill grate and cover, there was a white, medium-sized, styrofoam cooler on top of the metal table which was full of ice, but was minus its lid. Only seconds after the women went back inside, for the first time, Bertie stepped around the grill and grabbed two cans of Tecate beer from the cooler for himself. "Help yourself," he said unceremoniously to me. He then went back to where he'd been standing. Holding one beer in his right hand, he set the other one down on the square, wire mesh platform, almost at ground level, under the grill bowl. There was one white plastic chair in front of and to the left of the grill. I grabbed a beer for myself and sat down in this chair. Bertie took no advantage of the white plastic chair behind him, but continued to stand where he was at the grill, drinking his beer and poking about, every now and then, with the stick. We didn't say much (—Bertie certainly didn't—) as we imbibed our cold Tecates. Though, outwardly, I made an effort to be sociable, inwardly, I felt depressed, to a degree, and was growing more irritated by the minute at having to keep company with such a pompous bore, who obviously had no great liking for me. I felt like a penguin alone with another penguin who I could barely tolerate, on a small, moving ice floe. I said, under my breath, "Well, it's my own fault for coming."

After ten minutes or so, as Bertie was starting in on his second beer and I was polishing off my first, the women reappeared accompanied by Mike, Belinda exclaiming, "Look who I found!" I got up. Mike was dressed, characteristically, in a worn and faded, old pair of blue jeans and a nondescript, long-sleeved, brown shirt, and he had on a pair of considerably creased and old-looking brown boots. The jeans looked a little too short for him. He also had at least a day's growth of grayish beard. Altogether, he looked like an aging ranch hand down on his luck. (I also noticed Evelyn giving him a sour look.)

Mike came up to me smiling. "Hello, Chris! Long time no see!"

We shook hands. "Yes, it's been awhile."

"How've you been?"

"Fine Mike—just fine. How've *you* been?"

"Never better! And *Evelyn*!"

They shook hands. "Nice to see you again, Mike," she said politely.

During this exchange between the three of us, Bertie had come over from behind the grill, and he now greeted Mike with, "Hi, Mike! Welcome to our so-called garden party!"

They shook hands. "Thank-you, Bertie! Great to be here!" I couldn't help but notice that Bertie was much gladder to see Mike than he had been to see Evelyn and me. It must have been awhile, also, since Mike had seen Bertie, for he exclaimed, giving Bertie the once-over, "What—have you enlisted in the Army or something?"

"Not hardly. This is my new look. What d'you think?"

After a moment, Mike replied, "Bertie, my boy, there's no one who can wear it quite like you." There was a pause. Bertie gave Mike a look. I gave Mike a look. Was that a compliment? Belinda (—I think, just to say something—if not also, perhaps, to rein in Mike—) abruptly exclaimed, "Would you just look at that moon! Isn't that splendid?" The rest of us looked towards the eastern sky. A big, golden, full September moon floated just above the distant mountains, looking, in all its grandeur, like a mellow version of the sun.

"Now that's what I call a real harvest moon!" Mike exclaimed.

"That is one beautiful moon," I said, really just to Evelyn, who stood beside me.

"It is!" she agreed. "I think it's the biggest moon I've ever seen."

Belinda said, thoughtfully, "It seems so close—so real—like you could land on it by plane in thirty minutes. It's hard to believe it's actually hundreds of thousands of miles away."

"I know what you mean," I said.

Mike, following his own train of thought, put in, "You know, I've always thought the loveliest but saddest song I've ever heard is, 'Full Moon and Empty Arms.'"

This remark was so unexpected that Evelyn, Belinda, and I just looked at each other. As for Bertie, he'd gone back over to his same spot at the grill while this mutual lunar admiration was underway; and only seconds after this remark of Mike's he cut in by saying, with a hint of sarcasm, "Look, folks—I think it's about time we be putting the meat on."

Belinda responded with, "Oh, right Bertie! Evelyn, my dear, come with me." The two of them went back inside. No sooner had they done so than Bertie said graciously, "Help yourself to a beer, Mike."

"I believe I will," Mike said, and he reached into the

cooler and pulled out a Tecate. I did the same, helping myself to another. Bertie was still working on his second can. After taking a sip, I asked, "How long have you been back, Mike."
"About a week."
"And how are things in Texas?"
"Expensive as ever!"
"I'll bet."
Mike elaborated, "I've been thinking lately about living down here permanently from now on . . . selling my apartment in Austin. I really don't enjoy it much there anymore. Not only are prices for everything through the ceiling, but it's getting so congested. It's not the Austin it used to be. The highway—you know, I-35—is a bumper to bumper parking lot, for miles, during morning and evening rush hour, and the city streets aren't a whole lot better. I'm also getting too old, I guess, to put up with the horrible Texas heat. This summer it was over 100 degrees in the shade every day for three weeks straight, with, of course, not a drop of rain. Then, living in Austin, there're those idiots at the state capital always in the paper and on the local news. What a confederacy of dunces! What a crazy gang of fascists! Would you believe there's this woman legislator there—a Republican, naturally—who's seriously proposed her own original plan for solving the illegal immigration problem, bombing the border, on the Mexican side."
Bertie cut in, with a sneer, "They'd be better off bombing the American side."
Mike let out a laugh—but not in amusement—and said dismissively, "Somebody should drop a bomb on her."
I chuckled.
Mike gave me a questioning look, and a smile, and asked, "What d'you think about it, Chris? You're a Texas good ol' boy."
I hesitated a moment. "Old I am—and a Texan—for what it's worth—but as to how *good* I am--that's open for discussion." This elicited a laugh from Mike, and even from Bertie. I continued, "It doesn't matter what I think; and I

hardly think about it, at all; but I will say that of the millions upon millions of illegal immigrants in the United States, not one one of them would've set foot on American soil if they hadn't been welcomed into the country by American business interests in the first place as ready and available cheap labor—labor that can be paid for under the table, and laborers who don't have to be provided with any benefits, no matter how many hours they work. What a deal! What a way to maximize profits! All this political talk about stopping illegal immigration is nothing but flag-waving hypocrisy, that's only said to get votes from the angry and displaced American workers. Only, instead of this anger being directed at the poor Mexicans, it should be directed at the greedy and Un-American American businessmen and politicians, in bed together, who've sold these workers down the river."

There was a silence for a few moments. Then, Mike spoke up, "You should run for office—on your own ticket. What a speech!"

"I didn't think I was making any speech," I said. "Maybe I got a bit carried away."

"That's OK," Bertie said. "Everybody's entitled to their own opinion." Though Bertie said this in a gracious enough manner, I sensed a certain coldness (and condescension) in his words.

I decided I needed a break, if only to get away from *mein host* for awhile. "You two go ahead and talk," I announced, "I'm gonna take a stroll about the yard and stretch my legs a bit." They said nothing; and I turned and walked off, beer in hand.

CHAPTER 19

Enter A Couple

I walked towards the tall, broad oak tree in the middle of the backyard (—and the only tree in the yard—) under which, around its trunk, three black, round, wrought iron tables and accompanying, armless chairs were set up for the garden part of the dinner party. The tables and chairs were arranged in a semi-circle facing the house, one set to the left of the trunk, one set to the right of it, and one set in front of it. There was an already lit candle in a short glass in the center of each table. The leafy lower limbs of the big tree extended outwards far enough to provide a canopy over the tables. I was nearly at the tables when I heard a "Here we are!" behind me. I stopped and turned around to see Belinda approaching the grill carrying a platter of steaks. She deposited the platter on the metal table—said something to Bertie I couldn't make out—then promptly went back inside.

I took a seat at the front table, facing my compadres. It was such a lovely spot to take a seat, an outdoor table sporting a glowing candle, under a green, leafy canopy, and with a drink in hand, like a scene out of Renoir. All it needed were some violins, or maybe a mariachi band. I sipped my beer as I observed Bertie putting the steaks on, and carefully adjusting them, with a long barbecue tong. He'd gone around to the opposite side of the grill to do so, since that's where the steaks were on the metal table on his right. Mike stood close by on this left. The point is, that though they were both facing me, engaged in quiet conversation about something, never once did either of them specifically look in my direction.

After some minutes, Belinda and Evelyn reappeared carrying trays—Belinda, of plates and glasses/Evelyn, of napkins and silverware—and they were accompanied by an older Mexican couple. The man was plainly dressed in a dull yellow, long-sleeved shirt and brown pants, and the woman was as plainly dressed in a short-sleeved, brown dress. They were both gray-haired and on the corpulent side. From where I sat, my immediate first impression of them was that they looked like a nice couple. Salutations were made all around between them and Bertie and Mike. Belinda and Evelyn lingered there while this transpired, then continued on towards the tables.

Approaching the tables, Evelyn right behind her, Belinda asked me, rather brashly, "What are you doing over here all by yourself?"

"Oh," I replied, "I decided to stretch my legs a bit—take a stroll about the yard—and I ended up here."

Belinda put her tray down on my table, but before she could do anything, Bertie called out,

"Belinda! Can you come here a minute!" She made a face.

Evelyn cut in, "Go ahead. I can put everything around."

Giving Evelyn a weak smile, Belinda said, "Thank-you, my dear," and—taking two of the empty glasses with her, in either hand, for some reason—she walked back towards the grill.

As Evelyn placed the contents of the trays around, I asked her, "Are you having a good time with Belinda?"

"Oh yes. We've been talking about many things."

"Such as?"

"Oh, nothing that'd interest you—women talk."

"Uh-huh. Who's the couple?"

"The Hinojosas—Lupe and José—neighbors from down the block. They seem like a nice couple."

"I suppose they speak little to no English?"

"Oh, I don't know about that."

We didn't talk anymore as she completed her chore, as efficiently as a waitress. Once this was done, she grabbed the chair on my left and, setting it closer to me, sat down.

We were silent for a spell, both of us staring at the group at the grill, all of them chatting and laughing away. I took a sip of my beer. She took a sip of my beer. Finally, turning to me, Evelyn said, quietly and mysteriously, "I'll bet you don't know what the date is today."

"It's September 14th," I answered.

"September 14th," she repeated decisively. "Does that—what's the expression?—'ring a bell' with you—I mean, concerning you and me?"

I thought about it for a few moments. "No, I can't say that it does . . . the first time we made love?"

"No," she said, almost indignantly. She looked towards the group at the grill. After some seconds, she said, "It was on this day, twenty-two years ago, you proposed to me."

It was a jolt. "Really!"

"Yes," she said simply. She looked back at me. "You remember that, Chrisito, the Hotel Royalty restaurant in Monterrey?"

I smiled, in spite of myself, at the memory. "Do I! I wish I didn't—I mean, what happened. I've never been so embarrassed in my whole life—reaching across the table—taking your hand—popping the question—your "Yes"—then releasing your hand and knocking over your whole glass of orange juice into your lap! Talk about spoiling a moment!"

Looking down at the table, exhibiting merely a faint smile, she commented, "You know what? Somehow that makes the memory all the more precious to me."

I took a sip of my beer. "It's *precious* all right."

Looking towards the grill group again, she sort of half-exclaimed, "How the years rush by! It seems like only yesterday. I know people are always saying that—but it's true . . . It's funny—when you're living your life, day by day, life feels long; but when you look back on your life—on all you've gone through—it feels very short—like just a day almost."

I was impressed by what she said. "You could say just the opposite—but, in a way, the same thing—about the future, it looks long, before you, but it isn't. I don't recall who, but a famous person once said that life's 'nasty, brutal, and short.' I don't know if the 'nasty' and 'brutal' part's especially so—unless you work in a coal mine, or for a drug cartel, or maybe as an assistant manager at McDonald's—but life's certainly 'short.' I guess it's all over before you know it."

Evelyn gave me an odd look, then, unexpectedly, reached over and gave my hand a squeeze. We were silent for a bit, gazing at the animated group at the grill as if we were watching a play, until, at length,` she asked me, about as unexpectedly, "We *are* happy together, aren't we?"

For a couple of moments I "heard" a few bars of that song "Happy Together" by the 60s group, The Turtles, where they're singing the actual words, "We're happy together." "Yes, of course," I said.

She explained, "It's true I still have my girlfriends in Monterrey, going all the way back to my college time—Silvia, Lupita, María Luisa, Alejandra—but I'm not as close to them as I think you think I am. They have their own lives. They have their children. They even have their grandchildren now. No, Chrisito, you're the only one I really have in the whole world."

I felt a pang of sadness. "I could say the same thing. I *do* say the same thing."

There was a long pause. Where some feelings are concerned, words don't matter, the heart feels no need to speak. I took a sip of my beer, and, after maybe half a minute, another. Finally, Evelyn said sincerely, looking at me, "Two are better than one," as if she was the first person who'd ever said it. She smiled affectionately at me.

"Yes, that's true," I agreed, "unless you're stuck in an elevator with Hillary Clinton."

She laughed, loudly. Though she didn't notice it, I noticed that her outburst attracted the attention of those at the grill, who all looked our way, momentarily. Once she recovered herself, she said, "Oh, Chrisito—never tell me again you don't make me laugh!"

A white dove (una paloma blanca) suddenly appeared from out of nowhere, alighting on a fence post opposite us, to our line of sight, a little to the left of the tree. It sat (or, rather, stood) there very still, facing the yard, and looking at nothing in particular, apparently not even aware of our presence. We were both surprised and enchanted by its appearance, (as pure white doves are a relatively rare sight on any day in Saltillo); and we both instinctively sat as still as it did, not wanting to attract its attention and cause it to fly off. Evelyn only exclaimed, under her breath, "¡Qué hermosa!" ("How beautiful!"). After maybe thirty seconds, the dove cocked its head to the left and looked directly at us for a few seconds (—not that we'd moved a muscle—) then, with a flap of its wings, it took off and disappeared as suddenly as it had appeared.

"Did you see that?" I exclaimed. "It looked right at us!"

"I saw that."

"How curious! D'you think that's supposed to mean something?"

"Quién sabe?" ("Who knows?") Maybe it knows something we should know."

"What's that supposed to mean?"

"There's a famous Spanish song, "La Paloma," that says the dove's a messenger of love. Maybe it was just reminding us of that."

I wasn't sure if I grasped her meaning, and didn't say anything. She reached over and gave my hand another squeeze.

CHAPTER 20

Enter Paula

    Belinda came out of the kitchen carrying a big (and full) glass salad bowl, followed by a young woman carrying a plate of stacked high with tortillas in her right hand, and a plate of what looked like "extras" for the tortillas in her left. Perhaps because of their burden, they didn't bother to linger at the grill, but walked straight towards the tables. They set their stuff down on the table to the left of the tree.
    I couldn't help looking—really, downright staring—at this young woman, who looked to be somewhere in her twenties. Taking nothing away from Evelyn, in all the years I'd lived in Mexico, as well as Texas, I'd never seen such a beautiful Mexican woman. She unavoidably put Evelyn and Belinda in the shade. She was of medium height, with a slender yet curvy figure, and a face—what a face!, dark, glowing eyes, arched eyebrows, rosy, perfectly-shaped lips, and a pert little nose all framed by a mass of jet black, wavy hair pulled back and secured in back with a tortoise shell hairpin, from which a thick, braided ponytail trailed down her back. She wore a white muslin, short-sleeved dress which hugged her body and set off her light brown skin to nice advantage. She also had on a thin silver necklace around her neck from which hung a tiny silver cross. I felt a strange mixture of awe and gladness. It wasn't everyday you saw such a paragon of feminine beauty. She noticed my reaction, which was something she evidently was accustomed to, for she gave me a little, friendly—but, at the same time, rather distant—smile.

Introductions were called for. Belinda took the young woman by the hand and brought her over to stand right before us. We both stood up. Belinda, all smiles, announced, "This is Paula Cuello!" as if she was showing us her brand new, shiny corvette. Shaking Paula's offered right hand, Evelyn said, "Mucho gusto, Paula. Me llamo Evelyn Steer" ("Nice to meet you, Paula. My name is Evelyn Steer"), and Paula responded agreeably with, "El gusto es mío" ("The pleasure is mine"). As I, in turn, shook her hand, I said, "Me llamo Chris," and Paula, face to face with a gringo, smiled back at me and responded, with a slight accent (and slightly shyly) with, "Nice to meet you." For a woman, she had firm handshake, in spite of her delicate hand. "Oh, you speak English?" I asked, surprised. Before Paula could say anything, Belinda cut in (—more like butted in—) with, "Paula's from Piedras Negras. She went to an English Academy there. She's now working for me as a translator-helper." (Belinda runs her own translating service, Traducciones de Belinda, Inc., out of a small office in town, not far from the Cathedral Plaza.) "Where are you from?" Paula asked, in general, to either of us. Evelyn spoke up for us both, "Fort Worth, Texas—though I grew up in Linares, south of Monterrey." "Oh I know Linares," Paula said. "I have a sister who lives in Montemorelos," (a small town close to Linares.) Evelyn's eyes opened wide as she exclaimed, "¡De verdad! . . . Montemorelos es famosa por sus naranjas." ("Really!. . . Montemorelos is famous for its oranges." It is. From the highway, you can see thick orange groves full of orange oranges stretching to the horizon.) "Oh, lo sé," ("Oh, I know,") Paula agreed, looking at me.

Belinda, (who'd been sidelined, temporarily,) suddenly announced, dramatically, "Ah—looks like dinner is served!" Evelyn, Paula, and I looked towards the grill to see Bertie walking towards the tables carrying a platter of steaks, followed by Mike and the Hinojosas. Mike was carrying the cooler.

CHAPTER 21

Dinner-1

After introductions were made between Paula and Mike, Paula and the Hinojosas, and the Hinojosas and me, we all sat down. There were four chairs set up per table, as in a cross. Evelyn and I stayed where we were, (though Evelyn moved her chair a little back to the left), and Mike and Paula sat down opposite us, Paula across from me, and Mike across from Evelyn. Belinda and Bertie and the Hinojosas sat down at the table to the right of the tree, Señor Hinojosa with his back to our table, his wife opposite him, Belinda on his left, and Bertie on his right. Our two tables were close enough so that any normal conversation easily flowed between them. The other table, to the left of the tree, served as the serving table, it was where the platter of steaks were, the tortillas and fixins, the salad, and the cooler. While the introductions were going on, I'd asked Belinda if she could bring me some water. She exceeded my expectations by bringing back a whole six pack of bottled water which she placed on my table. Once we were seated, I took one, as did Evelyn and Paula. Mike stayed with his beer, as did Bertie and the Hinojosas. Belinda stayed with her glass of wine; and she'd brought along the bottle for reinforcement.

We hadn't been seated for long, engaging in pleasantries, when Belinda, tapping on her wine glass with her fork, announced, "Everybody—please! In just a second, you can go and serve yourself—but first I'd like to say a little prayer." We all dutifully bowed our heads, except for Mike, who only half-bowed his. "Let us thank the good Lord for the food we are about to receive as we remember and pray for those millions who don't have such food, or are surrounded by such friends." She instantly repeated the prayer en español for the benefit of the Hinojosas, then said, "Amén." Everybody repeated "Amén" (except Mike.) After a moment, she exclaimed, "Everybody—help yourself!" Everybody did. Interestingly, as we all milled about the table, filling up our plates, I noticed that Paula, on my right, passed by the large platter of steaks and helped herself to the salad, instead. Mike, opposite her, noticed this, too, and commented, "You don't want any steak, Paula?" Putting some salad on her plate, she replied, "I'm a vegetarian. I don't eat meat—dead animals— if I can help it." Mike gave her a look which was practically a sneer, for a moment, (unnoticed by Paula, but not by me,) but said nothing more.

A few minutes after everybody was seated and eating, Mike, on his own initiative, stood up, picked up the remaining six pack of bottled water, walked over, and put them in the cooler. He brought back another beer with him. When he sat back down, he popped the top on his beer, took a good gulp of it, and said, really, just addressing the air, "I guess I'm like W. C. Fields, who said, 'I never drink water. I'm afraid it will become habit-forming.'" This provoked laughter from Bertie, Evelyn, and myself, but not from Paula, Belinda, or the Hinojosas.

Paula asked innocently, "Who was W. D. Fields?"

Mike answered authoritatively, "W. *C.* Fields—a famous comedian—and big-time drinker—long before your time."

"Oh," Paula said.

"You have to realize something, Paula," Bertie interjected, "Mike goes *way* back."

Mike smiled complacently. "That I do."

Belinda spoke up, with some spirit, and with an airy disdain, "I really think that we can find something better to talk about." She then turned to Lupe and started talking confidentially to her, en español, about something.

Mike, chewing on a piece of steak, asked Paula, "Tell me,

Paula, how long have you been living in Saltillo?"

Paula, for some reason, shot me a little smile, just for a second, before she answered, "I've only been here six months."

"What brought you here?" Mike continued.

"Things are bad in Piedras Negras. Not many jobs. There's much more opportunity here."

"I would think," Mike said, "being right at the border, you could cross into Eagle Pass and get a good job there."

Paula imperceptibly stiffened. "No, it's just as bad there as in Piedras."

Mike seemed surprised by this, and was about to respond, when Evelyn spoke up, "So you're here all by yourself?"

"Yes," Paula answered. "I have an apartment not far from Belinda's office."

"So, you're a single working girl!" Evelyn exclaimed, with, it seemed to me, a forced cheerfulness.

"Yes," Paula replied.

Evelyn's face went expressionless for a moment. Paula continued, "I can walk to work and back every day."

"How nice," Evelyn said.

"Yes, that is nice," Mike agreed.

"Saltillo's a great walking town, any day of the week—especially around The Cathedral," I put in.

"Yes, it is," Paula agreed, smiling pleasantly at me.

That seemed to conclude round one of the questioning. We were silent for a bit, concentrating on our meals. This information made a curious impression on me. "All by yourself." I found this hard to believe, such a beautiful young woman being unmarried, in a country where girls marry very young, and a lot less attractive than her. It made me wonder. Paula certainly had a boyfriend—or boyfriends. Then again, maybe not—at least, not steadily. After-all, she had come alone. Besides, there was something about her—a certain haughtiness—well, not exactly haughtiness—more like a look and spirit of independence which seemed to say that she would be very choosy about who she went out with, (like most extremely attractive, single women,) if she went out with anybody. At the same time, she wasn't at all remote, but cheerful and pleasing, and even somewhat shy.

At length, I asked her, as pleasantly as possible, "How do you find working for Belinda, Paula?"

"Very nice. There's a lot of work to do. I really enjoy the work. It keeps me busy."

"I guess you have a lot of"—here, Bertie cut in, to my great irritation, with the uncalled for remark, "I'm sorry, Chris, but Paula doesn't have the time to teach you Spanish."

Without giving him so much as a glance, I said, "I wasn't going to ask her to."

Paula looked embarrassed.

Evelyn picked up the thread, "You must love the buen clima (good—more like wonderful—weather) here after Piedras"

"Oh, I do," Paula earnestly replied

"We've never been to Piedras Negras," Evelyn continued, "but the other border towns we've been to—Laredo and Reynosa—are absolute infiernos (hellholes) in the summer."

Paula looked serious for a moment, as she looked down at her plate. By implication, Evelyn was saying that Piedras Negras was a hellhole as well, which perhaps Paula rather resented. In any case, her serious expression dissolved as he she responded to Evelyn by saying, with a thin smile, "Of course, it's hot in Piedras in the summer, but you get used to it. This was my first summer here, and I couldn't believe it, sometimes, at night, I had to use a blanket!"

I think Mike was beginning to feel the effects of his beer. He blurted out, "Up where we live—Chris and Evelyn and me—you sometimes need *two* blankets!" This was an exaggeration.

Seeing the question on Paula's face, I explained, "We live in a colony called Lomas de Lourdes, on the southern edge of town, up in the foothills. It's at a higher altitude than the city, so it's cooler up there in the summer. You frequently need a light blanket, too, at night."

"It sounds very nice," Paula said sincerely, smiling at me. Like with all very beautiful women, her smile was the icing on the cake.

Evelyn changed the subject—or, rather, went back to the subject—by asking Paula, "So, Paula, all your family's in Piedras? Well—no—you said you had a sister in Montemorelos."

"Yes," she answered, "and I have another sister who lives in Ciudad Juárez. My youngest sister still lives at home with my parents in Piedras. I don't have any brothers."

"I see," Evelyn said.

Then, Paula asked Evelyn directly, "Do you and Chris have any children?"

Evelyn sort of froze. Mike smiled to himself. I answered, "No, we don't have any children." Then, feeling suddenly defensive about it, I added, "We never really wanted any that much."

What can you say to that? Still, realizing that she had to say something, Paula said, "Then you have all that much more time for each other."

And what can you say to that? I merely smiled at her. I thought it was a sweet thing to say.

Bertie put in, "I think people should have all the children they like. Serves 'em right."

You could have heard a fly fly by. Belinda was not amused, and coolly said, "So that's the way you feel about it, is it, señor? Saying such a thing in front of *me*! My, my—you're just full of surprises tonight, aren't you? . . . I take it, señor, you know where the sofa is?"

Mike grinned. I lowered my head to try to hide *my* grin.

There was a pause. Then, Paula asked, "May I say something?"

"Certainly, my dear," Belinda answered.

Paula now hesitated, as if she'd changed her mind. Then, looking straight at me, but rather abstractedly, like a student might look at her teacher, she said candidly, "I'm not married—but to me, it's not the children, it's who you marry."

Evelyn looked at Paula with distinct admiration, "I'm glad to hear you say that, Paula. That's just the way I feel."

"Wait till you have children," Belinda said dryly. Then, contradicting the tone of this remark, she said, "Some day, Paula, you'll find the right man and get married, and'll have a simply beautiful wedding, I'm sure!" She paused for a moment, before adding sentimentally, "I always cry at weddings."

Bertie put in his two cents by saying, with a sneer, "If they knew what they were in store for, it'd be the *bride 'n groom* who'd be crying."

That fly flew by again. Mike, Evelyn, and I—and even Paula herself—let out a laugh; but Belinda found no humor in this remark whatsoever, and said haughtily to Bertie, "You just never stop, do you?"

Mike and I smiled at each other like a couple of conspirators. Bertie tried to make amends by saying (to my mind, with a touch of anxiety,) "I'm sorry, honey. I wasn't talking about us—about you and me—but about marriage in general—about many of the unhappy marriages I've seen—about *my* first marriage—I mean, you know, not all marriages are made, or *lived*, in heaven."

Belinda was obviously neither impressed nor moved by Bertie's roundabout and rather evasive explanation, and just stared straight-faced at him. Mike, slowly turning his beer can around on the table with his right hand, asked Paula, in a low voice, "Paula?"

"Yes Mike."

"You're an extremely attractive woman."

"Why, thank-you, Mike."

"You say you have a sister in Montanamorelos?"

"In *Monte*morelos—yes?"

"And another one in Ciudad Juárez?"

"Yes."

"Are they married?"

After a moment, Paula replied reservedly, "Yes."

"And the one still living at home"—

"What about her?"

Mike looked and sounded a little irritated. "Is she married, too—or has a boyfriend?"

Paula looked like she could've burst out laughing. "No, Mike, she's only thirteen."

"Oh. Well, I was just asking."

I couldn't believe Mike's effrontery towards someone who was virtually a complete stranger. I thought to myself that he really must be drunk. I felt sorry for Paula, and said, against my natural inclination, and with a false humor, "Everybody knows what you're 'just asking,' Mike—Paula, most of all."

At this, Paula let out a high little laugh, which caught the attention of Belinda, who stopped talking to Lupe and José for a moment to ask, "What's so funny?"

"Nothing!" Paula answered. Mike said, not very convincingly, staring down at his plate, "I'm sorry if I offend anyone. I was just asking."

Paula said diplomatically, "Thank-you for your interest, Mike. Anything's possible. Maybe in three or four years, if she's interested, I can put you into contact with Teresa."

Mike, giving Paula a quick sidelong glance, merely nodded his head. End of round two.

CHAPTER 22

Dinner-2

And the dinner/garden party rolled on. People talked about different things. We seemed, though, to keep coming back to the subject of the weather, no matter what we talked about. I remember Bertie saying, "Did you know there are more people living, or *packed into* Mexico City, alone, than in all the ten provinces of Canada, from the Atlantic to the Pacific? That's Canada, plenty of room—and more."

"That only shows," Mike said, "not a great many people wanna live in a country that's an icebox most of the time."

"Personally," I said, "I prefer the cold to the heat. Texas can be absolutely unbearable in the summer. You can literally 'fry an egg on the sidewalk,' as they say. It can get to where you *hate* to go outside."

"That's a fact," Mike said, nodding his head in agreement. "That's why I love it here in the summer."

"You're right there," I agreed.

Bertie sat up straight. "Ignorant people have this ignorant idea that Canada's nothing but a frozen-over wasteland. It's not true! Speaking of the summer, Canadian summers are even better than down here. You don't know what you're missing."

Paula spoke up, "Maybe because I've always lived there, until recently—the heat—and it gets very hot in Piedras—has never bothered me that much. Maybe it's because of my darker skin." She said this simply matter-of-factly. She paused for a moment, then continued, "I used to love it when I was a girl how, on a hot day, me and my friends would cool off by the big fountain in the plaza, eating ice cream cones."

"That's charming." I said, giving Paula a smile.

She looked intently at me, giving me a returning smile, but said nothing.

Belinda said, with some impatience, "All this silly talk about the weather. Why don't you talk about some real differences, like living in Mexico compared to the US and Canada. I can tell you, I'd never go back to The States today. Everything's too expensive!"

"I'll drink to that!" Mike said—and he did. "Yes, whenever I go back to Austin, I'm shocked at the high prices. I can barely pay the rent and bills on my small apartment; and they're going up all the time. It's downright ridiculous!" Just the thought of this seemed to affect him, he took a rather aggressive gulp of his beer, and stared down at his plate, looking like a just-fired undertaker.

"You don't have to tell me about it," I said. "Try losing your full-time job. And if you're over fifty, heading towards sixty, good luck trying to find another one in The States today. Nobody wants you. You can just go roll up in a corner and die like an old dog, for all that society cares. Even once you get your Social Security, you're little better off. Who needs it? That's why we're here."

"It's no picnic in Canada, either," Bertie said. "We have universal health care, like here in Mexico, which helps—a lot; but everything else is very expensive—especially food. If you own your own home, the taxes are outrageous. And, like you're saying, once you get on in years—unless you're Gordon Lightfoot or somebody—life definitely doesn't get any easier. Older people get little respect, and even less employment."

Evelyn asked, "Who's Gordon Lightfoot?"

"Yes!" Paula chimed in.

"Ol' Gordy"—Bertie pronounced his name with a kind of slow relish—"he's a very popular Canadian folk singer who had huge hits in the 60s and 70s. Maybe you've heard of the songs "Sundown" and "Early Morning Rain."

"I think I know "Sundown," Evelyn said.

"I'm sure you'd know if you heard it," Bertie said. "Many other artists have covered his songs. He really did write some great songs. Anyway, he's up in his seventies today, and looks like hell, after all the booze and women, but he's a very rich man, and is practically a Canadian institution nowadays."

"You have some CDs of his, don't you?" Bellinda asked.

"Yes," Bertie replied.

"Maybe you can play them for us later," which Belinda said almost like an order.

"Please do!" Paula exclaimed.

Bertie smiled at her. "I can do that."

"I remember Gordon Lightfoot," Mike said.

"So do I," I said.

This didn't quite close the subject, as Bertie came out with, "See—Canada *has* contributed something to the Arts, in spite of what most of you *Americans* think."

Clearly directed at Mike and me, Mike made the cutting reply, "Oh, come on, Bertie, get down off your pedestal! Nobody's denying that."

I could've slapped Mike on the back. I couldn't have said it better. Bertie didn't say anything.

Evelyn changed the subject, "Paula, now that you're living and working here, you think you'll stay in Saltillo from now on?"

"I'm not sure," Paula replied. "Probably. I really don't have any reason to go back to Piedras, except to see my family. I like Saltillo, and I like working for Belinda a lot."

Belinda put in strongly, "Paula's an excellent worker. I'm very glad to have her."

There was a pause. Then, Evelyn, sort of boldly but shyly asked, "Paula—forgive me for asking you this—but I find it hard to believe such a beautiful young woman as yourself isn't married . . . especially, here in Mexico."

I wasn't quite positive I knew what Evelyn meant by that last part, but it didn't sound exactly kosher to me. Paula, definitely taken aback, sort of drew into herself, and there was a cold look in her eyes for some seconds, before she relaxed and almost smiled as she replied, "I haven't found the person yet I want to marry; and I'm not in any hurry. I have my job, and my apartment, and it's enough for now."

Bertie started to say something, and actually got out the words, "Not everybody"—but then shut up. End of round 3. We went back to our meals, and talked about other things.

P.S. About a half hour later, Bertie brought out his portable CD player on a very long extension cord (or two cords) from the kitchen, making to set it down on his table, but Belinda told him to put it over on the serving table, instead. He popped in a CD, Gordy's Gold, *and we were provided with background music as we conversed. G.L.'s smooth, catchy tunes created a pleasant atmosphere.*

CHAPTER 23

Dinner-3

Contrary to my expectations (and fears) the party didn't go the route of a typical Mexican party, after-all. This was partly due to the fact that nobody else arrived; and partly due to the fact that Mike and Paula left "early"—that is, at around twelve forty-five. It always seems to be the case, party-wise, that the more people who show up, the longer the party goes on. When, on the other hand, you have a small group of people, like we did, the sooner does everybody go home. This is due, no doubt, to the fact that at large gatherings, if one or two people leave early, it hardly makes a dent in the proceedings; but if the same thing happens at a small, more intimate gathering, it can produce a domino effect, "Well, I guess it's about time I be going to," and so on. In our situation, it was this "early" departure of Mike and Paula that started the ball rolling. It certainly took the zing out of the party, speaking for myself. It wasn't long after their departure that we left, too.

Mike let out a big yawn. "Well, this has really been swell—so swell I feel it's time to call it a night. Don't wanna spoil a good thing."

"What?" Belinda exclaimed.

"No, really, I've got a lot to do tomorrow. Best be gettin' on home now." Mike rose slowly to his feet. He suddenly looked like the old man that he was. Turning to Belinda and Bertie, he said, "Thanks for everything."

Belinda looked somewhat taken aback, but politely replied, "Anytime, Mike. Drive carefully."

Mike made no reply.

Bertie spoke up, "Let me show you to the door, Mike," and he rose to do so.

"Nice to meet you, Paula," Mike said with a smile.

"Nice to meet *you*, Mike," she said, smiling back.

Evelyn, smiling, spoke for us both, "I hope we see you again, Mike."

"Oh, you will," Mike said seriously. "I'll drop by sometime, or you can always drop in on me."

"It's a deal," I said.

Mike gave a little wave to the Hinojosas, which they returned; then he and Bertie headed (—Mike, a little unsteadily—) for the kitchen door.

Even as they did so, Paula announced that she, too, needed to be going.

"So soon?" Belinda asked, her voice rising.

Paula glanced sharply at her. "It's pretty late for me. I have to get up early tomorrow—I guess it *is* tomorrow!—and start cleaning my apartment. That's how I spend my Saturdays!"

It seemed rather incongruous to imagine such a beautiful young woman with her sleeves rolled up doing such a mundane thing as cleaning her apartment.

"Well, if you have to go, you have to go, I guess," Belinda said, prosaically, like a mother talking to her teenage daughter. Let me show you out." She rose to do so.

Paula rose. "So nice meeting both of you," she said, smiling at us.

"Igualmente" ("The same to you"), said Evelyn, returning her smile.

"Igualmente," I said, smiling as well. For a moment, her dark, glowing eyes lingered on mine. Then, like Mike, she gave a little wave to the Hinojosas, adding, with a smile, "¡Adiós!" which they responded to by repeating "¡Adiós!" smiling back at her. Belinda then escorted her to the kitchen door, where they almost collided with Bertie coming back outside. Paula and Bertie bid their good-byes, then she and Belinda went through the door.

Bertie resumed his seat, and, in a few minutes, Belinda

hers. Upon sitting down, Belinda almost immediately got into a deep discussion with both Lupe and José, en español, about something. This hadn't been going on long before Bertie got up and, without a word, walked back to the grill, walking right past us as if we were invisible. Thus, Evelyn and I were left to ourselves at our table of (now) two.

Like an old married couple, we know how to "read" each other, without saying a word. Bertie hadn't been at the grill very long before I gave Evelyn a look, which she mimicked back at me. She then announced, "Belinda, I think we better be going, too."

Belinda broke off her conversation to inquire, "What's that, my dear?"

Evelyn repeated, a little more forcibly, "I think we better be going, too."

Belinda looked genuinely surprised. "Oh—no—you don't need to leave yet!"

"Yes," Evelyn said, "I'm afraid we do. I've got a lot to do around the house in the morning. And tomorrow afternoon, we may be going to Monterrey."

This was news to me.

" I see," Belinda said, with thinly-veiled disappointment. "Well, here, let me show you out," and she rose to do so. We exchanged good-byes with the Hinjosas, then followed Belinda towards the kitchen door, stopping, momentarily, at the grill to exchange good-byes with Bertie. I noticed that Bertie didn't appear to be doing anything in particular. Once we'd exchanged good-byes with him, Bertie made the parting shot (or stock statement), "Nuestra casa es su casa" ("Our house is your house"), which he said with about as much feeling as a prison warden would to a new inmate.

CHAPTER 24

Heading Back

The streets were almost deserted at this hour, which made it an easy drive home. With all the lights shining along Luis Echeverría freeway, lighting it up like day, it seemed like an awful waste of electricity, with hardly anybody on it—or, rather, it was like the whole freeway was solely lit up for our (and a handful of others') personal convenience. Saltillo, for all its considerable size, is still very much a provincial town, in spirit. People rise and go to be early, unless there's a party to give or attend. Thus, in the wee hours of the morning, as we had, you have the streets and freeway more or less to yourself/yourselves.

We weren't very long on our way before I turned to Evelyn and said, "Well, Evelina, you can't blame me for leaving early. I saw the look on your face."

"No," she said, keeping her eyes on the road, "I saw the look on *your* face. I figured we might as well go. That's why I said that thing about Monterrey."

"I don't wanna split hairs over it, but I think it was a mutual feeling."

She didn't respond to this, for the moment. I said, "Well, Bertie was his usual ever-annoying self. Actually, if you don't take him seriously, he's really kinda comical . . . and the things he says! That remark about the *bride 'n groom* cracked me up!"

"I sense a lot of anger in him, though I can't imagine about what," she said.

"I don't know if it's so much that," I said, "as just the fact that he has a pretty unpleasant personality."

"I'd say that's about the same thing."

"Maybe. I don't know what Belinda sees in him."

"He's not *that* bad," she said strongly, and even a shade sarcastically. "He's just the way he is."

"'He's just the way he is' all right," I said, then added, under my breath, "for a kept man."

"What's that?"

"Nothing." I stared out the side window.

We were silent for a few moments, until Evelyn returned to our previous subject of conversation by saying, "In a way, you're right—I mean, about our leaving. I could've stayed longer, but after Mike and Paula left early it suddenly felt empty."

"That was the thing," I agreed.

"I thought more people'd be there," she continued. "It really wasn't much of a party. You don't know, because you don't speak the language, but the conversations Belinda was having with the Hinojosas were so silly! Mostly, Lupe and José were talking about their new granddaughter and how she had this problem with sucking her thumb, and how she gurgled and burped when they poked her tummy, and how she giggled when they tickled her feet, and a whole salad bowl full of other fascinating facts. I was having a nice time talking to Belinda before *they* showed up . . . It sometimes really irritates me—Mexicans' pathological obsession with their *family*—and everyone in it—like nothing else matters in the whole world . . . They can go on and on and on." She let out a short, bitter laugh. "Babies, babies, and more babies! . . . They should replace the eagle and serpent on the Mexican flag with a baby carriage."

There was a cold sarcasm to her words that kept me from reacting with any amusement towards them, and I only commented, "You and I are alike in that, not having any real interest in children, or in family, like other people—like most people—certainly like most Mexicans. Of course, we both come from small families, and they're all gone—and have been for years. I guess if we'd had children, or even had just one child, we'd feel differently."

"I'm not so sure about that," Evelyn said, staring out at the road. "My grandmother said to me once she wished she'd never had any of her children. Honestly—as I think I've told you—I've never had some big burning desire to have children, like most women. Maybe I'm strange that way."

"I think Paula'd agree with you."

She gave me a suspicious look. "What d'you mean?"

"Well," I replied, matter-of-factly, "a beautiful young woman in her twenties living the life of an independent, single woman in a country where girls a lot younger and a lot less beautiful than her are already married and changing diapers."

"Yes, and I was exactly like her in my twenties, living in Monterrey."

I smiled at her. "And just as beautiful, I'm sure."

"Yes, I was," she said, looking in her side mirror. There was a pause. Then, in a barely audible voice, looking straight ahead, she said, "I wasn't born on a carro de burro (a donkey cart). I saw the way you were looking at her."

"What's that?"

She turned for a moment to look at me, and repeated, more strongly, "I saw the way you were looking at Paula, and she at you."

"I'm sure I don't know what you mean."

"Yes you do."

I looked out the side window. I had this sudden impulse to laugh out loud. "How could I not look at her? She sat right across from me."

"That's not what I mean and you know it."

After a moment, I looked at her, with her profile set like stone, and made the comment, "Do I detect the green-eyed monster?"

"The *what?*"

"That's from Shakespeare. You're jealous—of Paula."

"I'm not jealous of Paula. It's you we're talking about."

I lit up a cigarette, and cracked the window. "I haven't done anything. I've nothing to say." I wanted to stick my head in the sand, like an ostrich.

Evelyn relaxed a bit. "Well, as far as you're concerned, I guess you couldn't help looking at her. No man could. At least you didn't act as ridiculous as Mike. It just makes me close to crazy to even think about you with another woman."

"Then don't think about it."

Evelyn didn't miss the implication of this remark, though I didn't mean it that way. She gave me a hard look for a moment. We were silent for awhile. She drove, and I looked out the side window at the crowded, passing city, thanking my lucky stars that I lived in Lomas. Then, she suddenly laughed lightly to herself.

"What're you laughing at?"

She glanced at me. "Oh, Chrisito . . . you really are such a child—especially when it comes to women." She coughed. "You can't even see it yourself, it seems."

"See *what?*"

"That Paula's attracted to you."

I felt a tingle in my shoulders for a few seconds. "That's ridiculous. I'm old enough to be her father."

Evelyn didn't look at me, but only at the road. "I agree—but trust me. I'm a woman. I know. Some women like older men. Some *prefer* married men. I hate to say this to you—to puff up your ego—but you don't look and act like a man in his sixties—like an old man—like Mike. You look like you're in your middle forties—even a little younger."

"So? I can't help that."

"No, you can't. I'm glad you do, but I need to be careful with you," she said, looking in the rear view mirror.

There seemed to be something slightly sinister (and controlling) in this remark which I couldn't help but resent. "You're just seeing things."

"I certainly am."

"Look—can we just forget this whole conversation! Your imagination needs to wear glasses. I didn't even know Paula *existed* until tonight, and I'll probably never see her again. Why and where would I? In a city of well over a million people . . . and we hardly ever leave Lomas!"

Evelyn rapidly said, "There's Belinda's office."

My jaw stiffened. I kinda (a-la-Cagney) wished I'd had half a grapefruit with me. "Madam, in the whole seven years we've known Belinda I've been to her office once—with you, if you'll remember—to have my birth certificate translated. I can't foresee any reason to ever go there again. And you can put that in your pipe and smoke it!"

Evelyn looked at me for a moment like a child might at the equation, $E=mc2$. I don't know whether or not she was pacified by my words, but she didn't say anymore on the subject for the rest of the drive home.

CHAPTER 25

When I Saw Grandma

I don't know whether or not it was the aftereffects of the alcohol, or whether or not I just felt like livening up a dull auto trip (or both), but I asked Evelyn, when we were about two-thirds of the way home, "Did I ever tell you about the first time I saw a naked—well, nearly naked—woman?" knowing full well I'd never told her a word about it.

"No, you never have," she replied, like the Church Lady. "I swear, I never know what you'll say next."

I let out a chuckle. "It's an interesting story . . . I was eight years old, and was at Grandma and Mort's house in Dallas. The memory's kinda hazy, like in a cloud—with no real beginning or ending—except for its central focus, which is as vivid in my mind today as it was "live" fifty-four years ago. I mean, I don't remember why I was there, just that I was in the central hallway of their ranch style house—perhaps having just come out of, or just going into the middle bathroom—when, looking down the hall, I saw Grandma in the back bedroom, barefoot and in her underwear. At this time, Grandma was in her early fifties. She'd left the bedroom door open. Perhaps she thought I was watching TV in the living room, or playing outside. She (fortunately) didn't see me seeing her. She was only in my line of sight for around ten seconds as she moved about the room getting dressed. She'd come over to get some stockings out of her dresser drawer, and, at this point, only had on a pair of beige, lace-topped, sheer panties and a white corset replete with hooks, straps, and ribbons, the tight corset hugging and pushing her breasts upwards and outwards. She'd obviously not gotten around to doing her hair yet. Grandma always wore it pulled severely back into a snug rear coil (which bore an uncanny resemblance to some of the snakes I'd seen at the Dallas Zoo;) but now, unpinned and liberated, it fell, in a brown cascade, partway down her back, and made her look younger than her years, in spite of the fact that she hadn't gotten around to doing her makeup yet, either. I'd never seen her hair like this before, and had no idea it was so long. I'd also never seen such an outlandish-looking contraption as her corset, and couldn't imagine what its purpose was. It looked very uncomfortable. All in all, it was a true shock and a wide-eyed surprise. I'd never seen a woman half-naked before—even if, as a middle-aged woman, Grandma exhibited a less than perfect body; though she still looked pretty good—shapely—for her age. And this was my *grandmother*, for Pete's sake! Always so prim and proper, who never let liquor touch her lips, who always wore plain, dark dresses—seldom slacks, and certainly never jeans—who never laughed out loud, never gave hugs or kisses, and who'd give me the stare if I absent-mindedly put my elbows on the dinner table, (which was a stare she'd sometimes accompany, unsmilingly, with the rhyme, "Mabel, Mabel, if you're able, keep your elbows off the table.") *This* grandmother was a revelation. There was a sort of wildness about her. What really struck me, though, more than anything else, was the disassociation between a woman's body and her conventional, clothed appearance. There was something strange and exotic, and even a bit frightening about seeing a woman, for the first time, so womanly . . . I'd never look at Grandma in quite the same way again."

"That's some story," Evelyn said—and that's all she said—and no sooner had she said it, than we were at the exit from the freeway to the colony.

CHAPTER 26

Back Home

Once back at the house, we pretty much promptly retired to our rooms. Still a bit keyed-up from the evening, it took me awhile to drop off to sleep. I lay there in bed thinking about the party, about my conversation with Evelyn on the drive home, and about Paula—particularly the latter two. I had to be honest that I hadn't been totally honest with Evelyn, which she probably suspected, anyway. This boy wasn't a complete fool. I did see the way Paula was looking at me—smiling at me—(which was not like any saleswoman, saint, or sister); and it goes without saying, it did warm the cockles of my heart, as they say. I suppose there was also an element of ego in it—an element flattering to my ego—that a gorgeous woman of her age should look in such a way at a man of my age. Her very youth and vitality were like drinking a glass of sparkling champagne after drinking nothing, for ages, stronger than water. There was an attraction there, no doubt about it, (and it was all I could do to keep from looking at her;) but, even so, it didn't mean it would ever lead to anything. In fact, I didn't even want to think along those lines right then (—like Scarlett, I'd "think about that tomorrow"—) and, shutting such thoughts out of my mind, I gradually dropped off to sleep; though, just before doing so, a final thought went through my head, which was actually the quote by the famous old-time actor of stage and screen, John Barrymore, "No man ever thinks he's too old to play Romeo."

P.S. Funny how the only word that rhymes with "cupid" is "stupid."

CHAPTER 27

At The Alameda

The first Monday of the month is the major cleaning day at our house, when Evelyn employs a local Lomas middle-aged housewife/part-time maid, one Pilar Cantú, to clean our house, room by room. Pilar, (with, sad truth to tell, a face that could stop a bus,) is short and stocky, with jet black hair which she keeps cut short in a bowl cut, making her rather resemble, poor soul, Moe of The Three Stooges fame. To her credit, Pilar always launches into her task with gusto (as Evelyn critically supervises); and this industrious enterprise lasts for most of the day, and includes rolling up rugs and taking them outside to scrub with detergent and hose down, cleaning out cupboards, washing walls and baseboards, sweeping and moping every room, (necessitating moving furniture,) deeply dusting shelves, and polishing furniture. To keep Pilar happy, Evelyn usually plays ranchero music for her on her CD/Radio player as Pilar cleans away—music which (for me, at least,) with its standard, repetitive, "cheery" nature becomes really obnoxious after awhile. I'm always so tempted to go change the station. It's a day that I dread. There's no real peace for me anywhere in the house; and it seems that whichever I room I move to, that's the room where Pilar's coming next. What's more, though Pilar's a nice enough woman, she's ignorant as a brick; and, on occasion, she does something that really gets to me. For example, in my bedroom, in my bookshelf, I have my books of literature precisely arranged chronologically, beginning with the ancient Greeks and Romans (in English translation) and continuing up to the 20th century, from Homer to Hemingway, you could say. Well, the first (and last) time that Pilar did a deep cleaning of my bookshelf, she took out and put back these books all out of order, and with many of them upside down, which totally enraged me. I knew she didn't know any English, or history, or literature —or literary history—but it enraged me just the same.

On this particular Monday, following the B&B gala, it being a nice, sunny day, I decided to get away from the house for awhile and leave Evelyn and Pilar to their doings. I called and took a cab from the house to downtown—to the old colonial part of town known as El Centro—specifically to The Alameda Zaragoza park, (universally called simply "La Alameda" by the locals,) where I planned to stroll about and eventually sit down and read a newspaper or a magazine. They're kiosks in the park which sell a nice selection of newspapers and magazines in both Spanish and English. It being a crisp Fall day, I was dressed accordingly in blue jeans, brown loafers, and the same long-sleeved tan shirt that I'd worn to the garden party.

The Alameda is the largest and oldest park in Saltillo. It's in the oldest section of the city, only four short blocks west of The Cathedral Plaza. It's no Central Park, by any means, being maybe a fourth the size of that New York City landmark; but it's still a good size, and makes for a pleasant and peaceful oasis in the midst of the bustling downtown area. It's full of tall, shady trees of every variety—oaks and maples being especially predominate—and many of these thick-trunked trees are very old, going back well over a hundred years. On the other hand, the park is no forest, and spread across it are areas of smooth, grassy lawns, flower beds, and rose gardens. Criss-crossing the park, in every direction, are wide, bush-lined walkways covered with plain, worn, 12 inch tiles of the dull, reddish-orange color which has made "Saltillo Tiles" a byword for tiles the world over. There's not a lot to really do or see in the park, entertainment-wise. It's mainly just a place to relax in (on one of its many black wrought iron benches) and walk around in and enjoy nature (—there're colorful birds everywhere—) though in the southern sector of the park there's a fairly large and famous lake in the shape of The Mexican Republic, bordered by towering palm trees, where you can rent a little boat and paddle about on the water if you like, perhaps alongside some of the quite tame white and yellow-beaked ducks which inhabit the lake.

The long walkways, coming from every direction, inevitably lead into a number of modest, circular plazas spaced out across the park. In the center of each plaza is some sort of fountain or monument, and around its perimeter are the black wrought iron benches. My favorite plaza is the one that's not too far from the southern edge of the park, and is characterized by a faux-Egyptian, slender, white marble obelisk (without any hieroglyphics) rising up some twenty feet in the center of the plaza. This obelisk was, historically-speaking, (so I've read,) a gift to the city of Saltillo from the administration of Mexican President Porfirio Díaz in 1910, given only a couple of months before The Revolution erupted, to honor the one hundred year anniversary/birthday of the Mexican Republic; and it's been standing right where it is ever since. Once I got out of the taxi, I strolled off in the direction of this plaza.

As I approached this plaza at a leisurely pace, at around twelve-thirty, it appeared to be deserted except for someone sitting on one of the black, wrought iron benches, a woman, on the bench just to the right of the incoming walkway. I soon froze in my tracks. The thick, braided, black ponytail and the tortoise shell hairpin. I very stealthily stepped some feet further forward to get a glimpse of her face. The left side of her face, sure enough, it was Paula. She was sitting there reading a book, dressed in a dark brown, short-sleeved dress. For some seconds I stood there as if paralyzed—unsure what to do, advance or retreat? (Actually, it wasn't that much of a struggle.) Finally, assuming a carefree air, I stepped forward and around up to her, saying, as nonchalantly as possible, "Señorita Paula Cuello, I presume?"

She started, and looked up at me—quite surprised, but instantly breaking into a smile. "Ch-Chris! Hello!"

"Buenas tardes" ("Good afternoon").

"Buenas tardes," she replied, after a moment, with mock-solemnity, still smiling at me. "Please—sit down."

I did, a few feet, judiciously, to the right of her.

We both asked, at exactly the same time, "What are you"—then laughed together. I let her complete the question, "What are you doing here?" even as I looked into her beautiful face and noticed that she was wearing the same thin silver necklace with the tiny silver cross around her neck.

"Oh, I decided to get away from the house up in Lomas for awhile. Today's housecleaning day, if you know what I mean."

"Yes."

I elaborated, "When I can—when it's a nice day like today—and I'm not doing much at home, I like to come down here to the park and walk about or sit and read under the trees for awhile, and watch the people passing by. Even take a break from Evelyn for awhile." I smiled. "For some reason, this particular plaza's never very crowded, and I can always get a seat here. And you—what brings you here?"

"Like you, I like this plaza. It's never crowded. It's also the closest one in the park to Belinda's office. My lunch time's from twelve to two; and I sometimes come here to eat my lunch and read for awhile, if it's a nice day. Today, I don't have any lunch; but I thought I'd sit and read for awhile before going back to my apartment to fix myself something. My apartment's only a few blocks away." She made the last remark quite casually, as if she were merely talking about the weather.

"What's that you're reading?" I asked.

She gave me a look that bordered on embarrassment. Then, instead of answering me, she somewhat hesitantly simply handed the book to me. It was a small, hardbound book, covered in a plain, sea green cloth, looking neither old nor new. I opened it to the title page to read, *Los Poemas de Manuel Acuña* (*The Poems of Manuel Acuña*). I didn't know quite what to say. I made a show of thumbing through the pages, for some moments, as she observed me; but I wasn't seeing anything (—it was all in Spanish, anyway—) no, I was really thinking to myself that there was more to this young woman than met the eye, (and *that* was a lot.) Reading a book of poems—of all things!—not some silly romance or some trashy tabloid. And *serious* poems! I was familiar with Manuel Acuña, probably Saltillo's most famous native son, who has a whole plaza named after him not far from The Cathedral Plaza, and only blocks from where we were sitting. I'd heard about his tragic life, and how he'd committed suicide over some woman when he was in his twenties, way back when, in the 19th century. Actually, I did notice one thing as I thumbed through the pages, even if I didn't know what it meant, on one page there were two stanzas of a poem underlined in pencil. Finally, I couldn't resist asking Paula, "You really enjoy reading this?"

"Yes, I do," she said with conviction.

"Manuel Acuña . . . I've heard about him. I guess he's about the most famous person to have ever come from Saltillo."

"Probably so," she agreed.

"I've always been meaning to read some of his poems, but have never gotten around to it. I guess I could get some of them in an English translation somewhere . . . maybe on the internet."

"I'm sure you could."

Turning to that page, I said, "I see that some lines from one of his poems here are underlined. Did you do that?"

"Yes. They're my favorite lines of his."

I instinctively sensed that Paula was reluctant to go any further, but, seeing the question on my face, she plunged ahead, "They're from one of his most famous poems, *"Adiós a,"* which, in English, would be "Good-bye To." He's complaining about his—his—well, in English, I don't think you really have a word for it. It's not like only his "girlfriend" or "sweetheart"—it's more than that. It's like what you say in Spanish is his "enamorada"—like his "great love." He's anticipating her leaving him forever; and he compares her to a bird flying away." She gave me a serious, but also shy look. "I can do something for you, Chris, if you'd like me to. Give me back the book. I will read the lines to you in Spanish, then give you the English translation, as best as I can."

"OK." I handed her back the book, with the book open to that page. She read,

> "Después es necesario
> que tú también te alejes
> en busca de otras torres
> y de otro cielo en pos.
>
> Que te alces de tu nido
> que te alces y me dejes,
> sin escuchar mis ruegos
> y sin decirme adiós."

She paused. "In English, it would be,

> Then you must also
> leave me
> in search of other bowers,
> and in search of other skies.
>
> For you will arise from your nest,
> will arise and leave me,
> not hearing my pleas,
> or telling me good-bye."

She closed the book and asked me, as if she was asking an invisible person standing in front of her, "What's your opinion?"

I looked down at my hands. "Hmmm . . . It's not exactly 'all's well that ends well,' is it?"

She let out the slightest laugh. "No, it isn't!"

"I like the line, 'in search of other skies.' I've been doing that all my life."

"So have I—so have I," she said in a diminishing voice.

I looked at her, smiling. "Paula, may I ask you something of a personal nature?"

She arched her eyebrows. "You may."

"Is that your favorite passage because it means something special to you?" I instantly regretted having asked her. She gave me a stony look, and said nothing. I was about to say something when, all of a sudden, two mockingbirds fell out of the trees together from somewhere overhead onto the tiled pavement in front of the obelisk, (as if they were violently thrown down there,) and proceeded to get into a horrible fight, viciously jabbing at each other with their beaks, wildly flapping their wings, and erratically rolling around on top of each other like a rolling, gray and black ball. Oddly enough, they didn't make a sound, except for the wild flapping of their wings. This continued for some seconds, until they just as suddenly broke apart, stepped proudly about a foot away from each other (while looking straight at each other), then abruptly up and flew off, at the same time, in different directions.

"Talk about two angry mockingbirds!" I exclaimed. "Mother o' Mary! . . . Have you ever read the book, *To Kill A Mockingbird*, or seen the movie?"

"No," she replied, as if regretting the fact.

"Well, it's considered a sin to kill a mockingbird; but I think they're perfectly capable of killing each other."

She gave me a knowing look. "And why's it considered a sin?"

"Because they do nothing but sing their little hearts out for everybody's enjoyment, and do no harm to any living creature."

"And you agree with that?"

"No, I don't. When I was a child, living in Dallas, they used to dive-bomb (—seeing her look, I added, "you know, like a descending fighter plane"—making a quick swooping motion with my right arm—) if I ever happened to come anywhere near their nests. They've been known to actually injure cats and squirrels. They're pretty aggressive birds."

As if none of this "mockingbird talk" had ever occurred, Paula gave me an engaging smile, (so that she looked at her most beautiful,) slightly cocked her head to the left, and asked me sweetly, "Chris, you haven't had lunch yet, have you?"

"No, I haven't."

"Neither have I. I have a suggestion to make. My apartment's very close by. If you're in no hurry, why don't you let me fix lunch for us both, before I have to go back to work."

There was something about the way she said this that made my refusing her out of the question, which, perhaps, says more about me than Paula. "Why, thank-you, Paula! That's very nice of you. I am kinda hungry." I stood up. Extending my right arm, I exclaimed, "Lead the way!" Even as Paula stood up herself, I noticed, for the first time, that the clear, bright sky was beginning to cloud over a little.

CHAPTER 28

Into Paula's Apartment

We made our way out of the park, talking mainly about the garden party. Paula's apartment was, sure enough, close-by, only two blocks south of the park, down Bulevar Carlos Salazar (Carlos Salazar Boulevard), a street I'd never been more than a little ways down before. Proceeding down this street, we took a left at the second narrow side street, Calle Luis Gutiérrez, and her apartment was on the left in about the middle of the first block. I'd never been in this neighborhood before. Actually, to the eye, you'd never guess there were any apartments here, as apartments go. Not only this block, but all the blocks down Luis Gutiérrez, as far as you could see, in either direction, comprised nothing but a monotonous extension of solid cement, mostly two-story row houses, on both sides of the street, generally of a dull white color, and with very little exterior decorations, like balconies or columns or whatnot; and the houses butted right up against the sidewalk. The main and immediate impression they made on me was that they were of great age and great heaviness. As if to accentuate the former, a number of the houses had their apparently original, thick, wooden front doors (going back God knows how far,) which, unpainted, weather-beaten, and heavily-grained, (some with little holes in them, here and there,) looked so old that they looked like they'd fall right off their hinges if you made to open them. Paula's apartment house was a good example. It's ancient, brownish, bare front door, which looked like it might have come off of Santa Ana's outhouse, had a big, rusting, iron keyhole. I couldn't help but stare as Paula pulled an old, pretty enormous iron key out of her black purse with her right hand and, with a little effort, unlocked the door. Once we were inside, she immediately locked it again.

We were now in a little foyer whose walls and ceiling were painted a very pale (or very old) blue. The floor was bare cement. Immediately before us was a narrow cement staircase flanked, on each side, by a short aisle leading to the two downstairs apartments, one on each side. Though the sides of the staircase were of the same pale blue color, the steps themselves, like the floor, were just bare cement. The staircase, which contained no handrails, didn't go up very far—maybe twenty steps—before it ended at a cement landing, its sides also pale blue, which extended from wall to wall in about the middle (both vertically and horizontally) of the foyer. This landing was bordered, on each side, by a black iron railing, with each individual, twisting rail sporting a ping pong ball-size, white porcelain ball in its center. As I approached the landing up the steps right behind Paula, I saw that there was one maroon door on the left and one maroon door on the right. Paula simply opened the door on the right and we entered her apartment. This surprised me. As we entered the apartment, I commented, "You don't lock your door?"

"No," she replied, "I know all the neighbors. That front door's enough. I think it'd take a cannonball to get through it."

I let out a laugh. "What a nice apartment!"

"Thanks. I guess you're the first real man to ever be up here."

There was a somewhat creepy ambiguity to this remark, it seemed to me, which left me speechless, so I didn't say anything. It'd been years—since I was in college—that I'd been invited into a single girl's apartment; and I immediately felt a little awkward, like I didn't quite know where to "place" myself, or what to do. There was a sudden, loud, sharp "crackle" outside, for a second. Paula went over to the window and looked up and down the street, but apparently it was nothing. She made no comment about it, but, coming back to where she'd left me standing, near the door, and setting her purse down on the coffee table, (and perhaps sensing my awkwardness,) said, "I need to go to my bedroom for a minute. Why don't you sit down on the sofa, Chris, and relax. I'll be right back." She tossed me a smile, then disappeared down a hallway.

I sat down on the sofa—a simple, plump, double-cushioned piece of work, covered in brown cloth. In fact, "simple" was a good word for the whole apartment, or for what I could see of it from the sofa, to the left of the front door. Against the wall opposite me was the TV on a (tacky) brass-barred "TV table" (looking like it came right out of the 1950s,) with a DVD player on its single lower shelf. To the right of it was a pine bookcase of four shelves, maybe five feet high. Across the large room, a small, round, pine table and four matching, armless, slat-back chairs were set up in front of the fairly large window looking onto the street below and across the rooftops in this section of the city. To my left was a hallway which obviously led to the bedroom and, I assumed, the kitchen and bathroom. The walls and ceiling (of cement) were all white, and the floor was covered with the aforementioned Saltillo tiles; though, if anything (and paradoxically) they were of an even duller reddish-orange color than those in The Alameda. And that was about it, except for some nondescript pictures on the walls—well, with one exception, on the wall over the sofa there was a framed picture-poster of Vincent Van Gogh's famous colorful and magical "Starry Night" painting. The glass-topped, redwood coffee table in front of me contained some magazines and some knick-knacks, the most conspicuous one being a rearing glass horse on a square, black onyx pedestal, in the center of the table, maybe six inches high. It was very realistically and beautifully carved—especially its long, flowing mane.

Paula was gone for more than a minute. Out of curiosity, I got up and went over to the bookcase to have a look-see. The two bottom shelves were filled with various objects—women things, like a collection of music boxes, and painted china figurines of cats, birds, and ballerinas, and whatever—but the two top shelves were filled with books. I saw immediately, by their spines, that they were all in Spanish, with the exception of five books in English, here and there, (which, to me, really stuck out from the rest,) which were, *A Christmas Carol, John Lennon, The Lone Star State, The Poems of Emily Dickinson,* and *The Old Man and the Sea.*

I was about to take out and take a look at *The Lone Star State* when Paula reappeared from down the hallway. "Well, I'm back!" she exclaimed, smiling. I noticed right away that though she was basically dressed the same, she'd taken off her flesh-colored stockings and black pumps and was now wearing a pair of brown sandals prettily decorated with a row of alternating white and azure rhinestones across their single bridge. Noticing this, I also couldn't help but notice that on the right side of her right leg, a few inches above her ankle, there was a small, very red tattoo of a heart with a black arrow piercing it diagonally downward, from left to right. Her bare lower legs, though quite shapely, as a mature woman's legs, still also looked somewhat like those of a young girl. She came up to where I was standing and said, "I see you've been looking at my books."

"Yes," I replied, "I was just curious."

"There're some in English in there."

"I see that." I really wanted to change the subject, and said, sort of surveying the room, "You've got a nice place here, Paula—lots of light—and (stepping a little in that direction) a great view of the city. Just the thing for such an attractive single girl as yourself!" I gave her a smile and couldn't believe I'd actually said that. Man, I was as bad as Mike.

She looked archly at me. Then, in a flash, she became serious for a moment as she glanced at the little cuckoo clock on the wall over the bookcase. "One twenty-five. I need to fix our lunch . . . Do you like quesadillas?" she asked me brightly.

She seemed so intent on pleasing me. It was touching. "I love quesadillas!" which seemed to make her even brighter. (For those who don't know, quesadillas are two flour tortillas with cheese in-between, warmed up until the cheese melts, and often, then, sliced into triangular slices.)

"They're quick to make in the microwave. And I have some cokes, and I think"—

"Paula, just some water'll be fine."

"I have some bottled water."

"That's perfect."

"OK. Just give me a few minutes."

"Can I be of any assistance?"

"Oh no," she said, in a bashful manner. "You just stay right here." As if on an impulse, she stepped over and, pulling *The Lone Star State* out of the bookcase, she handed it to me with the words, "Here's a book in English about Texas with pictures maybe you'd like to look at. You can sit down here on the sofa." She made this last remark in a rather commanding tone which made me smile inwardly. "I'll be back with the lunch soon," and she disappeared down the hallway again.

I sat down on the sofa again, but didn't look at the book, after-all—at least, not then. Placing the book on the coffee table, I got up and went over to look out the window. It was quite a view over the flat, mostly white roofs of houses and buildings stretching all the way to the blue mountains on the horizon. The view itself was grand, even if the view of the city from here wasn't very interesting, it being nothing but a "sea of roofs," more or less, except for some exceptions, in the middle distance, on the left, two modern, twin, bluish glass office buildings/towers rose up into the sky, looking very out of place; in the middle distance, on the right, there was a wide-footed radio tower of alternating sections of red and white (which, if not for these bright colors, would've been ugly;) and in the center distance, almost to the slopes of the Sierras, two white, triple-decked, Spanish baroque bell towers of some church soared up above the low-slung town; but the church was so faraway that they looked like toy towers. I also noticed that, to the south, the sky was a long, darkening cloud mass above the mountains in that direction, meaning (I figured) that Lomas was about to be hit by rain. No sooner had I "figured this" than I heard a low rumble of thunder coming from that direction. Well, it would be good for the garden.

I went back over and sat down on the sofa again. I picked up *The Lone Star State*, and hadn't been looking at it for very long, when Paula reappeared carrying a large plate of quesadilla slices and napkins in her right hand, and a bottled water in her left. She set them down on the coffee table—said, "Let me just get my water"—and disappeared again. Presently, she reappeared; but just at that moment there was an extended, rolling peal of thunder in the distance, loud enough to be almost startling. She shot me a glance/smile, then detoured over to look out the window, setting her water down on the dining room table. After a few seconds, she said, "Chris, come over here a moment." I did. "Look at that," she said, nodding towards the south. I did. The sky over the mountains was no longer as dark as it had been; rather, a long, solid sheet of grayish rain, looking like a tremendous curtain, completely obscured the mountains, and looked like it was more or less stalled in that area. More rolls of thunder, which weren't deafening, by any means, but were still fairly loud. Suddenly, there was a long, bright yellow flash of lightening, looking like a great, jagged rip in the "curtain," gone about the second it appeared. "Wow!" I exclaimed. This was followed, after maybe ten seconds, by a booming roll of thunder.

"That's where you live, isn't it?" Paula asked.

"Yes."

Looking at my empty shirt pockets, she inquired, "Do you need to call home? You can use the phone in my bedroom. I don't have a cell phone." (I *had* left my cell phone at the house.)

"No, it's nothing," I assured her. "We get rain like that all the time." This was a lie. A thunderstorm of this magnitude was a rarity up in Lomas.

"I hope it doesn't come down here," she said concernedly. "I have to walk back to work . . . Maybe I'll have to take a taxi."

I looked up at the sky. It was clouding over. "It's hard to tell . . ."

She looked into my eyes for a moment with a particularly searching and even sultry look (—"My God," I thought, "she really *is* beautiful"—) then, looking away, said, matter-of-factly, "We need to eat." Giving me a sideways glance, she said, "Come, Chris!" She grabbed her water, and I followed her back over to the sofa.

CHAPTER 29

Lunch With Paula

Taking slices of quesadillas on our napkin, and sipping our water, we proceeded to eat our lunch. We chatted about different things. Being only a two-sectional sofa, Paula sat pretty close to me, and for the first time that afternoon, I detected the faint fragrance of her perfume, which rather reminded me of sweet peaches. Perhaps she'd put some on when she'd gone to her bedroom.

It was a novel experience for me. It wasn't that I'd never been alone with a young, attractive, single girl before, but, as I've said, it had been so many years ago that it virtually seemed like a whole new experience for me, and a very delightful one. Paula's great beauty, together with her intelligence for one so young, made me feel special just to be in her private company—and, in my case, at my age, very special. On the other hand, it puzzled me, and also intrigued me, (not that I was complaining.) Why? Why me? I'd met any number of "pretty señoritas" in Saltillo; and, though always nice and considerate towards me, there had never been the slightest interest shown towards me on any personal level by any of them, even though I might have sort of wished there had been. Perhaps I had a too low opinion of myself. Perhaps Paula saw some quality in me I couldn't see. Perhaps, as an "educated gringo," I was a novelty to her. Perhaps she was lonely, (though I found this hard to believe; but then, we always think attractive people never are.) Perhaps she just *liked* me. Still, why was such an extraordinarily beautiful young woman in her twenties still single and, apparently, had nobody else?

Don't ask me how I knew (or sensed) that she had nobody else, but I did. She hadn't brought up Evelyn's name once the whole afternoon, except indirectly, by implication, when she asked me if I wanted to call home. She knew very well I was married, and had been for years; yet, here I was, by her own invitation, sitting close to her, and there was a subtle electricity flowing between us. Perhaps more to the point, I found myself slowly, and even inevitably, being drawn to her. It was kinda scary, in its own way; and it made me feel, sitting there alone with her in her apartment, like I was a bird out on a limb, being watched over and waited for by an expectant cat. Perhaps that's not a very good comparison; and is being unjust to Paula; but it expresses, I think, the way I felt. Evelyn was right.

While these things were going through my head (and heart), I attempted to make light conversation as we ate our lunch. I mentioned that I'd noticed the book *John Lennon* in her bookshelf, and asked her, "So, you've read all of that book?"

"Pretty much." She said this somewhat self-effacingly.

"You like The Beatles—their music?"

"Very much."

"What's your favorite song of theirs?"

Without any hesitation, she answered, "The Long and Winding Road."

I thought this was a curious—even an odd—favorite, but only said, "Really?"

"Yes." She then immediately asked me, "What's yours?"

I hesitated. "There're so many great songs . . . I guess maybe "Penny Lane," or "I Feel Fine". . . and I like a lot of their single work, too, like Harrison's "What Is Life." Their music'll live forever."

"I guess that really is the music of your youth—of your time. I mean, for me, I just like it."

I gave her a look. What a perceptive comment! "Yes, you've no idea . . . Back in the 60s, every new album of theirs was a major cultural event. How we used to rush down to the music store! I don't think there's ever been anything like it since, or ever will be again."

There was another long roll of thunder in the distance, louder than previously. Though we both naturally heard it, neither of us commented on it, though I did notice that the light outside seemed to be growing darker.

"I could tell you"—I said, but dropped it.

"Tell me what?"

I gave her a small smile. Actually, I was starting to feel ambivalent about all this "Beatle talk." It suddenly seemed silly. This was 2015, and here I was discussing The Beatles with a girl who hadn't even been born until twenty years (or more) after the group had disbanded. And how did that make *me* look? "I was gonna tell you a little Beatles' story—but maybe we don't have the time. It must be getting on to two."

"Just forget about that," she said, with some impatience, as if getting back to work was the last thing on her mind. She gave me a sort of "sweet 'n serious" smile, and said, "I just love listening to you talk, Chris. Please tell me the story."

"Well," I began, "I guess many people from my generation have a Beatles' story to tell. Here's mine—though it doesn't directly concern me. It was in the Fall of 1964. I was only eleven years old and wasn't much into The Beatles yet; though I would very much be three years later with the release of *Sergeant Pepper*. (It's funny, when I listen to *Sergeant Pepper* today, some of the songs seem rather forced and mechanical, even though it's still a great album.) I was growing up with my mother and older sister, Carol, in the little rental house we lived in in the Oak Cliff section of Dallas. Carol was a devoted Beatles fan. Yes, in January of that year, all of her Elvis Presley pictures in their place of honor on the wall over her bed had been discarded for those of the Fab Four. In fact, I'll never forget that night of nights when The Beatles first appeared on The Ed Sullivan Show in February of '64. It was their first appearance on American TV and really, in effect, their introduction to America. They weren't unknown, though, their records (and faces) had gone before them; and a great army of teenage girls from all over America tuned in that night with hearts pounding with anticipation to see them singing and playing *live* for the first time. Carol was no exception. I can still see her, sweet fifteen, sitting Indian style, in blue jeans and a pink sweater, on the living room floor right in front of our black and white TV—totally transfixed—so thrilled that she barely showed it—watching John, Paul, George, and Ringo singing and playing away as if she were witnessing The Second Coming of Christ." Paula laughed. "Later on, in November of that year, as part of their '64 American Tour, The Beatles made their one and only stop in Dallas, at the old Memorial Coliseum in downtown Dallas, torn down years ago. Of course, Carol went; but she did so with my mother, who said, "I'm not about to let you attend such an *orgy* all by yourself." She, perhaps inadvertently, used that very word in front of us at the dinner table; and, though I had no idea what the word meant, (nor, I'm sure, did Carol,) there was something about the way she said it—or stressed it—that didn't sound good. When I asked her, "What's an orgy?" she replied stiffly, "Never you mind."

"It was strange, but after they'd returned home from the concert, and all the next day, Carol said very little about it. I do remember her making one observation. She said, "It was the most unbelievable thing I've ever gone through." Carol was a rather reserved and not a very communicative person, normally; and my impression was that it was such an overwhelming experience for her that she couldn't find the words to describe it. My mother, though, talked about it readily enough. She told me she remembered when *she* was a teenager, in the early 40s, going once to see a young Frank Sinatra in concert—back when he was the slick heartthrob of America—and how many of the girls in the audience went nuts; but she said that was *nothing* compared to this. She told me the coliseum was packed to the rafters, and that the crowd was relatively quiet until the emcee announced, "And now—The Beatles!" When the Beatles ran out onto the stage in their monkey suits, she said, the whole place erupted, and a roar of screaming started and continued, without letup, until the end of the show, with girls jumping up and down in their seats, pulling their hair, crying tears of joy, and screaming out the names of John, Paul, George, and Ringo. She said it was really pretty frightening; and that she herself felt, sitting there "as your sister's mother" in the middle of the arena, among all the pandemonium, like a nurse on a battlefield. I asked her how Carol had acted; and she said Carol was thrilled and excited, but was as much in shock as her at the rest of the crowd. Music-wise, she said it wasn't much of a concert because you really couldn't hear or enjoy any of the songs too well for all the constant, wild screaming. I asked her if any of the individual Beatles said anything to the audience. She replied that John said, at the very beginning, "Hello, Dallas!"—but that after that, he couldn't have said anymore. Many years later, after Carol had been divorced for some years, I stopped by her house in Dallas one Saturday afternoon to visit her. Cindy, my niece—her only child—was off with her high school friends somewhere, and it was just the two of us in the house. We sat at the kitchen table and got into reminiscing about old times over iced tea and delicious chocolate chip cookies which Carol had baked herself. By and by, the subject of that concert came up, and I asked Carol to tell me about it again—not that she'd told me hardly anything about it, in the first place. This time, though, she went into a little more detail—a little more rather boring detail. At length, I asked her, like an overly inquisitive reporter, "But what did it feel like? What was it *really like* seeing The Beatles?" She gave me a penetrating look for a couple of moments, then replied, totally uncharacteristically for her, "It was like 10,000 teenage girls all having screaming orgasms all at the same time, that's what it was 'really like.'"

Paula looked at me with wide-open eyes and with her mouth half-open. I suddenly felt a bit like a dirty old man. I said, apologetically, "Lo siento, Paula. There was no need for me to tell you that." A horn honked down on the street.

"No, no—that's all right," she said quietly. "That's a

wonderful story. I wish I'd been there."

I didn't really hear her. Glancing at her tiny cross, I said, "I've forgotten, I guess, how to act around a young woman such as yourself . . . I've never told that story to anybody—not even to Evelyn."

"I'm glad you told me."

"Are you?"

"Yes, I am." She gave me a frank smile. After a moment, she asked me, "And your sister, Carol—she's still living in Dallas?"

"No, she died about twelve years ago from cancer, quite unexpectedly."

"Oh. I'm sorry to hear that."

"Yes, and two years after her, my mother died. My father's been dead for years. I don't wanna sound morbid, but his ashes were scattered over the Shenandoah River in the Shenandoah Valley of Virginia, one of the most truly beautiful places I've ever seen. It should be on everyone's list of the *100 Places to Visit Before You Die*, in my opinion." I looked down. "They're all gone now." Suddenly feeling sorry for myself, I added, "Gone, as well, are any friends I ever had, my career, and so much else . . . You don't understand, Paula. You can't. You're too young. Lucky you! You're fresh. You have your whole life in front of you. Mine's all behind me, with the added burden of all my memories. You can't imagine what that means." I let out a quick laugh. "Yes, a life left to just tending the vines and roses." I added, as an afterthought, "When you don't have much of a present, you don't have much of a future."

"But you have Evelyn."

"Yes, I have her."

"And now, I hope, you have me."

I gave her a long look, like a nervous bridegroom might look at his soon wife-to-be comin' down the aisle. She calmly met my gaze with the trace of a smile. It was like they say in the melodramas, "a look that seemed like an eternity." Her killer beauty was like some kind of power. She reached over and took my hand in hers—or, rather, rested her right hand on top of my left one, even as we continued to gaze into each other's eyes.

Talk about melodramatic! At that very moment, believe it or not, there was an extremely bright flash of lightening right outside, which quite startled us, and caused her to back her hand away. This was followed, a few seconds later, by a terrific thunderclap. We got up and went over to the half-open, horizontally-sliding window. Through this window the faint but pungent smell of tortillas, with a smell like dark toast, drifted into the room from a tortilla maker's shop occupying the first floor of the house to the left, right next door. Also, reaching up almost to the window, just below us, was a tall and thick bougainvillea bush, which hugged the wall, and whose many, many big, bright, vivid purple blossoms, as delicate as if they were cellophane, almost hurt the eyes to look at. I heard a low, trembling buzz, and, looking down, saw an iridescent hummingbird darting from one blossom to another, sipping the nectar with its needle-like beak, at the top of the plant. "Look," I said to Paula, "a hummingbird!" After sipping maybe the third blossom, it drew away a foot or so and halted, in a holding pattern, in mid-air like a tiny helicopter for a few seconds, then took off like a shot arrow and vanished from view. "Yes, they seem to like that bougainvillea" was Paula's only comment. The sky was uniformly gray now, extending all the way to the mountains. It was the same to the south, where the rain appeared to have played itself out. Gray though the sky may have been, the view was as clear as could be, as far as you could see, in whichever direction. On the other hand, there was an ominous silence in the air which you could almost feel, that reminded me of how deathly quiet and still it would become outside in Texas when there was a tornado coming your way. After about a minute or so, as we stood there, the whole sky before us suddenly opened up and rain loudly poured down in torrents, accompanied by more thunder and flashes of lightening here and there. The wind also picked up.

CHAPTER 30

Belinda Calling

Paula slid the window nearly shut, as the rain was sort of obliquely spraying, through the screen, into the dining room. It was like the whole apartment was under siege from the hard rain, particularly as it made a relentless, dull roar as it pounded on the roof. Paula said, "Just a second," and went over and glanced at the cuckoo clock, returning to say, with a long face, "It's two-ten. I don't remember that clock striking two—do you?"

"No. I don't think it did."

"That's something else I'll have to get fixed, I guess." These words were no sooner out of her mouth than the phone rang, sounding faraway against the pounding rain. She went back to her bedroom to answer it.

I remained where I was by the window, looking out glumly at the strong downpour, which showed no signs of letting up. Glum as I felt, superficially, deep inside, it was like I was lit up by a warm light. I couldn't help but sense the contrast. Normally, for sure, looking out at such a glum sight would've made me feel nothing but just that, glum; but this feeling was now counter-balanced by a sort of newfound joy that made the rain, though still a melancholy sight, a rather inconsequential one. Paula had reached over and placed her hand on mine, and I had let her. The bridge had been crossed, for better or worse. Not that anything had really happened. Still, the bridge had been crossed.

Paula came back and up to me to say, seriously, "I have to go back to work—*now*. That was Belinda. She wanted to know where I was. She wants me back there now—rain or no rain. She says there's an important translation she wants me to get right onto—that has to be finished this afternoon, as soon as possible."

She looked down at the street for a few seconds. "There're always taxis on that street, even in the worst weather." She was thoughtful for a few moments. "What we can do is take a taxi down there. You can come along with me to the office. You can get out and say hi to Belinda if you like, or take the taxi on home, or wherever you want. How does that sound? Unless you'd like to take your own taxi?"

"No, no—that sounds fine—only I won't get out and say hi to Belinda. You and I walking into her office together?"

Paula let this sink in for a couple of moments. Giving me a knowing smile, she said, "Oh, I see what you mean. OK, we'll do it that way. Let me just get my purse. There's an umbrella around here somewhere we can share. . ."

Before she could move away, I said, "Paula!"

She looked into my eyes. "Yes?"

"When will we see each other again?"

She looked smilingly at me, with a warm and open look, like a woman might look at a man who's just presented her with a bouquet of red roses. "Whenever you want to, Chris."

"How about this Thursday, same time, same place—at the obelisk."

She considered this for a moment, then said firmly, out of her smile, "I'll be there."

"If it happens to be raining, expect me around the same time down there at the old door."

"OK." She looked past me, for a moment, at the pouring rain, then said, "Come—we need to go." She turned and walked over to the coffee table as I followed her, picked up her purse, and switched off the ceiling light. Then, exclaiming, "Oh, just a second!" she disappeared down the hallway. I remained standing by the coffee table. She returned, shortly, carrying a black umbrella in her right hand, her black purse having slid down to her right elbow.

She walked past me to the door, opened it, and we were out of the apartment.

CHAPTER 31

So

Nobody loves their neighbor.
Very few people know who they are, what they really want, why they exist, or where they're going.
God isn't dead, Man is.

CHAPTER 32

The Days Before Thursday

Naturally, once back home, I mentioned nothing about my meeting or lunch with Paula to Evelyn, merely telling her that I'd sat in the park reading until the rain forced me to take a taxi home. The fact that she accepted this explanation without any comment (—not that she had any reason to doubt it—) made me feel ashamed of myself for so smoothly telling such a lie. Still, I could hardly tell her the truth, unless I wanted nothing more to do with Paula—but I *did*—that was the whole thing. Sure, we'd "held hands." Big deal, that was nothing, really. The bridge may have been crossed; but it was still totally possible to retreat back across it if I wanted to; except I didn't want to. At the same time, to carry this "bridge" metaphor a little further, I may have crossed the bridge, but I was walking into a minefield. I was a married man, married to a very married woman; and I couldn't forget the conversation I'd had with Evelyn on the drive home from the garden party. Like a hound dog, she was already "on the scent"; and it'd be impossible for Paula and I to "play the fox" for long, that was certain. I recalled, with a shudder, what Evelyn had told me once (and, I was sure, still absolutely maintained,) "If I ever catch you with another woman—that's *it*—you're history." Even logistically, just seeing Paula presented me with all kinds of problems. What's more—and most importantly—I felt bad—very bad—about doing anything to jeopardize my marriage, in which I was relatively contented. I'd never been unfaithful to Evelyn in twenty-two years, and had never seriously wanted to "trip the light fantastic"; but it was like I couldn't help myself—like I was bewitched or something. In short, I felt very conflicted. What I needed was someone to talk to about it, an "understanding ear." I decided to go and talk to Mike.

At Mike's House

On Tuesday afternoon, around three-thirty, as Evelyn was doing the ironing in her bedroom, I told her I was going to visit Mike for awhile. "Have a good time," she said. I didn't dress up for the occasion, which is of no importance when it comes to hanging around with Mike, but just wore the everyday clothes I already had on, blue jeans and a long-sleeved, brown shirt. I didn't call Mike first, but simply showed up at his front door, figuring he'd be there. He was; and he answered my knock on the door with a grin, and invited me in. By an odd coincidence, Mike was dressed virtually like me, in blue jeans and a long-sleeved brown shirt which was just a fraction of a shade lighter than mine, so that we looked, apparel-wise, almost like twins, with the only noticeable difference being that if I looked like my clothes came not too long ago from maybe Walmart, Mike's looked like his came from the Salvation Army—or, to put it another way, they looked like my clothes after wearin' 'n washin' for a couple of years. By another odd coincidence, we both had on black tennis shoes.

Mike invited me in, and then out again, that is, we passed through his small living room and out a sliding glass door onto his patio, which consisted of a cement slab—maybe ten feet by ten feet—surrounded by a bare pine fence, like Belinda and Bertie's, some five feet high. The fence was right at and almost touching the edge of the slab, so that there was no ground or a blade of grass within the precinct of the patio; though there were four large, plain clay pots in the patio's four corners, each one sporting a fairly big and multi-blooming red geranium. In the center of the patio there stood a black, round, wrought iron table with four accompanying chairs, identical to the tables and chairs at the garden party. On the table, in front of the right-hand chair, there was about a half-full glass of beer, a can of Tecate to the right of it, and a crossword puzzle book and a pencil to the left of it.

As we'd passed through the living room, I'd said, "I just thought I'd drop by and chat for awhile, Mike, if that doesn't take you away from something," to which he'd replied, "Not at all. I wasn't doing anything." Now, I said, looking down at the table, "I didn't know you were into crossword puzzles, Mike."

"Yes, I like to sit out here on the patio and work on them," he replied. "It relaxes me. I'd just poured out my beer, and was about to start in, when I heard your knock on the door."

"Oh—well—I'm sorry"—

"No, no—think nothing of it. They can wait. Would you like a beer?"

"Sure."

"Pull up a chair. I'll be right back."

I sat down in the chair to the left of Mike's, with my back to the door.

Mike returned soon with a beer and a glass, set them down before me, and sat down himself. He immediately topped off his beer, then set the empty can down in front of me with the words, "I know you smoke. You can use that as an ashtray."

"Oh, thanks." I popped the top on my Tecate and poured some into my glass. As the foam was flattening out, Mike leaned back in his chair and asked me, "So—what's up?"

Maybe it was just my imagination, but Mike looked at me with the slightest smile, as if he already divined what I was going to say.

"Well, Mike, I especially dropped by because I wanted to talk over something with you." I took a sip of my beer.

"That so? Anything you want to talk about, I'm all ears!" He took a sip of his beer.

I asked him, "You remember the garden party the other night?"

"Of course."

"Well, you'll also remember who all was there—especially Paula."

He smiled at me with his eyes through his black horn-rimmed glasses. "Oh yes, I remember especially Paula. How could I not? How could any man?"

"Yes—well—that's what I wanted to talk about."

"What? Paula?"

"Yes."

"What about her? You like her? That's no news to me. I saw the way the two of you were looking at each other."

It was like Mike had instantly taken all the wind out of my sails. (I like to flatter myself that I appear as inscrutable to others as a Chinaman; and it continually surprises me how most people can see right through me like a windowpane.) For a couple of moments I was speechless. Talk about cutting straight to the heart of the matter! (in more ways than one.)

I wanted to sort of build up to it gradually. Well, forget that! I took a good gulp of my beer, then said, "I'm afraid it's more complicated than that."

"Yes, I can see how it would be—for you. What's happened?"

I told Mike about meeting Paula in the park, and the Manuel Acuña thing—about being invited to her apartment and having lunch and talking with her—about the "holding hands" incident—and about our making a date, so-to-speak, for Thursday. I also mentioned something of what Evelyn had said (—the "Paula" parts—) on the drive home that night. It took some time to relate all of this; and Mike listened to me attentively, occasionally taking a sip of his beer. I concluded my tale by saying, "This is what's happened—and not happened—and, to tell you the truth, Mike, I'm in a quandary about what to do, or how to proceed—or even if I should proceed. I know it's no concern of yours; but I'd appreciate any thoughts you might have on the matter."

Mike looked thoughtful. "Hmmm . . . I must say, Chris, you certainly lead an interesting life. It's only been two days since the garden party. You move fast."

"Meeting Paula at the park was just a coincidence," I said, with some self-righteousness.

"*Was* it? From the way you've told me, you could have turned around and gone back, and not met her."

"Maybe," I granted him, "but why shouldn't I meet her? How was I to know she'd invite me up to her apartment?"

"You didn't have to go."

I started to say something, but Mike cut me off with, "Look, Chris—you're just putting up a smokescreen. You did what you did because you *wanted* to. You still want to. Why not be honest about it? It's me you're talking to, not your mother . . . Lord knows, Paula's enough to make a saint sweat." He took a sip of his beer. "You like Paula, and she obviously likes you—and not just as any friend. I was there at the table too, you'll remember. The die was cast before you ran into her at the park. Your problem—your dilemma—can be summed up in one word, Evelyn—or, in a larger sense, your marriage."

For some moments I didn't say anything. That man was right. In a sense, it was that simple, I wanted to be with Paula, even if only whenever, and I felt she felt the same way—except that it wasn't that simple. Another person was involved—a person I absolutely didn't want to hurt—not that this seemed to be of any concern to Paula at all. This, in itself, made me wonder. While these thoughts were going through my head, Mike asked me, "How old are you now, Chris?"

"Sixty-two," I replied reluctantly. I guessed where this was heading.

"And Paula?"

"How old is she? I haven't asked her and she hasn't told me. Somewhere in her twenties."

"OK, just for the sake of argument, let's say she's twenty-five. That makes you old enough to be her father—practically her grandfather—not to mention the fact that you're a married man."

"I realize that."

"*Do* you? You don't know what you're walking into, my

friend."

"In the first place, you're not me and her. In the second place, there's something you don't understand."

"What's that?"

"I think maybe I'm falling in love with her."

Mike looked at me like I'd told him I only had six months to live. "Oh my . . . That's bad."

"What's 'bad' about it?"

"You don't know? I think you do. If you just wanted to have a fling with Paula, I could understand that. I wouldn't mind having a go with her myself—though, in your case, even doing that presents all kinds of difficulties and dangers; but "falling in love" with her, that's a woodpecker knocking on a knot in the wood. "Where do you possibly think it's gonna go?"

"Yes, that's the real problem," I said gloomily. "The deeper I get in, the harder it's gonna be to get out"—

—"short of running off with her. And, believe me, it won't last, there's too much of an age difference. There's no future in it. She's barely out of her teens; and you, like me, are light years beyond that, heading towards the outer limits." He looked up at the sky for a moment, and he wasn't smiling.

My blood rose. "And who are you, the world's authority on women and relationships? You've never even been married. You're not in my situation."

"Thank God for that!" he exclaimed. "Maybe I've never been married, but I've been around—more than you think. I know what I'm talking about." He took a sip of his beer. "I'll go even further. I could be wrong, but I doubt if you're really that much in love with Paula after only two times together with her. You're just greatly attracted to her, and greatly fascinated by her."

"It's more than that."

"*Is* it? I doubt it."

"You have a one track mind, Mike." He grinned at me at that. "She has other qualities."

"Oh—her intelligence—her literary interests? . . . OK, you

told me about the poetry reading. Let me ask you this, What if—instead of the Paula that is the Paula that she is—she was fat, wore glasses, and had the face of a truck driver? Even if she was a graduate of Harvard and could quote Shakespeare till the bats leave the barn, would you still be attracted to her, you think, and still find yourself 'falling in love' with her? Now, be honest."

I resented being cornered like this, and grudgingly answered, "Put it that way, probably not."

"*Probably not*, indeed!" Mike exclaimed triumphantly.

"But that's just the point, she *is* beautiful *and* intelligent"—

—"*and* young."

"Yes, and that, too. There's also such a thing as feelings. Let me ask you a question, Mike, Have you ever been in love?"

He looked at me quite seriously, for a couple of moments, like a loan officer might look at someone who'd just asked for a personal loan of $100,000. Then, without changing his expression, he said, stressing each word, "No, I never have." After a moment, he added, "I've sometimes felt that I was, but it always turned out that I wasn't."

I looked at him about as seriously and with some pity. "Then I feel sorry for you."

"I feel sorrier for you! You don't know what you're getting yourself into. Have you thought about Evelyn?"

"Yes, I have." I took a sip of my beer.

"I'd suggest you think again—real hard. Do you want to ruin your marriage, after all these years, and all you've put into it, and all you've gotten out of it? What has it been, now, twenty-five years?"

"Twenty-two—and no, I don't."

"Like a lot of men in a similar situation, you wanna have your cake and eat it too, to enjoy the best of both worlds. I don't think, knowing Evelyn, you're gonna get it. It's more like your gonna get the cake thrown in your face and be kicked out the door into the street!" He let out a deep laugh.

I didn't laugh. "I've thought about that."

"I bet you have. You should. You need to seriously consider your marriage. Girls like Paula are a dime a dozen—well, not usually as strikingly beautiful—but a wife isn't. I should know, having never been able to find one. Another thing, What do you really know about Paula —her background—her past—even her present? You say she doesn't have anybody—you *think*. Why is that? A girl so gorgeous. It doesn't make sense. I'll just bet you there's a dark secret lurking around there somewhere, or else you're just not seeing everything. You most definitely, before you do anything else— if you do anything else—need to get to know her better. You might be surprised. That's my advice to you. My better advice'd be to forget about her altogether. This is a game you're not at all skilled at playing."

I had the disheartening feeling that all this talk was just so much talking in circles. There was no easy answer. With women, is there ever? It rather disturbed me and also made me rather mad, Mike's rather sinister comment about Paula's "dark secret." Still, Mike was right about one thing, I needed to get to know Paula better. That was OK by me. I wanted to. Still, the last thing I wanted to do was to destroy my marriage. What a dilemma! We were silent for a bit, just sipping our beers, during which a very big (for its size) blackbird, as black as night, suddenly landed from out of nowhere on the fence post directly opposite me. It looked straight at me with its hard, jet black eyes for a second, let out a single loud, harsh screech, then, with a flap of its big wings, took right off and disappeared. It all happened so fast, I don't think Mike much noticed it. I poured the remaining beer into my glass, and, after a few moments, smiled at Mike and said, "Thanks for listening and talking with me about it, Mike. I really appreciate it. You've given me some things to think about and consider. It's a big relief just to talk about it."

"Anytime. You can leave the money on the table."

I laughed.

He got up. "Want another beer?"

"Sure."

"Be right back."

I lit up a cigarette, leaned back, and relaxed. I was tired of the whole subject. When Mike returned, we talked about other things, and drank our beers. I might mention one little exchange we had, at one point, I asked Mike, "Don't you sometimes feel strange here?"

He looked curiously at me. "How d'you mean?"

"I mean I sometimes feel strange here among all these strangers—Mexicans. I don't mean that they're not nice people—they are—but they're not—how shall I put it?—they're not Americans—culturally, psychologically, or even emotionally. You know what I mean?"

"I know what you mean, but I don't let it bother me."

"It bothers me sometimes. For example, in all the years I've been around Mexicans, including in Fort Worth, I've never once seen a Mexican get really mad, or throw a fit about anything, publically or privately, even when they'd be wholly justified in doing so—in a situation where I'd probably go ballistic. In a way, you have to admire it—their stoic composure and complacency—*no matter what*—but I don't understand it, their incredible passivity. Neither does Evelyn. Then, Evelyn isn't completely Mexican. She's part—I guess you'd call it Caribbean—her mother was from Santo Domingo; and those people from down there are famous for their volatile tempers!" Mike smiled at me. "One day this summer we took the bus to Monterrey to visit one of Evelyn's girlfriends there. Though it was a coolish morning as we left Saltillo, it got progressively warmer as we drew ever closer to Monterrey. All the windows on the bus were shut (and couldn't be opened, anyway,) and the driver was apparently *not* going to turn on the air conditioning. It got to be very uncomfortable inside the bus. I was getting angrier by the second. So was Evelyn. We were sitting ten rows back from the driver. None of the other passengers said one word to him, but just sat there, though a few people were rapidly fanning themselves with a paper or a magazine or something. Perspiration was forming on my forehead. It's times like these when I wish I could speak

Spanish fluently—at least, all the *bad* Spanish." Mike laughed. "Finally, Evelyn, who was sitting on the left aisle seat, without getting up, screamed, en español, down the aisle to the driver to turn on the air conditioning. For some moments, he did nothing. She screamed again, louder and much madder. After maybe another fifteen seconds, suddenly, we heard the low hum of the air conditioner as it started flowing through the overhead vents. Evelyn leaned back in her seat, sighed, and commented, with acid sarcasm, "These people'd pass out and *die* before they'd say anything . . . I don't know how they *ever* got a Revolution started." It was true. That unbelievable passivity. This would never happen in Texas on a bus full of a bunch of gringos and gringas. I don't know . . . I've read that Santa Ana and Pancho Villa used to fly into rages all the time; still, I've never witnessed any such behavior among the Mexicans I've ever been around. What really got me was the reaction of some of the other passengers on the bus the first time Evelyn screamed down the aisle, they turned their heads to look at her and grinned, as if she were an escapee from a lunatic asylum. This, of course, (which she didn't fail to notice,) made her even madder. I've noticed this amazing passivity in other areas of their behavior. Then, you know, there's the famous "mañana" syndrome, 'don't do today what you can put off till tomorrow'—and that "tomorrow" could be four weeks away. Just wait till you need to take your car to the garage for repairs. Better buy a bicycle. When the plumber says, on Monday morning, when your kitchen sink's all stopped up, that he'll be there at one p.m., that "one p.m." may very well be on Tuesday or Wednesday; and it'll probably be more like six p.m. Their chronic lateness—even in just coming to dinner—is enough to drive you up the wall, and across the ceiling. I've read on the internet that most Americans who decide to move to Mexico decide to move back within two years or so, they just can't take it anymore, the differences between the two cultures."

After a few moments, Mike responded with, "America's a dynamic society; but Mexico's a static society where any significant change, in anything, is a long time comin'. You can't push Mexicans very hard; nor do they push themselves. The biggest difference I see is the difference in time. How often do you ever see a Mexican wearing a wristwatch? Not very often—at least, among the everyday Mexicans. Time's not a priority with them. Things move much slower here than in the States. Things are done when they're *done*, and people arrive when they *arrive*, whenever that may be. Personally, being retired, and not pressed for time, it doesn't bother me that much. I'm more than contented being out of the rat race. I've always found the Mexicans I've ever been around to be, generally speaking, the friendliest and gentlest people I've ever known, unless they're behind the wheel." I laughed. He made a fist with his right hand for a moment, then stretched it out flat on the table as he said, "I like the laid-back, easygoing lifestyle of Saltillo. I would think you would, too."

"I do, for the most part. I think it bothers Evelyn more than me."

"You know, if I'd been in you alls' shoes, I'd never have taken the bus, in the first place. I would've driven myself. Mexican buses are proverbial."

"We take the bus because it's cheap, and Evelyn doesn't want to drive all that way and back, and especially in the traffic in Monterrey."

"I understand that, but I'm just saying . . . Anyway, you ain't gonna change their mentality. I guess you get adjusted to it or you don't. I still like it better here, in every way, than in Texas."

"So do I," I agreed, almost wholeheartedly.

Eventually, after being there around three hours, after the sun had slipped behind the mountains, I bid Mike thanks and good-bye, and returned home.

Wednesday

I puttered around the house and garden for most of the day. Evelyn spent most of the morning, after breakfast, washing, drying, folding, and putting away the clothes. In the early afternoon, after lunch, she drove into town to do some necessary grocery shopping, leaving me by myself for a couple of hours.

My conversation with Mike about Paula had had a curious effect on me. On the one hand, it was like drinking down a cup of strong black coffee, without any cream or sugar, or taking a cold shower, it certainly made me take a sober look at the situation—the whole situation. On the other hand, like I'd told him, he didn't understand. I still planned on seeing Paula the next day at the appointed time and place, and we would see. And I did most definitely plan "to get to know her better."

Wednesday evening I received an email informing me that my friend Thomas in Fort Worth was dead, at sixty-three, from a sudden heart attack. It was from his sister-in-law, Helen, wife of his older brother David. They live in Waxahachie, ("WALKsuhHATCHee") a small, picturesque town about thirty miles south of Fort Worth, famous for its grandiose Victorian, gingerbread homes, most of them dating to the 1880s and 90s, and some of them to the Civil War, or right after. Waxahachie has also been used as a movie set for such films as the 1984 *Places in the Heart*. Thomas's current roommate had called Helen with the news; and Helen had taken it upon herself to write to me. It so saddened me (and Evelyn) to hear of his death. Another loss to chalk up. (Sometimes I think I've only lived this long just so I can, apparently, outlive everybody else I've ever known and/or loved.) Thomas and I went all the way back, over forty years, to when we were in college together. Our friendship was never really much of a "friendship" as it's commonly defined—more like just a long-lasting acquaintance. Particularly in our twenties and thirties, we palled around together, talked about everything under the sun, and took short and long road trips to the quaint, small towns all over North and Central Texas, both of us enjoying rummaging through antique shops, especially for old books and records; but, at the same time, we were never very close to one another, emotionally. I guess it was both our faults. If I was an introverted extrovert, Thomas was a nut. Tall, thin, and wearing wire-rimmed glasses, Thomas was an intellectual person, with a passion for history, who knew more about ancient Rome than he did about modern-day Fort Worth, and who had the most amazing record collection of anyone I've ever known, (and who thought "And Your Bird Can Sing" was The Beatles' best song;) but he also had a hair-trigger temper, was as moody and could be as waspish as a woman, and he was a compulsive talker—a motor mouth. I don't know why he was like this, but he was. I've sometimes wondered if Thomas was—not mentally but emotionally retarded. He was eternally the rebellious adolescent harboring a smoldering and implacable hatred towards the Establishment. I guess what I liked the most about him, and the reason why I continued hanging out with him, was that he was very knowledgeable and never boring. He also was one of those high-strung people you meet sometimes who can eat like a horse and never gain an ounce of weight. He could never hold down a job for very long, and was continually storming off or getting fired from his job due to his anger at his boss or because of his outrageous behavior. (He once told his boss, on being fired by him, "I could tell you to go to Hell, but I wouldn't want to ever meet *you* there.") He had a degree in History, but, of course, this got him nowhere; and he survived by doing just about anything that was above the level of a street cleaner. He periodically went through long periods of unemployment. He always lived in cheap apartment complexes in Fort Worth with, off and on, an endless succession of male roommates, each one of whom he would always eventually clash horribly and part company with. He never had any money to speak of, and, as far as I know, never had a girlfriend; though, once in a lunar eclipse, he might go out and pick up a girl for a night at a bar or a strip joint or somewhere. He had a stubborn streak that made a mule look like a model of flexibility. For example, even though his parents, his brother, his roommates, his neighbors, and even I tried to persuade him to let his sandy hair grow out—at least, a little—so he'd look like a normal human being, it only made him all the more determined to wear it like he forever did, which was in a burr that was more than a burr, in that all the bone formations in the back of his skull were visible, making him look like a neo-Nazi freak, or a member of some bizarre religious sect. Mostly, he talked—and talked—about something/about nothing—just talked. Unless he was listening to music, watching TV, reading, eating, or sleeping, (and, I suppose, on his job, working,) he literally never shut up. It could get to the point where you wanted to scream. Going on a long trip with Thomas could actually cause you to contemplate murder. Sometimes, if he was in a blue mood, (which wasn't uncommon,) he might be relatively quiet; but, paradoxically, he might just as well, in such a mood, be at his worst. Thomas was also a terror on the road, looking upon all the other drivers as his natural enemies; which is why most of the time we went anywhere—certainly on a trip of any distance—I did the driving in my Chevette. Thomas would tailgate; would angrily pass "slow" drivers on two lane roads, even against oncoming traffic, while sometimes shooting the bird to "the offender"; and would rudely honk his horn if the car or truck in front of him didn't promptly move when the light changed. His roommate Craig once told me, when Thomas wasn't around, "Happiness is *not* seeing Thomas in your rear view mirror."

After I eventually got married, we saw less and less of each other, which, I suppose, was only natural; and by the time Evelyn and I moved permanently to Lomas, our relationship was just a once 'n awhile thing. Back when I was still single, in the mid-80s, I taught six grade remedial English for two school years for the Waxahachie ISD, and resided in a small rental house in the town. As a result of this, I got to know David and Helen quite well, and was often invited over to their modest house for dinner with them and their two boys. If my relationship with Thomas gradually dried up, over the years, mine with David and Helen never has. Evelyn and Helen have become good friends. We visit them when we take trips back to Texas, and we keep in touch, which explains Helen's email.

Anyway, once, way back in the late 70s, after spending a particularly trying couple of hours with Thomas at his apartment, after I got back to my apartment, I sat down and wrote the following poem, which I've never shown to anybody. Oddly enough, for some reason, I wrote the poem in the past tense; but now, oddly enough, it seems appropriate as a sort of epitaph for Thomas. Here it is,

Thomas

His hands were in his mouth,
and his heart was in his head.
He talked and talked and talked,
only, most of what he said

was just said to be said,
(or was just said to be heard.)
Yes, he could talk and talk
and not ever say a word.

His present was just pennies,
and his future was past due,
which made him rather nervous
with not having much to do;

and so he talked and talked,
and became one of the birds
of life, whose constant song
was just words, words, words, words, words . . .

CHAPTER 33

Thursday-1

The day dawned on "all things bright and beautiful." There wasn't a cloud in the sunny heavens or on the horizon, and the leaves barely trembled in the gentlest breeze. It was a perfectly lovely Fall day, with a slight but crisp bite in the air which seemed to give an added zest to the day, like a slice of lemon in a glass of iced tea.

Thursday is Evelyn's "rosary day," (a point which wasn't lost on me when I suggested this day to Paula.) Not that Evelyn's particularly religious, in any formal sense. She may have been born and raised a Catholic (like most Mexicans), but she has an ambivalent attitude towards the Catholic Church itself, regarding the Pope as more or less a joke, and looking upon going to confession as something of questionable benefit. And there're other things. I gather that much of her irreverence is a result or a reflection of her grandmother's attitude, which was, apparently, anything but devout. On the other hand, sitting around the kitchen table at a friend's house praying the rosary is hardly going to church, which we rarely attend anymore, except on special occasions like a wedding or a funeral or Christmas or Easter; and, above and beyond the religious aspect of it, (if not more importantly,) it's an opportunity for her to get out of the house for awhile and socialize with her other women friends. The reading of the rosary is always held at the house of her friend Constanza, (a middle-aged, childless widow,) in Lomas, and is always attended by three or four other women—housewives, of various ages—who live in the colony. Aside from praying the long-drawn-out, complete rosary, they also enjoy refreshments and conversation afterwards, which can go on for even longer. In short, she's usually gone for a good four hours, leaving the house around eleven-thirty. She once invited me to accompany her, which, against my better judgment, I did, for the first and last time. I just don't have the patience for it, the seemingly endless praying followed by the seemingly endless "girl gab." Besides, being the only man there I felt pretty out of place, like a pirate in a bingo parlor or something.

I didn't say anything to Evelyn about my going anywhere. As far as she knew, I'd be around the house for the rest of the day. About twenty minutes after she'd departed I called for a taxi. I figured I'd be back home before her; and, if not, I'd think up some excuse. So, I guess you could say that if she went off to pray, I went off to play, in a way.

But before coming to Paula, I think this would be a fitting place to interrupt the narrative for a few minutes by inserting something I once wrote in thinking over the whole subject of Christianity, specifically, the "career" of Jesus. Like "Thomas" I've never shown it to anybody. Here it is,

Jesus the Loser

Jesus, by any earthly standard, was an almost total loser.

Here was a young man, in his early thirties, in apparently excellent health, with a brilliant mind and a magnetic personality, who, nevertheless, had no home or even a room of his own, no family ties, no possessions, certainly no wardrobe, no formal education, no job, no money, no wife (or girlfriend—indeed, no sex—) no children (obviously), no pets, no hobbies, no favorite food or drink—a man who expressed no interest in music or literature or art or the theater or dancing or sports or traveling (outside Judea) or business or industry or science or education or the emancipation of women or the question of slavery or making money or poverty (really) or politics—in fact, in *anything* (save in one thing)—who had to walk wherever he went because he also had no personal means of transportation; though he did reportedly ride a borrowed donkey on Palm Sunday.

Aside from the marginal types he habitually hung around with—beggars, paupers, prostitutes, and other unemployed losers like himself—Jesus received no love or respect from, and had no influence on, the greater society around him.

The State feared him, the mercantile classes ignored him, and the religious leaders, with a few exceptions, hated and despised him.

Far from being granted any hearing for his message of peace and love, he was regarded by the authorities as an unbalanced and dangerous rebel.

Eventually, betrayed by one of his very own disciples (for thirty pieces of silver), he was arrested, brutally beaten, and hauled into court where he made no effort whatsoever to defend himself.

Meanwhile, while this was going on, one of his closest disciples, Peter, on being confronted and questioned on three separate occasions, denied, each time, (even vehemently, the third time,) knowing Jesus at all.

Sentenced to death, to the great satisfaction of the crowd, a crown of piercing thorns was jammed down on his head as "King of The Jews," and Jesus was then taken out and cruelly crucified like a common criminal—in fact, between two criminals.

As a final indignity—to add insult to injury—

his stripped-off garments were gambled over right under his nose by his crucifiers.

When his mutilated corpse was finally taken down from the cross and deposited in an unmarked tomb carved out of the rock, not one of his remaining eleven disciples attended the ceremony.

Yes, this was Jesus, a weird, and quickly-forgotten-about loser who changed the entire course of Western civilization.

I was dressed virtually the same as on Tuesday (—I don't have much of a wardrobe, either—) with only the addition of a brown sweater over my tan shirt. The taxi dropped me off at the same spot in front of the southern entrance to the park, and I strolled off in the direction of the obelisk. It was twelve-twenty by my watch. . .

I didn't notice one person anywhere. It was like I had the whole park to myself. This very emptiness made me (irrationally) fear that Paula might not be there, too, for some reason. I quickened my step.

Approaching the obelisk plaza down the same path as before—déjà vu!—there she was, same girl/same place, there was the same thick, braided, black ponytail and the same tortoise shell hairpin. Though, this time, I absolutely knew it was her—like before, my step slowed to a crawl as I sort of tiptoed closer. I observed her for a full minute. She was just sitting there, legs uncrossed, wearing a long-sleeved, deep purple dress, staring straight ahead, with her hands resting, right over left, in her lap, looking like she was listening to Beethoven's Ninth Symphony. If I thought she might have been casting a glance around, now and then, to see if I was coming—well, she wasn't. She was as motionless as the obelisk itself. I made me suddenly feel lost and intimidated, like the foreigner that I was (in more ways than one); and it took a certain degree of courage to casually stride up to her and present myself.

"Paula! ¡Buenas tardes!"

She was as beautiful as ever. Without moving a muscle, but simply lifting her eyes, which did seem to darkly-brighten, (if that can be imagined,) she looked into mine and replied, "Buenas tardes, Chris. As you can see, I'm here."

"Me too." I motioned with my left arm towards the bench. "May I?"

"Por supuesto." ("Of course.")

I sat down on her right—once more, a few feet away from her. I noticed that she wore no necklace. She looked at me curiously, as if I was a rare and exotic species of bird. She almost looked scared. Actually, I think she was just nervous—as nervous as me. Neither of us seemed to quite know how to proceed.

Looking down at her hands which, at the same time, she drew slightly apart, she said, "I thought maybe you wouldn't come."

"Why would you think that?"

She didn't say anything for a few moments; then, looking directly at me, said, "I feel we need to talk, Chris, but why don't we do so taking a walk through the park? It's such a lovely day. There's practically nobody here. What d'you think?" She gave me a smile.

"That's fine with me." The words were no sooner out of my mouth than she stood up. I stood up. We started off, side by side, (I still on her right,) making a turn onto the same tiled walkway down which I'd approached the plaza.

P.S. I've heard people ask, in words like, "If Jesus really was—or is—then why hasn't he returned once in two thousand years?" I have an answer for that, simple as it may sound, If I'd been treated the way he was, I wouldn't return, either—ever.

CHAPTER 34

Thursday-2

In spite of what she'd said, we actually slowly walked for some distance as silent as if we were members of a funeral procession. On either side of us were open, green spaces; and the sunlight brokenly lit up our path as it streamed down through the leaves of the tall trees bordering the walkway. Somehow the faint hum of the traffic and the occasional horn made the silence of the park seem that much stronger.

Finally, Paula stopped, which made me to stop, too. We looked into each other's eyes, and she asked me, "Tell me, Chris, what d'you expect from me?"

The question was so direct—so general and, yet, so specific—that I didn't know what to say. She apparently guessed as much, for she followed it up by saying, "I don't mean to put you on the spot."

"No, no," I finally said, "I just wasn't expecting such a question. You know, Paula, I could ask you the same thing."

Now, *she* was silent. We gazed into each other's eyes, neither of us betraying any emotion. Then, turning her face away, she commenced slowly walking again, as I did, too. After some seconds, she said, with some shyness, looking straight ahead as we continued walking, "I know you're married. I know you're older than me. I know you're not Mexican—and I don't really care." She glanced at me. "Maybe you do." I didn't say anything, even so much at meeting her glance. She added, as we both stared down the walkway, walking on, "I like you, Chris, very much. I like your company, and I feel you like mine." She glanced at me again. "What d'you think we should do about it?" There was, it seemed to me, a hint of innocence in her voice.

This time, I stopped. We looked at each other. "I must say, Paula, you're nothing if not direct."

"Why not be?"

"I've never met a woman like you."

"I've never met a man like you. You can be sure of that." She looked calmly (and unsmilingly) at me, her dark eyes glowing. Her drop-dead beauty seemed to make the whole park around me a more beautiful place. There was one of those black, wrought iron benches a little ways ahead, bordering and facing the walkway, on my side. "I think I'd like to sit down a minute," I said, nodding towards the bench. "OK," she said, and we went over and sat down in the middle of the bench, I on her left this time, but close enough to her so that you couldn't have placed a kitten between us.

We were silent for a spell, sitting there rather stiffly, our feet planted firmly on the ground and our hands in our laps like we were, indeed, listening to Beethoven's Ninth Symphony. Sitting as close as we were—even closer than we'd been on her sofa—it made me feel like we already were "a couple," even if that was, of course, premature.

A little distance away, on my right, two brown and greenish-purple necked pigeons were strutting about on the walkway, not far apart, their heads bobbing this way and that as if they were searching for something, but weren't even coming close to finding anything. Paula asked me, "You don't have anything to say?" Staring at the pigeons, I answered, "I probably have too much to say."

There was a long pause. I suddenly felt shy and uncommunicative, as if I'd already said too much, when, in fact, I hadn't said anything. Paula, obviously judging that I wasn't—at least, for the time being—going to elaborate any further, finally broke the silence by saying, "If you have too much to say, you probably have a problem; and the problem's probably Evelyn." I could've stuck my finger in a light socket. I started, and started to say something, but she raised up her left hand, for a moment, like a fan, and said, "Please, let me finish first." I conceded to her wish. She went on, in a roundabout manner, "I may be a beautiful—even very beautiful—woman. So what? Everybody thinks that because I *am* beautiful I have a wonderful life. No problems, no worries, no loneliness. And I have an easy life, everything comes easy to me because of my beauty. I can get whatever I want. The truth's a little different. I have to face other women being jealous of me, and who usually keep their distance from me, as do most men—not because they're jealous of me, but because my beauty makes them act shy around me—or else they look at me as one thing only. She interrupted herself to make the comment, "When I first met you, you seemed shy to me; but obviously you're not."

"I think I am kinda shy in the company of women, generally speaking," I replied, "but, at the same time, I don't care."

This brought forth a little laugh from her. She continued, "But this is just part of it. When you're especially beautiful but also have *brains*, then you're really—what's that expression I've heard you Americans say?—oh, 'up a creek.'" She let out a weak laugh. I smiled, but didn't interrupt her. She smiled at my smile, as if reassuring herself that I understood her meaning. "Sure, I've had boyfriends. Why not? *That* actually *is* very easy for me, if I feel like it. Not one of them has meant anything to me, really. They wanted me—that's all. I can't remember having an intelligent discussion with any of them about anything." She paused for a couple of moments, then continued, "Then, you have to understand where I come from, poverty. I've never had a car. Really, when I think about where I come from, it's a miracle I'm the kind of woman I am, or am not. Piedras Negras isn't Paris, France. It's a hot, provincial, Mexican border town, bigger than a pueblo, but not what you'd really call a *city*. Most people are poor, with little education. Many have almost none. As you probably know, there's no compulsory education in Mexico, if you don't go to school, you don't go to school. Many don't—or barely do—especially among the poor people. My father can sign his name and read the monthly bills, and that's about it. My mother can read a little if it's not too difficult; but she never really reads anything."

I interrupted her, "What's your father do?"

"He's a plumber." This seemed to silence her for some seconds. She then went on, "My sisters and me all received a basic education—better than our parents—but my two older sisters have never done anything with it. All that ended when they got married—very young—and started having babies. And our family's typical of most of the poor families in town. My father was fifteen and so was mother when they got married. I think there's some hope for my little sister, Teresa. She's like me. She's in no hurry to get married, and wants to continue with her education and do something with her life first. It probably won't happen. There's lots of pressure on girls to hurry up and get married and start families, a lot of it coming from the other girls around you who can't wait to do so, or 've already done so.'"

I interrupted her again, "It's called 'peer pressure.'"

"Oh, yes—I know that expression—yes, it is." She said this with a slight haughtiness, even as the two pigeons suddenly took off with a whoosh—one, a second after the other—to parts unknown, which we both noticed. She looked up at the sky for a few seconds (which was an unchanged, cloudless, strong blue), then continued by saying, with a complete about face, "Chris, I haven't had lunch yet, and I'm not really hungry. Are you?"

"Not especially."

"We can go back to my apartment and I can fix something for you . . ."

"No, don't bother. I'm fine. I'd rather we stay here and continue talking."

"Yes," she said, as if I'd told her exactly what she wanted to hear. She picked up the thread of what she'd been saying as if talking confidentially to her father confessor, "You see, I'm different—really different—and I know it. Sometimes it bothers me. Most of the time it doesn't. I've accepted it." She let out a fast laugh. "I never asked to be born; but I might as well make the best of it! . . . Maybe I'm too much for any man—even you." She smiled at me. "I hope not."

"Just what are you trying to say, Paula?"

She was silent for a little bit, before she responded with, "Maybe I'm too assertive for a little Mexican woman; but I don't meet a man like you every day—someone I feel a bond with—who's intelligent and educated—and interesting—and who knows Mexican women. I mean, you're married to one." She paused for a moment. "I think maybe you have no idea of just how special you are to a woman like me. I'll admit it, I'm very lonely, at times, believe it or not. I have nobody here. I've been here six months, and the only men I've met so far are the same kind as those back in Piedras. None of them can speak hardly a word of English, except for Bertie; and they have nothing interesting to say, anyway, anymore than those back home. I refuse to settle for that. I have a horror of becoming like my parents and my girlfriends back in Piedras. I want more out of my life than that. That's why I came here in the first place. I have a good, professional job, a nice apartment, and my independence; and I don't miss havin' babies, slappin' tortillas, and washin' my husband's dirty underwear." I let out a laugh, which brought a corresponding laugh out of her. "Yes . . . but I'm still a woman. I could continue to live like I do—no problema—but why should I let a man like you get away? I know you're attracted to me, Chris. I'm glad. You and I can have a wonderful relationship together. I won't make any demands on you. We can meet when we can. Who needs to know about it?" She added, as an afterthought, not without a little rise in her voice, "Everything'll be all right, I think."

This was a lot for me to digest—almost overwhelming. It was hard to tell if Paula was either very worldly-wise or very naïve—very, for want of a better word, romantic. I stood up and stepped a few feet forward. This caused her to exclaim concernedly, "Where're you going?"

"Nowhere. I'm just stretching my legs for a second." I could've no more left her sitting there than I could've stopped breathing, and I knew it. I gave her a sheepish look, and sat back down. She now became quite quiet and still, leaning back in the bench and calmly gazing at me, apparently satisfied that she'd said all she wanted to say, and content to wait for me to say whatever I wanted to say, sure, no doubt, that it'd be to her liking; and her very tranquility made her look almost transcendentally beautiful, like a (dark-haired) angel. And I was quiet and still for a full minute, at least.

Finally, I spoke up, looking at her, "I must express my feelings, which isn't easy for me. I know how I feel, but it's hard to put it into words. You, it seems, have no problem with that." I smiled at her; but she didn't change her impassive expression, continuing to gaze at me with her dark, glowing eyes. I went on, "I've never felt—exactly felt—about a girl—about a woman—like I do about you, Paula—even when I married Evelyn. You see, she was thirty-seven and I was forty . . . When I was a young man—when I was your age—I never had a girlfriend, and for a long time afterwards. I was always doing and interested in other things. Yes, while other guys my age were out happily chasin' girls, I was alone in my room, propped up in bed, reading *Crime and Punishment*." A suggestion of a smile played across Paula's face for a few seconds. "Oh, I might enjoy a girl every now and then—but that was about it. My nature, I guess, always was—still is—and always will be too serious for women. It scares them off—not to mention my tendency towards sarcasm. And I can't—and won't—be what I'm not. I won't 'play the game'—play the clown—like other men—are forced to do—never have—never will. A woman has to come to me, or at least meet me halfway. Few ever have . . . especially when you're poor and ordinary-looking, with little prospects of ever making it big, and drive old, used cars like I always have—still do. Evelyn was different, she saw past all that; but she was older and wiser by then. That's what amazes me about you, Paula, that you're so wise for being so young. I really never have known a woman—a young woman—such an *unconventional* young woman—like you, in my whole life, anywhere . . . and certainly not one so very beautiful." I smiled at her. Without changing her expression, she merely commented, "I think you're pretty unconventional yourself. If you weren't, you wouldn't be here." I looked intently at her for a moment, then, not saying anything, turned my head to gaze out across the wide lawn facing us. There was a pause, during which a long and lean, black and brown, white-speckled roadrunner zipped across the lawn. I continued, still gazing across the lawn, "Well, I'm goin' the long way round the barn, I guess—I mean (—figuring that she might not be familiar with this expression—) saying everything but what's to the point." I looked at her. "Paula, you're not going anywhere. You're settled down here, with your job and your apartment. From what you say, I don't think you have any desire to go back to Piedras. I'm settled down here, too, and have no desire to go back to the States. In other words, we're not just 'two ships passing in the night.' Forgive me, I seem to be always talking in clichés. It's a habit of mine. The point is we both have lives here in Saltillo, different as they may be, in so many ways. You want to share some of your life with me; and, of course, I'd be thrilled to share some of mine with you." I smiled. All of a sudden, there was an odd, brief, strong gust of wind, which lifted her ponytail for a moment. "Should we, or shouldn't we, that is the question." She smiled slightly at me at that. "You, obviously, are 'ready to go.' I'm ready—most men are unless they're dying—but I don't want to do anything to cause any pain to Evelyn."

"I'm not asking you to," she said plainly.

"It'll have to be 'our secret,' I guess."

"That's up to you . . . I just want to be with you when I can." She said this, it seemed, like a young girl, under her mother's custody, might say to her divorced father. This struck me. I looked deeply into her dark, glowing eyes. Her supernatural beauty was like some kind of magnet. I leaned towards her. She met my leaning. We kissed—deeply and passionately. It may sound corny, but it really was like an electric current raced through my whole body, to my very finger and toe tips. It was a kind of bliss, for sure. I didn't see stars, but I felt them. Though we'd gotten to know and feel close to each other, through communication, we were now suddenly—physically—joined to each other as if we were one throbbing body, (even if it was just a kiss,) which raised our relationship to a whole new level. It was a long kiss; and it was I who finally broke it off, against her desire, as she instinctively resisted the parting, whispering, "Oh, Chris . . ." Nevertheless, once "the deed was done" she pretty quickly recovered her composure, (as I did, more or less,) not the least of which was because, at that very moment, two nuns in all black habits, (two long, cool women in black dresses,) strolled past us on the walkway, giving us the eye. Paula stared out at the wide, green lawn before us as if it had been the Saltillo Cemetery. We were silent for some time, as I stared out across the lawn as well.

At length, I looked at her, and, to my surprise, she was crying, not sobbing, by any means, but her eyes were "full of tears," and, even as I looked, a single tear slid down her left cheek. Otherwise, her expression remained unchanged as she stared impassively out across the lawn. I asked her, "What's the matter?" She made no reply. I said, "Most of the girls I've ever kissed have simply kissed me back—a few have slapped me—but I can't remember my kiss ever reducing any of them to tears." She let out a laugh, through her tears, in spite of herself. "Oh, Chris," she said, "I feel so happy—so safe—so secure—with you. You're such a change—a welcome change—from any of the men I've ever known." I didn't know quite what to make of this, which she said so earnestly. I said nothing; but she added, "And I'll make *you* happy. You just wait and see." It suddenly dawned on me that I'd gotten myself into something much deeper than I ever thought possible. Who was this girl, really, who'd come into my life? There was something mysterious going on here; but, strange to say, in general, I just felt fatalistic about the whole thing, "what will be will be." And I was, deep down, very happy, too. It was like the years had rolled away and I was in my twenties again with the girl of my dreams.

I said to her gently, "Please don't cry, Paula. There's nothing to cry about."

"No, no—I'm not really crying," she said unconvincingly. She reached into her black purse on her right on the bench, pulled out a white handkerchief, and dabbed her eyes and cheeks with her right hand. Replacing the handkerchief in her purse, she said, "I'm glad we had this talk, Chris. I feel better now."

"Me too." There was a pause. "I'm afraid it must be time for me to be getting back to work," she said like she hated having to say it.

I glanced at my wristwatch. (She wasn't wearing one.) "Yes, it's almost two."

Though we were both now aware of the time, neither of us stirred, but just sat there silently, like we were glued to the bench. A colorful blue jay landed in about the middle of the lawn, but it didn't stay there for very long at all. Facing in our direction, it stood there and proceeded to preen its white breast feathers, for maybe fifteen seconds, before it suddenly flew off. On an impulse, I said, "Paula, how about this coming Monday afternoon I meet you here—by the obelisk—same time—and take you out to lunch? I know a nice little café not far from here, around the corner from The Cathedral. It was shown to me by Mike. I know you're a vegetarian; and they make a very tasty tostada there." (Tostadas are hard tortillas typically covered with a layer of refried beans, on top of which are sliced or diced lettuce, tomatoes, and chicken, all lightly salted, and the whole thing topped by a generous couple of spoonfuls of cream.) I knew for a fact that Evelyn had a noon appointment Monday to have some dental work done.

Paula instantly brightened. "That will make me so happy!"

"We have a date, then?"

"Sí —Yes!"

"Good."

On an impulse of her own, she leaned over and gave me a light kiss on the cheek, then stood right up. I stood up as well. She took me by the right hand, but I (perhaps being the neurotic that I am) discouraged this by saying, "I don't think we should do this, Paula. You don't know who might be around," and let go of her hand. This actually caused her to let out a laugh. So, we walked out of the park as "chaste" as a brother and sister (not from Alabama); but, her mood revitalized, she chattered away about this and that like a vivacious schoolgirl as I escorted her back to Belinda's office, only a few blocks from the park. Once there, she gave me a quick but bright smile, a long kiss on the lips, exclaimed, "Monday!" then quickly turned and went up the few steps and through the front door. I hailed a passing yellow cab, (nearly stepping on a dead, brown sparrow on the sidewalk,) and was promptly on my way back to Lomas.

CHAPTER 35

Home Almost Alone

If I'd intended to find out more about Paula, I both had and hadn't. By her own words, without my asking, she'd told me much about herself; but I still felt uneasy about her, in general. There was still something missing—something that didn't add up. I had the instinctive feeling that she was holding something back, or was holding a card she had yet to play. Her very frankness seemed almost too frank, at such an early point in our acquaintance, as if she was coming on to me but putting on an act at the same time. Maybe I was all wrong, and being unfair to her. It's pretty impossible to analyze women. Even Sigmund Freud himself said women were "a dark continent," (which is practically an admission of defeat.) Women are so complicated, like the delicate inner workings of a watch, which seldom tells the correct time. Paula was really pretty outrageous, but also so sweet and straightforward that I didn't know what to make of her. Apparently, a "relationship" with her (—perhaps like a train wreck—perhaps, hopefully—not—) was right there, waiting to happen. Maybe I was too old-fashioned. It wasn't the 1950s anymore . . . Modern girls. Good-bye Donna Reed (Who's *that?*)/Hello Madonna, and her like. It made me wonder. And I wanted Paula—now, more than ever. I also felt sorry for her. There was something ravishing and extraordinary about her, for sure, but also something sort of tragic. I smiled to myself. If anyone was "tragic," it was probably me.

These were some of the thoughts I thought and the feelings I felt as I hung around the house by myself after returning from my "rendezvous" that Thursday afternoon. It was around two-twenty when the taxi dropped me off in front our house. I knew I couldn't expect to see Evelyn until around four.

Alone in the house after my "high time" with Paula I felt listless and somewhat depressed. I fixed myself a cup of hot tea and took a seat on the sofa, a plump, two-sectional sofa similar to Paula's, except upholstered in a material consisting of a rich fantasy of medium-sized maroon and corn yellow flower blossoms on short stems with deep green leaves all set against a dark blue background. After taking a sip of my tea, I put the cup and saucer immediately down on the "coffee table" in front of me. I'd made it too hot, as usual. Let it cool down a bit. I say "coffee table" because, though it functions as such, it's in reality nothing you'd find at your local furniture store, it being an old, olive green, WW2 Army footlocker that belonged to my step-grandfather Mort, second husband of the same grandmother who I "saw down the hall." Stenciled across its top-center, in white lettering (—the tall letters an inch high, and the small letters and numbers half an inch—) is, "S/SGT Morton T Iler," and centered right below this is, "15048777," his serial number. The rank, name and serial number are still quite clear. Though a bit beat up, with its strong front clasps all rusted (but still workable), the footlocker remains a "solid box," and serves its purpose. I have a special affection for it, and keep its top generally free of anything, except when needed, so much the better to see it and let it be seen. Inside it there are various important papers and documents, as well as photo albums concerning Evelyn and myself, (together and separately.) There's also a pair of black WW2 German binoculars in their original black leather case which Mort took off a captured Nazi officer late in the war, so he told me when he gave them to me when I was a youngster. He also explained, in giving them to me, that you could take anything off a captured soldier that was of a military nature, but not of a personal one, such as his jacket, his wallet, his wristwatch, or any rings he wore. The outside of the case is pretty scuffed up, but the binoculars themselves are still in good condition and function perfectly well; and I sometimes use them, when the mood strikes me, to look out the window at the city in the distance. I bet that Nazi officer would've never *dreamed* they'd ever end up here in Mexico.

Relaxing on the sofa, thinking my thoughts and feeling my feelings, after a few minutes I picked up the cup and saucer and set it on my lap. I took a sip. Better. I thought that maybe I wanted a cigarette; but I didn't have them on me—didn't see them anywhere—and didn't remember where I'd put them. Since I don't smoke that much (anymore), I spend half my life, it seems, either looking for the pack or (especially) the matches or lighter. It's ridiculous. It's enough to make you quit for good—not because of any health reasons—but just to save yourself the aggravation. I sipped the tea and gazed about the living and adjoining dining room on my right, gazed at the things everywhere that made our house a home—that were a true reflection of our interests, such as Evelyn's decorative plates, many of them from her grandmother, hanging on the dining room walls showing colorful birds, (one showing a glorious peacock with spread feathers,) equally colorful flowers, and scenes of old, colonial Mexico, such as cobblestoned streets, colonnaded walkways, arches, rococo church towers, brown-robed, strolling friars, and more—which are so many plates that I sometimes joke to any guests we ever have, (and always to Evelyn's cold amusement,) that we have more plates on the walls than in the kitchen cabinets. There was the simple pine bookcase of four shelves against the wall opposite me, going back to my childhood, containing both her books and mine (in English and Spanish) and various little objects of hers and mine; and on whose top is displayed, in the center, in a plain silver frame, our dark background, studio wedding picture showing her, from about the knees up, in her white wedding gown and trailing veil, holding an enormous bouquet of white roses, with me on her right, (actually her left), without a mustache, in a navy blue tuxedo, also from about the knees up, standing just behind her, grasping her left arm holding the roses with my left hand, with my slightly tilted head just touching hers, which is slightly tilted towards mine. We're both smiling into the camera, naturally, but smiling with a difference, in that though she looks positively radiant, she also looks somewhat subdued, as if she's deeply contented; while I look, I have to admit, rather smug, like the cat that's just swallowed the canary. To the left of the bookcase, hanging on the wall, was the colorful poster, in a thin black frame, from the movie *Cinema Paradiso*, our favorite movie of all time. And, of course, there were other things of hers, mine, and ours here and there. The point that came home to me was that everything, taken together, represented a life together—of two lives joined together—of memories—stretching back over decades. "What's Paula to this?" I couldn't help but ask myself.

I looked down at the olive footlocker, "S/SGT Morton T Iler". . . Mort . . . I thought about him—and'll tell you about him . . . He was a strange man . . . I'd known Mort since I was in short pants, and I've never known anyone like him. He never seemed to especially need anyone or anything—even Grandma, really. He was completely self-sufficient, with an obvious yet also strangely subtle strength unto himself. I never knew where it came from. Of medium height and build, Mort was a quiet and serious man; yet he was invariably in a pleasant mood, and was always good company. Occasionally he could be witty, as when he said, "The preacher gave a good sermon today; though, I'm afraid, he was more like a teacher." I don't recall him ever once losing his temper, swearing, or complaining about his circumstances. (Towards the end of his life, when he was having recurring pains from his cancer, Mother and I would stop by twice a month to take him to his appointment with his doctor. It used to exasperate her how, when the doctor would ask Mort how he felt, he'd always answer, "Fine.") Though enjoying steady economic security as the branch manager of the Anchor Fence Company in Dallas until he retired—not to mention being married to a rich divorcée—Mort was the very opposite of materialistic, even bordering on the miserly. He could pinch a penny. His idea of changing the spark plugs in his car, back when plugs probably cost around 50 cents apiece, consisted of spending an hour or so in his garage taking out the old plugs, sandpapering them down, then putting them back in again. He was that kind of man.

Mort was an elder in his church. He was a long-standing member of the Lion's Club. He didn't smoke or drink. His post WW2/late marriage to Grandma was his first and only marriage; and I'm sure he never messed around with other women. He wasn't the type at all. He went to bed early and got up early every day. He went to work and came home, busied himself around the house and yard, regularly attended club meetings, and went to church on Sunday—and that was about his life. His marriage to Grandma produced no children. There couldn't have been a better role model for a lonely boy like me than Mort, considering the hard-living, self-centered, Dean Martinish father I had. The father I *had* was only very minimally in my life, anyway; while Mort was always there, and was always happy to give me his time. He was like a second (—really, a first—) father to me. He'd take me to ballgames in the summer, with him sometimes on the weekends when he'd go out to give fence estimates, and to the Texas State Fair every year.

After Grandma died from a heart attack in 1993, Mort was reduced to living all by himself in the big house in Dallas day after day, and lonely night after night. This didn't seem to bother him in the slightest. I would've been deeply depressed, I'm sure. I'd make an effort to visit him, from time to time, because I felt sorry for him. He'd always graciously greet me, and we'd spend a happy time together. And yet—yet—I always had the feeling that, as far as Mort was concerned, if I happened to drop by, that was OK; and if didn't, that was OK, too. Mort seemed to take whatever happened with a shrug and a smile.

Mort was odd. I could never fathom what made him tick.

I'll never forget the last visit I ever had with him, a couple of months before he died of prostate cancer in 1999, at ninety-one. I'd known since my childhood that he'd been in the Army in WW2—not that he ever talked about it much. (I'd also known something else about him, which Mort took some pride in, his father was a first cousin of the legendary Western lawman, Wyatt Earp.) Mort had been a staff/tank sergeant in the 20th Armored Division, originally formed up in Kentucky, where he was from. What I'd never known, though, until that last visit with him, (now that I was much older,) was about Dachau. Sitting across from me at the old, redwood picnic table in his backyard on that sunny, mild Spring afternoon, I remember him dressed in black slacks and a dark red, long-sleeved, flannel shirt, in spite of the weather, or maybe *because* of his age; while I had on blue jeans and a yellow, short-sleeved shirt. With his square-jawed, clean-shaven, genial face, and with his brown, horn-rimmed glasses, Mort looked little changed to me—except for his white hair—from when we first met, when he was forty-nine and I was four. As we sat there talking, next to the flowering pear tree—a miracle of beauty, as if the whole tree was covered in brilliantly white, shimmering snow—Mort started reminiscing, at length, (which was a first for him, with me,) about his wartime experiences. In talking about how the 20th Armored had fought its way across Nazi Germany, (in which he mentioned that the Nazi soldiers "were very disciplined and very determined fighters,") he dropped this bombshell, the 20th Armored had participated in the liberation of Dachau concentration camp in southern Germany. Mort described what he witnessed in gruesome detail, such as the long line of boxcars full of corpses. As he explained, he subsequently found out that around twenty six hundred men, women, and children had been crammed into thirty nine boxcars at Buchenwald concentration camp. With the American Sixth Army approaching, they started evacuating the camp. These Jewish "prisoners" were to be transported by rail to Dachau, two hundred and fifty miles away to the south; but due to sections of the track having been blown up by Allied bombing, and the consequent detours and delays, the trip took nineteen days, with no food or water for the overcrowded unfortunates locked inside the boxcars. This "Death Train," as it came to be called, rolled up to Dachau only shortly before the 20th Armored stumbled onto the scene to find the boxcars just sitting there on the tracks outside the camp, the engine having taken off. Busting the locks and sliding back the doors, to be greeted with a perfectly horrendous stench, they found each boxcar piled high with the dead and rotting, twisted and tangled bodies of men, women, and children. Even after half a century, Mort related what he saw to me with a good deal of anger—an emotion I'd never seen him show before—though it wasn't so much shown visibly as in his words. He even used some choice *bad* words, which I'd never heard pass his lips before. He told me he had photos in his Army footlocker in the garage that were too horrible to show me—or anyone. On a side note, before this topic of conversation was concluded, I asked Mort how the Nazis had been able to do such unspeakably evil things on such a scale. In a masterpiece of understatement, he replied promptly and simply, "They had all the guns."

As I drove back to Fort Worth, I thought about what he'd said. I recalled what I'd read somewhere what a veteran had said about war, that after going through all that Hell, the rest of your life is practically a holiday, for nothing which you subsequently experience or suffer will ever be as bad as *that*. Maybe, I thought, that explained a lot about Mort, his nonchalant acceptance of life, without complaint, and the singular way he was a sort of stronghold unto himself, content to just "do his own thing" and let the rest of the world do theirs, *howsoever*—not asking for much, not needing or wanting much, and not expecting much—glad just to be alive—taking nothing of society at large that seriously—just enjoying each day as it came in his own little corner of the world.

Mort left a simple will in which he left everything—money,

stocks, bonds, personal possessions, his car, his furniture, and the house itself—to my mother, his step-daughter, as if, by implication, he couldn't care less what happened to it all, likely knowing that she'd sell everything off, (which she did) though we kept some things for ourselves. My sister and I helped mother conduct two estate sales before the house was put up on the market. In doing so, we had to go through all the stuff in the house and in the garage. No such photos were found in that old green footlocker, (my present-day "coffee-table.") Perhaps Mort, knowing the end was near, with foresight, had destroyed them.

Here came Gigi down the hall, walking in that easygoing yet determined way that cats walk. She seemed to be coming up to me, but she stopped shy of me by a few feet, sat back on her haunches, and just looked at me. I said to her, "Well, Gigi, how's life?" As if she didn't care to answer me, she turned her head then her body up to the right and aristocratically strolled off towards the dining room.

P.S. I can't resist telling a funny story about something that happened at Grandma and Mort's house when I was a teenager. Their next door neighbors across the fence, on the west side, were the Coffee's, Harold and May, who were around their same ages. Like Grandma, May was, and always had been, simply a housewife. Mother, I haven't mentioned, was not. She was a legal secretary. For some reason, Mother never liked May. I never heard her say a word against her; but it was pretty obvious when she was around May, who used to walk over to visit Grandma now and then, that she didn't much care for her company, (which May undoubtedly saw and felt.) Mother would hardly speak to her. I never liked May much, either. She was the only person I've ever known who was both friendly and unfriendly at the same time. On the tall side, thin, with short gray hair and a hawk-like face, May did have a rather domineering and self-righteous personality; and it was perhaps her Fundamentalism, which she wore on her sleeve, that rubbed Mother the wrong way.

She was in the habit of "dropping pieties" on any occasion; and she had one for any occasion, such as the time I was boasting about hitting two home runs at a school baseball game that day in front of Mother, Grandma, and May at the kitchen table at Grandma's, which brought forth from May the comment, "Now—now—don't forget, 'Pride goeth before a fall,'" which I thought was an odd thing to say, and didn't really understand, anyway.

But to get to the story . . . We had a birthday dinner at Grandma and Mort's house for Mother's fortieth birthday, on July 20th, 1969, which consisted of turkey and dressing and all the trimmings. Seated around the table, there was Mort at the head of the table dressed in brown slacks and a short-sleeved, red robin-colored shirt around the collar of which was a black string tie whose circular, sliding silver clasp sported a bucking bronco—I sat on his right, wearing blue jeans and a shirt-sleeved, olive green shirt—Carol sat across from me in a short-sleeved, pink dress with white polka dots— Mother sat on her left in a short-sleeved, checkered dress of little beige and yellow squares—and Grandma sat on my right, across from Mort, in a long-sleeved, plain, chocolate brown dress, looking like she belonged at a funeral instead of a birthday celebration. The time came round, after the meal, to bring in the birthday cake. As Grandma did so, from the kitchen, followed by Carol with the serving plates and forks, she announced, "This birthday cake was made by May Coffee just for this occasion. She brought it over yesterday." Looking at Mother, as she set the cake on its china platter down in front of her, she said, "This is your birthday present from the Coffee's." Mother gave her a curious look, but said nothing. (May Coffee had never done anything like this before.) It was a circular, two layer cake covered in white icing and decorated, in the middle on top, with a single, thick, lighted white candle. We all sang "Happy Birthday"—Mother made her wish, giving me a smile as she did so—she blew out the candle—everybody clapped—and she then stood up to cut the cake. Applying the long silver cake knife, she sliced away.

Nothing happened. She tried again, applying more pressure. Still nothing. The knife didn't so much as make a dent in the cake. Mother gave Grandma a puzzled look. Grandma got up from her chair, came over, studied the cake for a few seconds, then, taking one of the forks in her right hand, scraped away some of the icing. Her expression froze as her eyes grew large. "It's a real SPONGE!" she exclaimed. She scraped away some more of the icing. Sure enough, the "cake" was merely two large, circular, yellow sponges stacked one on top of the other, hidden under the white icing. Mort and Carol looked at the "cake" with open jaws, but I started laughing. Grandma gave me a stern look. Mother gave me a furious look. I continued laughing, anyway. Mort, fighting to keep back a grin himself, said loudly (and unconvincingly) to me, "Now, Chris, this is something that isn't funny." I gave him a look like he'd said nothing and went on laughing. It was like I couldn't stop laughing. Grandma exclaimed, like Queen Victoria, "Young man, you can leave the table and go to your room!" I did. That is, I went down the hall to the middle bedroom, which was always "my room" whenever I spent the night at Grandma and Mort's. As far as Mother was concerned, (and my sister and me,) it was good-bye to May Coffee for forever; and it practically was, I think, for Grandma, too, who was not in the least bit amused by the "sponge cake." If May ever came over anymore after that, it was certainly never when any of the Steers were there.

CHAPTER 36

Goodbye Thursday

Well, Evelyn came home around four-thirty. Knowing that I had little to no interest in what she'd been doing, she didn't go into anything about her time spent at Constanza's house, and I didn't ask, except to ask, merely as a courtesy, expecting no explanation, "Did you have a nice time?" to which she replied, with a sort of proud firmness, "Yes, I had a *very* nice time."

For the rest of the day, I worked in the yard and garden until it was almost dark, then came in and had dinner on a tray (fried chicken and creamed corn) in the easy chair in front of the TV in the living room, as Evelyn did the same in bed in front of her TV in her bedroom. Actually, I watched one of my "classic" videos on TV, the John Wayne western, *Red River*, which is about a long and arduous Chisholm Trail cattle drive. Once it was over, I retired to my room to go to bed around ten-thirty, which was early for me, but I felt kinda tired after such a day. Evelyn was already asleep. Turning off the bedside lamp and settling my head into the pillow, Paula wasn't on my mind at all as I dropped off quickly to sleep.

CHAPTER 37

The Nightmare

That night I had a bad dream—a real nightmare. In it, I was attempting to climb over a split rail fence which separated a somewhat sunken dirt road from a wide, green field beyond, somewhere out in the country. It was midday, and a hot sun overhead beat down out of a blue, nearly cloudless sky. Thus, it was sometime during the summer. I was wearing blue jeans, a red, short-sleeved shirt, and white sneakers. At a little distance away in the field, some cows were grazing, more or less grouped together. In the far distance, stretching from one side of the view to the other, there was a cornfield; and the only tree in sight was a medium-sized live oak near the fence, maybe thirty feet down on my right.

I say I was "attempting" to climb over the fence because instead of just hopping up and over it, five rails high, I had to keep balanced, in making my climb, a large, circular, silver tray on which were stacked, in a pyramid-like fashion, whole, plucked chickens—the same kind you buy in the grocery store, but unwrapped and ready to cook—eleven in number. With my left hand thus engaged like a waiter in a restaurant, this only left my right hand to grab hold of the rails. Why I was doing this—carrying this generous chicken platter out into this field—is a good question. There was no house, or even a barn, in sight; nor, in the dream, did I ever feel or believe I was taking these chickens to anybody. What's more, this was no easy maneuver, trying to keep the heavy tray steady as I made my ascent. I felt that at any moment the tray would tilt and send the slick chickens tumbling over one another to the ground. It was slow, and even tortuous going. Perspiration ringed my forehead from the heat and the exertion. Of course, in reality, it'd be physically impossible to support such a load of hefty poultry with just one arm, unless you were Hercules, (which I'm not); but then in dreams the physically impossible is often magically possible.

The cows were apparently shaken out of their usual laziness and indifference by the singular sight of me and my pyramid of fresh, dead chickens at the fence; and they started to amble over in my direction. I hardly paid them any mind, though, concerned as I was with the task at hand. Only when they drew near, (pulling up maybe ten feet away from me,) did I notice that these were truly cattle with a difference, in that they had the brown bodies of cows, but *human heads*! Their faces were the white faces of men and women of different ages, none of whom I recognized. I wasn't so much disconcerted by the unbelievable appearance of these "people-cows" as by how they greeted me—different ones saying such things as, "Who do you think you *are*, coming into *our* field?" "If those are for *us*, we don't eat meat." "Looks like a bird in the hand really *is* worth two in the bush!" This brought forth a round of laughter from them all. And simply, "They're gonna fall!" "They're gonna fall!"

I managed to make it to the top rail during the course of this "welcome," but was so unnerved by the mocking words of the people-cows that, sure enough, I let the tray tilt too far, and the precariously-stacked up fryers went cascading to the earth, hitting it like a ton of bricks on the other side of the fence, in front of the people-cows. Then, to my absolute amazement, the headless, bare birds, upon striking the ground, instantaneously turned back into *real chickens* and started running around in every direction like a bunch o' nitwits, cackling, flapping their wings, and bumping into each other. The people-cows found all this highly amusing, and started loudly laughing. What happened then was unreal—outrageous—truly nightmarish. I couldn't believe it, the people-cows *wouldn't stop laughing*. The chickens soon settled down, once they found their own space, and proceeded to slowly strut about in that jerky, cakewalk manner common to chickens. A few of them even wandered off across the field. No matter. The people-cows kept right on laughing—the force of their laughter causing their heads to bob up and down, and from side to side. It was as if, once started, they simply couldn't stop laughing. Their laughter soon grew hard—vicious—exposing their teeth, wrinkling their foreheads, and almost shutting their eyes. I was dumbstruck. It made no sense. Having been sitting on the top rail since spilling the tray, bewildered by what'd happened and what was happening, I didn't know what to do. Anybody else, seeing that the "stupid cows" were now past all reason, would've simply left them to their convulsive fit and beat it off down the road, glad to get away from them. Not me. It was like I was glued to the spot. Suddenly, from behind me, a scarlet cardinal alighted on the top rail of the fence, some ten feet down from me, on my left; but, apparently taken aback by all the commotion, it only remained there for maybe five or six seconds before it flew off, over the cows, towards the cornfield, very quickly growing smaller and smaller until it was just a tiny red dot, and then was gone. Anyway, I just sat there, like a dumb Humpty Dumpty, with the result that the uncontrollable, obscene, howling laughter increased in volume and intensity to the point where (perhaps childishly/ perhaps overdramatically) I raised the tray up in front of me like a shield and, almost closing *my* eyes, screamed out a drawn-out, "PLEASE! . . ."

My eyes popped open like a Jack-in-the-box. I involuntarily sat/shot up halfway on my left elbow, and for some moments I was both shocked and confused by the utter silence of my room—its stillness and darkness—and, through the window opposite my bed, by the stars shining serenely in the sky.

For some minutes, once fully awake, I lay there in bed trying to make some sort of sense out of this grotesque, absurd dream—unsuccessfully. I didn't recognize, in the faces of those nasty cows, anyone I'd ever known, or perhaps had just seen somewhere. Ditto for that dirt road, fence, and field, which could've been a dirt road, fence, and field anywhere. Why raw/uncooked chickens, in particular? Obviously, I couldn't have been delivering them to anybody as food—as a ready-cooked meal. Then, as I've said, I never felt or believed, in the dream, that I was taking them to anybody. As for that horrible laughing fit, the effect was way out of proportion to the cause. Yes, that sudden "chicken change" from fryers into flyers was certainly startling and comical, and worth some astonished chuckles; but it wasn't all *that* funny.

As I lay there in the dark going over it, and trying to put the pieces of the puzzle together, the only thing that was clear was that there was no clarity. What did the dream mean? What hidden fears, anxieties, or conflicts did its different elements symbolize? I couldn't tell, or even begin to decipher. It was all too cleverly—too devilishly—disguised. I was just baffled.

Eventually falling back to sleep, I didn't dream anymore for the rest of the night.

CHAPTER 38

Chris's List

I woke up before Evelyn. She promised me before she went to bed that she'd fix me pancakes and bacon in the morning. I was gonna hold her to her promise. Forget about fixin' myself some humdrum cereal. I'd wait. I knew it wouldn't be long before she'd wake up, too. So, lying in bed, I decided to amuse myself, in the interim, with composing, in my head, a list of my favorite movies. I thought it'd be sort of a lark. It turned out it wasn't. Not only did I have to pull movies from here, there, and everywhere, so-to-speak, but I soon found that I couldn't simply make a Top Ten list. There were too many favorite movies. I tried for fifteen. Same result. Finally, I settled on twenty movies, though this still left me feeling dissatisfied. A really sufficient list would've probably been around forty movies. Still—hey—it was the first thing in the morning, and it wasn't gonna be evaluated by the New York Film Society. (I'm aware, as far as movie lists go, that the critics forever rank *Citizen Kane* as the No.1/ greatest movie of all time. I've seen it. So it has lots of fancy camerawork? I find it superficial and boring. Perhaps that's the whole point.) Anyway, I think this list is a pretty good representation of movies that I truly love, and can watch over and over again. The movies are in no particular order, they're all equally favorites. Well, here's what I finally came up with,
    1. *The Field*
    2. *Shane.* The greatest western ever made, in my opinion, with spectacular photography, and with Alan Ladd giving a subtly-shaded performance as the mysterious gunfighter.

3. *Valkyrie*
4. *West Side Story*
5. *A Hard Day's Night*
6. *Strangers on a Train*
7. *Sunset Boulevard*
8. *Angels with Dirty Faces.* James Cagney's powerful, electrifying performance turns an otherwise routine gangster film into a classic. I love the line, "I'll help you with the collection." Then there's that unexpected and unforgettable ending.
9. *My Favorite Year*
10. *Amadeus*
11. *Elmer Gantry*
12. *Cinema Paradiso.* A joy to watch, nostalgic and bittersweet, yet fresh and surprising. It's perhaps the most wonderful movie ever made.
13. *City Lights*
14. *Lincoln*
15. *Mutiny on the Bounty.* The one with Marlon Brando. Yes, I know the critics consider the movie to be dreadful; but I really like it. Brando's reaction to being *ordered* to go make love to Maimiti is priceless.
16. *Saving Mr. Banks*
17. *The Odd Couple*
18. *Birdman of Alcatraz*
19. *East of Eden*
20. *The King's Speech*

20½. *It's a Wonderful Life.* Though far-fetched and somewhat overly-sentimental, it has the most original plot of any movie I've ever seen; and it clearly shows the "lives of quiet desperation" and unfulfilled hopes and dreams that many, many men like George Bailey lead in our society. Lionel Barrymore's marvelously horrible as the mean Mr. Potter. It's a unique movie.

I think if I was laid up in a hospital bed for three or four days, after a major operation, and wanted something to get my mind off myself, these flicks'd do the trick. Even being (more or less) perfectly healthy, I can watch these favorites, as I've said, over and over again.

CHAPTER 39

Come Friday (YCTIWY)

I'd timed it pretty well. No sooner had I completed my list, than I heard Evelyn moving about in her room. Well, not exactly. Evelyn's frequently in the habit, upon waking up in the morning, of lying in bed for awhile longer, with the lights off and blinds closed, listening to music on her "positive thinking/self-help" CDs for a spell. On this morning, she'd popped in one of her Louise Hay CDs, and I was blessed with hearing the slow, deep, soothing, monotone voice of Ms. Hay floating out of her dark bedroom like Countess Dracula, her voice accompanied by a continuous, delicate, wind chime-like sound in the background. Though Ms. Hay, like all self-help gurus, tells you nothing but what you want to hear, like "love everybody" and "you're a special person" and "there's no such thing as evil" (—happy words which, of course, keep the dollars rolling in—) still, I suppose, it's harmless enough; and it does tend to put you in a good mood. I mean, it's better than listening to the song "Dust In The Wind" by the 70s group Kansas first thing in the morning. In any case, I don't begrudge Evelyn listening to such stuff if she wants to and likes to, which she obviously does.

As Ms. Hay leisurely went on, "You need to repeat to yourself, on a daily basis, 'I love my neighbors . . . I love my surroundings . . . I love my body . . . I love my job . . .'" I got out of bed, put on my robe and slippers, and went down the hall to the dining room. Looking out the dining room window, which is one of the first things I always do upon getting up in the morning, I noticed that the sky was overcast and gray, and that the city in the distance looked rather somber. It was like I'd told Evelyn once, "You never get tired of this view. It's always different yet always the same, if you know what I mean." She did. It's almost like the visible city has its moods, like a person, which are ever-changing.

While I was looking out, I heard the faint, garbled voice of Ms. Hay suddenly stop. A few seconds later, Evelyn came down the hall to the kitchen. I don't think she realized I was already up, for, after a few moments, in looking through the "window" between the kitchen and dining room, and seeing me standing there, she exclaimed, "Oh—good morning!"

Looking back at her, wearing her familiar gray robe, I replied, "¡Buenos dias! It looks like maybe it's gonna rain. I hate rainy days."

"Oh, you know it never rains very long up here."

I took a seat at the table, my back to the window. After observing her moving about the kitchen for some moments, I inquired, "Evelina, I hope you're gonna keep your promise."

She stopped and stared at me in wonder for a few seconds, then broke into a smile. "Yes, yes, I always keep my promises. Don't worry. Your pancakes and bacon are coming up." Breaking into an even broader smile, she added, "Chrisito, I spoil you too much!"

"*Do* you?"

"Yes, I do," she said forcefully, and even a shade exasperatingly. She turned towards the stove on her left and out of view.

I decided to leave her to her task, and didn't talk to her anymore as she went about making breakfast; while I changed my seat to my usual one looking out the window, and gazed out at the city in the distance—and, closer by—at two black hawks, fairly high up, who were circling over the foothill, side by side, at a good clip, and with their wingtips nearly touching (like two fighter escorts), which was something I didn't remember ever having seen before. I almost called to Evelyn—but didn't. I also noticed that one of the foothill's wild feral cats—this one totally jet black—was, curiously, strolling a little ways across the middle top of the low, white, cinderblock wall bordering the turnaround, then stopping—more like freezing—still standing—even as it stared down at the foothill for six or seven seconds—then doing the same thing over again. Something (some critter—maybe a mouse or a lizard—) must have caught its attention scurrying about over the brushy ground under the shrubbery. The cat's predatory nature, though held under control, was as evident as the daylight.

Well, Evelyn made four trips to the dining room table. First, she brought in the silverware and napkins, placing them appropriately around. Next, she brought in the glasses of orange juice. After that, she brought in the plastic bottle of syrup. Finally, she brought in the plates of pancakes and bacon, setting them down (mine first), then sitting down herself on my right. Even as she set the plate down in front of me, I noticed that the black cat suddenly leaped, like a lightening bolt, from the wall down to the foothill, and, thus, disappeared from sight. It seemed that all three of us were going to enjoy a meal. Also, no sooner had we started in our breakfast than the two hawks separated, flying off in opposite directions (to the east and west.)

We ate for a bit in silence, Evelyn not even looking out the window (or at me), but only down at her plate. I knew her changing moods well enough to know that this was probably a prelude to her opening up about something that was on her mind. Sure enough, she finally said, "Chrisito, I've been thinking about something lately."

"What could that be, I wonder?"

She looked at me through squinting eyes for a moment; then, relaxing her gaze, and letting out a sigh, she looked quite openly at me as she said, "I think the time's come for us to make out our will."

"And you say you never know what I'll say next! . . . I don't hear any ambulances comin' yet."

As if I hadn't said anything, she continued, "We can't just ignore it. We're not in our twenties—even our forties—

anymore. Anything could happen. What'll happen to everything—to this house—to my apartment? I can tell you, for a fact, that if you should go first, I won't stay by myself all alone up here in Lomas. I'll go back to my old apartment in Monterrey. I'll keep this place just as a weekend, or vacation home. If I should go first, you can't stay up here all by yourself, either. I really don't know what you'd do."

I started to say something, and got out the words, "I'll never"— before she cut me off, seemingly determined to get to her point, "But we can talk all about that later. The fact is someday—not that faraway—we'll both be gone. Who'll get everything?"

"Do you really care that much?"

"Yes, I do," she said emphatically, "and you should, too."

"I guess so." I let the words speak for me.

"What about all your books—my books—your ancient coin collection—your records—my jewelry—all the furniture, here and in the apartment—the apartment and this house itself—our"—

I cut her off, "OK—OK—I get the picture. I have a question for you, though, Who do you possibly think we're gonna leave it all to? Name one person."

She looked at me for a few moments as if I was talking Japanese; but then her expression became serious. There was a dead silence between us as I waited for what I knew she'd say. Finally, she said, "Well, the truth is, there isn't anybody . . . but I was thinking about leaving most of everything to maybe María and Pepe and their family. What d'you think?" María and Pepe Valencia are a middle-aged couple living on the corner of the block, next to Baby Diego. They have a twenty-something daughter and a teenage son still living at home, and two other married sons with children living down in town. Though none of them speak hardly a word of English, Pepe and María and the two children are nice neighbors, and we periodically go to their house, or they come to ours for a Saturday or Sunday evening get-together/party/barbecue. Pepe works for the government. María's a housewife. Of the two children still living at home, Pablo's an engineering student in college, while Gabriela's a secretary.

"Well, they're as good a choice as any. Pepe would love, and would take good care of the yard, I'm sure." Evelyn nodded her head. There was a pause, then I continued, "You know, it's pretty pathetic that we have nobody—no family or family members, or close friends—to leave our possessions to . . . We should go out and adopt some children before it's too late. A boy and a girl'd be nice—not babies—more like teenage orphans or something to solve the problem." Of course, I was only half-serious.

"Very funny. You must be crazy, *teenagers,* at our age! You don't know what problems are."

"It's just an idea." I smiled at her.

"A stupid one. We're not about to do that!" She paused. "No, I think my plan about María and Pepe's a good one." I could almost see her wheels turning. "Gaby or Pablo someday might want this house themselves—whether they ever get married or not—and they can have the extra income from the apartment."

"I think that's supposing a lot; but I agree that María and Pepe are probably the best choice we've got." I suddenly felt depressed. Gazing out the window at the somber city as if, truly, just gazing, with little interest, at a dull picture, I said, "We'll need to get a lawyer and have the whole thing done up right."

We have a lawyer. Don't you remember? Alejandro, who did our buying of this house."

"Oh yes."

"I'm sure he's still there. If not, we'll get somebody else. I don't think it'll be that expensive here in Mexico."

Evelyn's plate was back to being just an empty plate, while I was still working on my pancakes and bacon which I had more or less half-eaten. Evelyn's a fast eater, in spite of being, often, at the table, a big talker; while I generally take my time. She kinda attacks her food like a dog does his or her dinner bowl; while I kinda pick at mine like a bird, sometimes not even finishing everything. The only things I really wolf down are hot dogs. Anyway, having "cleaned her plate," and, apparently, quite satisfied with the happy conclusion of our discussion, (as most people are when you agree with them,) she gave me a pleasant smile and said, "I'm so glad we had this little talk. It sets my mind at rest . . . You go ahead and finish your breakfast," she said like my mother. "I need to do a wash."

"OK."

She stood up and, taking her plate, with the silverware on top, and glass, went back to the kitchen. Coffee, it seemed, wasn't gonna be served.

While she went about her business, I slowly finished my breakfast as I gazed out the window. Just because I'm a slow eater doesn't mean, necessarily, that I don't much like what I'm eating. The pancakes and bacon were delicious. I said that I suddenly felt depressed. Most facts *are* depressing; and our discussion only brought home to me the indisputable fact that I was much closer to the end of my personal journey than to its beginning. Oh, I might live another twenty years or so—*might*—but it was an equally indisputable fact that once you've reached a certain age—reached my age—the years go by very quickly. Yes, time was, indeed, *running* out. It was with a cold sadness (and an equally cold terror) that I had to face my own mortality. Young people can't comprehend this. When I was young the future seemed like my special, personal eternity; but when you've lived long enough you throw away your crystal ball. The future loses its glamour. In some respects, you come to dread it. You know this world too well. Each day is enough, (though I sometimes wonder how many more suns I'll see.) In essence, you come to take the future, like God, on faith; though, unlike God, not as seriously. I almost resented all of our possessions, in the end, there're just *things*, and don't mean anything, except for the memories attached to them, which are *yours alone*. Whoever gets them after you will form their own personal attachments to them (maybe). What they meant to you—if they have the slightest awareness of what they meant to you at all—will mean nothing to them. All really was vanity. It was even a pain and a bother to have to make out a will, and have to dispose of everything. It was enough to make me wish I'd lived my whole life in a tent, or on a mountaintop, like the saints of old.

What's more, this discussion also brought home to me, indirectly, the probable fact that this whole thing with Paula was something of a farce, though I only thought of it now, even as I observed another black hawk slowly circling over the foothill, fairly low. Mike was right. There was no future in it, for either of us, with the age difference; though this didn't seem to trouble Paula in any way. Then again, maybe I was taking it all too seriously. Just live for the moment. Enjoy life as it comes. Don't worry about tomorrow. You only live once. Go for it, etc . . . I only wished it was that easy.

As I stared out the window, in finishing my breakfast, I couldn't help but take the time to wonder what in the world I was doing here in Mexico. I didn't belong here, and never really would. Though I loved the house, with its beautiful location and enchanting, surrounding climate, and liked many things about Saltillo, I was, and forever would be *what* I was, a foreigner and an outsider. On the other hand, at my age, did it really matter? To a large degree, I'd had my life, for better or worse; and if this is where I'd ended up, for the little time still left to me, this place was as good as any, and better than most—certainly better than Texas—the Texas of today. Sure, my childhood in Dallas had been the happiest time in my life; but that was over fifty years ago when I was a carefree child, in a whole different, simple *Leave It to Beaver* era, which was long gone, (and was never gonna come back.) I remembered reading somewhere once that Mark Twain had once written (in a letter) that his childhood had been "a Paradise." Mine was, too, yes, truly, a *Paradise Lost*. Nothing in my adult life had ever measured up to it. The black hawk that had been slowly circling low over the foothill suddenly broke off his maneuver and dropped like a spear to the ground, disappearing from view below the turnaround wall, just like the cat had done. The hawk, like the cat, had doubtless pounced on its prey. I put Mexico (and Paula) out of my mind. I put Dallas out of my mind. I put the will out of my mind. I got up from the table, having taken my last bite of breakfast, and went to the kitchen to fix myself a cup of coffee. In doing so, I pressed the ON button then the RADIO button on my CD/Radio player on the counter, which came on in the middle of the song "Mind Games" by John Lennon. As I listened to the song while waiting for my coffee to warm up in the microwave, I thought to myself, "Yes, life consists, ultimately, not so much in trying to find happiness as simply in trying to avoid unhappiness."

CHAPTER 40

Must Be A Cultural Thing

    I drank my coffee and smoked a cigarette back at the table while gazing out at the silent city in the distance, not really thinking about anything; then, putting the cup and saucer and silverware on top of the pancake 'n baconless plate, I picked the plate up and headed back to the kitchen. It was just another Friday, little different, for me, than any other day of the week. I didn't do anything spectacular for the rest of the day, just worked in the yard and garden, washed the car, and looked at the internet while Evelyn washed the clothes, hung them up on the line to dry, (which is actually one of those 50s type, rotary clotheslines,) and eventually took them down and brought them inside, folded them, and put them away. She also spent some time on the internet and talked on the phone en español to who knows who. Speaking of that, it sometimes kinda riles me the way her apparent army of girlfriends brush me off like I was a total nobody. I mean, if the phone rings, and I'm lucky enough to actually answer it myself, (like when Evelyn's playing the piano or hanging up or taking down the clothes outside,) the person on the other end is almost always one of her girlfriends calling to speak to *her*—better believe it. Most of these girlfriends, like the ones calling from Monterrey, know me quite well, and speak some English—a few of them a lot. No matter. If I answer the phone and say, "¡Bueno!" ("Hello!"), they invariably say, without so much as a howdy-do, "Oh, Chris! (obviously surprised) Is Evelyn there?" followed by a dead silence. "Sí. Un momento," and I take the phone to her. I've found Mexican women to be tireless talkers, among themselves.

Around men, in social situations, they don't say much. Mexican men act the same way around women. Must be a cultural thing. Of course, Evelyn's an exception to the rule, she talks to everybody, without hesitation. I do, too; but I'm a much quieter person than her most of the time. After a rather late dinner, we watched one of my videos, *A Beautiful Mind,* on the TV in the living room, then went to bed.

CHAPTER 41

That Saturday

The day started with an argument. I woke up a little after eight o'clock; and a little while after I woke up, Evelyn woke up, which I knew because her CD player suddenly came on. It wasn't Louise Hay this time, but one of her Nature Sounds CDs, the *Tropical Rain Forest*, which combined the gentle sounds of a tropical rain shower with the occasional sounds of the sharp chirping of what I figured were some parrots, toucans, or macaws. As I listened to it, I pictured, in my mind's eye, William Holden grimly trudging through the jungle in the movie *The Bridge on the River Kwai*. It also occurred to me, for the first time, that *The Bridge on the River Kwai* is, in English, grammatically incorrect. It should be, *The Bridge on the Kwai River.* Nobody says, "the bridge on the River Mississippi." In fact, they'd probably say, "the bridge *over* the Mississippi River."

After a while, with the CD still playing, Evelyn appeared at my door, barefoot, and wearing her gray night robe. "May I come in?"

I noticed that she'd put on some red lipstick, which displeased me. Otherwise, she looked, indeed, like she'd just gotten out of bed. "Certainly," I said.

She sat down on my left, on the edge of the bed. "How do you feel?"

"OK," I replied.

She loosened the belt of her robe and shifted her position slightly, which caused the robe to fall back a bit, revealing some of her cleavage. "You wanna play?"

"Uh—not now. Maybe later."
"Why not now?"
"I don't feel like it."
"You said you feel OK."
"Not for that."
"Why?"
"Why must you always have a *reason* for everything?"
"'Cause there *is* a reason for everything."
"So?"
"If you can do it later, you can do it now."
I turned my head away on the pillow and mumbled, "Yea, I'm just a regular love machine."
"What did you say?"
"Nothing."
"I know what it is. I've seen it coming for a long time now, you're tired of me."
I looked straight at her. "I'm not tired of you."
She looked down at the floor. "You are—in that. You'd like somebody like Paula."
Talk about knocking me over, (if I wasn't already over,) with a feather! I collected my thoughts for a few moments, before saying, "Look, Evelina, Paula's a gorgeous girl, all right; but she's still just that, a girl, and one"—
She interrupted me with, "That's exactly *it*, she's a *young* girl. I no longer am. I don't think anybody'd call me 'gorgeous,' even if I ever was."
I was stumped as to what to say. What she said was—well—*true*. I suddenly felt like a heel. I looked at her, but didn't say anything.
She gave me a glance, then looked back down at the floor. "I wonder sometimes what you'd do if I suddenly died. It could happen. I'm no Spring chicken, and I do have a heart condition. I bet you'd marry someone like Paula—some young thing—before the grass started across my grave. You men are all the same. If you should die, I'd never remarry. Once is plenty enough."
"Thanks."

After four or five seconds, she airily said, looking sideways at me, "You take me the wrong way. You should take that as a compliment."

"I'll try."

She stiffened. "I do ask myself sometimes how or why we're still together."

"Because we love each other?"

She looked right at me. "See—that's just what I mean. You have to make a joke out of everything."

"I'm sorry. We don't love each other?"

"Words are words. I can't even begin to say to you the way I really feel; and I know you're never gonna say anything to me . . . I remember how you used to pick up Didi and hug her and kiss her again and again and say that you loved her. I'd drop dead if you ever did that with me. You've never said, 'I love you' to me once in twenty-three years."

I felt like I was in a rapidly falling, runaway elevator. After some seconds, I found the courage to say, "OK, Evelina, I love you."

"Very funny." She looked away.

Rather peeved by her response, I asked her, "Can you do me a favor? Please go over and turn off that CD player."

She gave me a hard glance, but got up, crossed over to her room, turned off the player—also brushed out her hair and put on some more lipstick, as well as her slippers—then came and sat back down on the edge of the bed. While she was doing these things, I recalled those lines from the movie *Zorba the Greek* where Anthony Quinn, as the earthy Zorba, says to Alan Bates, as Boss, "God has a very big heart, but there is one sin He will not forgive. If a woman calls a man to her bed and he will not go"—although, I thought, this probably said more about Zorba than about God (or women).

After Evelyn sat back down on the bed, the mild breeze that had been gently floating into the room through my half-open window suddenly stopped. After some moments, she stretched out her left arm and proceeded to run her fingers through my hair while looking abstractedly at me. This continued for a bit, with neither of us saying anything. Finally, with my left arm, I reached up, lightly grabbed her wrist, and pushed her arm away. This caused her to firmly pull her wrist out of my grasp and put her hand back in her lap. After maybe ten seconds, she commented, "I've always suspected that, deep down, you don't really like women very much."

"That's not true."

"You're the least romantic man I've ever known."

"So, you're finally admitting you've known lots of men!"

"No, I'm not . . . but I had my share of boyfriends when I was single."

"I'll bet."

This remark didn't phase her, and she continued in the same calm manner, "I mean, I've come to accept you for the way you are, over the years—being a loner—off in your own world—and it's nothing that big to complain about—there're many men a million times worse—but I wish sometimes you could show a little more feeling, and be a little more sensitive."

I looked at the ceiling. "Do you, now? Is that what you wish? . . . You women kill me . . . It's like on those talk shows where women sit around and cry crocodile tears over their numbskull boyfriends. Oh, how they *just wish* they could find a man who never raised his voice—was intelligent, considerate, kind, and full of feeling—who treated them like ladies—was romantic—and behaved like a perfect gentleman at all times. Meanwhile, this doesn't stop them in the least from going out and starting up a relationship with the biggest Neanderthal on the block."

She made as if to stand up, but she didn't. "How dare you say that to me! That's exactly why I married you, because you weren't some *estúpido*! Who do you think I am? Some bimbo? Your biggest problem is you're always opening your mouth without thinking. For such an intelligent man, I don't understand it." She started to calm down a bit. She stared at the wall. "That's because many women have little if any self-esteem . . . You don't know how lucky you are. I'd like to see you married to some women I know. ¡Ay Dios Mío! (Oh my God!) They've got *lots* of self-esteem. You'd have been in a homeless shelter years ago." There was a hardness in her voice.

"You take everything personally."

"Why not? Who else are you talking to? You did say 'you women.'"

"I can't even express an opinion. I wasn't talking about you, in particular, but about a lot of women in general . . . OK, just forget I said it. I shouldn't have. And I will try to work on my—uh—'emotional state.' There's always room for improvement. Things can always get better."

I think she accepted my clichés with some skepticism, for she said, "Like I said, 'words are words.' I hope you mean what you say."

"I do." There was a pause. Then, I said, "You know, Evelina, how, when we meet new people in this country, you sometimes take it upon yourself to explain that Chris is for Christopher, like in Cristóbal Colón, Christopher Columbus. Well, I must admit, when I married you, it really *was* like discovering a New World—yes, sir."

She gave me a blank look, as if she was unsure whether to take that as a compliment or not, (though I said it quite amiably, and meant it to be taken at face value.) After a few moments, she smiled thinly at me and said, "Yes, you were quite the little conquistador!"

Now I gave her a blank look, unsure precisely how to take *that.* As if she sensed this, she said reflectively, "I've never said anything to you, but I'd made up my mind, before I met you, that if I liked you, I'd marry you. I did, from the very beginning at the airport. So you really didn't have much work to do, though I let you play along, which you really did, you were like a different person."

"I was younger . . . Nice of you to tell me that, at last." She looked at me with raised eyebrows for a moment. "Yes, it did go smoothly and quickly. It surprised me. What was it, four days before I proposed?"

"Three. It was on the third day."

I looked critically at her, and commented, "We'd written to each other, exchanged photos, and talked on the phone a bit; but it was my finally flying down to Monterrey and our meeting, face to face, that was the thing."

She asked me frankly, "What did you think when you first met me?"

"What did I think? . . . You were taller than I expected, and *warmer*." She thought about this for some seconds, with the hint of a smile. Finally, she said, "I was happy the moment I met you."

"So was I with you." I gave her a smile.

Then, Evelyn spoke up, as if talking to both herself and me, "I remember those first years . . . I was so full of hopes and dreams and demands. I wanted it all. I wasn't ever satisfied. It must have been—I must have been—hard on you. Maybe it was because I married so much older than most women. I'd missed so much . . . I knew I could never give you a child."

"I've told you before that we didn't"—

She interrupted me with, "Please!" She placed her left hand over my lips for a moment, saying, "You don't have to say anything." There was another, good twenty second pause, during which a mourning dove, (a large gray dove,) started cooing outside, (I figured, probably up in one of the pine trees;) and its low, melancholy, clarinet-like cooing softly intruded on the silence all around. Then, Evelyn asked me, "Do you remember the time I threw the iron at you?"

"I certainly do. Never had that happen to me before."

She sort of seriously smiled and said, "You took a huge risk in marrying me. It was a risk for me, too; but I think it was more for you. You're so studious and quiet; but I'm *on fire* half the time—much more back then. You really do have the patience of a saint. I think, maybe unconsciously, that's one of the things that attracted me to you in the first place."

Though this was to be taken, no doubt, as a compliment, I wasn't much thrilled by it. No man really wishes to be called "studious and quiet," or be referred to as a "saint," unless, perhaps, he is one (uh-huh). I suddenly felt small; and, feeling so, blurted out, "Tell you what, honey child, after breakfast, and after I've taken my shower, we can do it, right back here."

She started, and said quietly, "If you want to."

"I do. It'll make your day."

She gave me a look. "You're pretty sure of yourself."

I merely smiled at her.

"Well, in that case, I better go and fix your breakfast." She emphasized the last word. She got up, tightened the belt of her robe a bit, shot me a smile, and headed for the kitchen.

CHAPTER 42

The Red Tricycle

Some things we remember, some things we only half-remember, and some things we don't remember at all. With me, I only half-remember many of the things from my past. With the passage of time, things that were once as sharp and vivid as a color photo become merely a watercolor—even, the farther back you go, a child's watercolor. As I lay there in bed waiting for my "breakfast call," I played a little mental game with myself, what was my very first memory in life? which was something I'd never taken the time to do before. Just trying to remember this was a mental effort in itself; but before long it came to mind. It really *was* like a child's watercolor, with the red tricycle being the only thing that was more or less clearly defined.

Here's the memory, as I remembered it, I'm riding my tricycle down the sidewalk, apparently in front of my house, but a little ways down from it. It's just started to rain, and raindrops are now and again hitting me. Thunder is heard. This doesn't bother me in the slightest. Suddenly, behind me, I hear the hard sound of the screen door of the front door slamming against the side of the house, and, a second later, my mother hollering out, like a lumberjack, and obviously concerned, "Chris! You come back here right now!" as if I'm riding my tricycle down the middle of the street or something. I'm very startled. Nevertheless, without looking back, I hunker down on the tricycle and continue pedaling down the sidewalk—even faster. I guess I was a defiant little bastard even then. Quick footsteps—shoes on the sidewalk—are heard behind me; and then the memory simply dissolved into nothingness. I could only imagine, as I lay there in bed, what happened next, no doubt, I'd mercifully put it out of my mind.

This memory takes longer in the telling than it did in the remembering. It passed through my mind in less than twenty seconds. Not long after it did so, Evelyn practically yelled down the hall, "Chrisito, you can come to breakfast now!" I got up, put on my robe and slippers, and headed towards the dining room.

CHAPTER 43

Saturday Breakfast With Jasmine

This morning, breakfast consisted of cereal (Cheerios), toast, blueberry preserves, (which I love,) and from-the-carton o j, for both of us. I sat, as usual, facing the window, with Evelyn on my right. The window was open, and, though there wasn't any breeze coming through it, the sensuously-sweet fragrance of a white-flowering, potted jasmine, on the walkway under the window, subtly filled the small room. The view wasn't much of a view this morning. The sky was a solid, silvery gray; and a whitish-tannish haze obscured the mountains, so that only the inner ring was only ghostly visible. As if in keeping with this drab view, the city itself appeared somewhat drained of its color, as if it was, Pompeii-like, recently unearthed after centuries. Indeed, it gave the impression of simply looking old—not in the least bit romantic—just old.

I brought up, for the first time, my people-cow dream, telling Evelyn all about it. Of course, when I was finished, I asked her what she thought it might mean, telling her that I couldn't make any sense out of it. She commented, rather nonchalantly, "You shouldn't be having dreams like that. You must've been worried or upset about something. It doesn't make any sense like being upset doesn't make any sense. About *what*, I can't say. I agree with you, it's disguised too well. It's just a crazy dream. Everybody has sometimes those. Me too. That's life. I'd just forget about it."

I could have said, "Thanks—for nothing," but said instead, "It seems that what we don't or can't understand we have no choice but to dismiss."

She gave my a sharp look, even making a loose fist with her left hand. "You're the great brain. If you can't figure it out—and it's your dream—why do you expect me to? Who do you think I am? Sigmund Freud?"

I was quite taken aback by her over-the-top reaction. After a couple of moments I said, in a conciliatory manner, "OK—OK—I'm sorry I brought it up. It isn't important. Like you say, it's just 'a crazy dream.'"

There was a pretty long pause as we ate our breakfast in silence. Finally, attempting to be cheerful, I smiled at her and asked, "What is important is what are we gonna do today after breakfast?"

Without so much as a crack of a smile, she replied, "I think you've already said what."

I imperceptibly started. "Oh yes . . . I mean, after that. Maybe we can go somewhere—get out of the house for awhile."

"Maybe. Where would you like to go?"

"We could go to the big flower market down in town across from HEB."

"Yes . . . and there're some things I need to buy at HEB, anyway. Only, we need to go early and get back before it's too late. I don't wanna stay down in town."

"Then that's what we'll do." Now, there were two mourning doves cooing outside.

CHAPTER 44

Except Maybe Tahiti

"I don't wanna stay down in town." This was an indirect reference to *crime*. Evelyn believes everything she sees on the internet, TV, and reads in the papers. (I don't.) She has more than a touch of paranoia about all the (supposed) crime in Mexico. What's more, she sees me as a sort of "white target" that she needs to keep an eye on. This is to say, though it doesn't bother her (much) if I drive about the colony by myself, or to the shopping center that's not that far outside of the colony, she always wants to accompany me, usually driving herself, if I need or want to go somewhere that's any distance down into town, as if being beside me will make a difference if "something happens." If someone assaults or kidnaps me I don't know how she thinks that being beside me is going to make any difference, short of her having a screaming, hysterical fit. Still, it seems to comfort her. Actually, speaking for myself, I don't worry about it, believing in what President Franklin Roosevelt said, "There is nothing to fear but fear itself." I also believe that what you fear has a tendency to come true. This doesn't mean I'm reckless or foolhardy about it. I watch where I go, and keep off the roads at night. We both live up in Lomas practically like hermits most of the time, anyway.

This doesn't mean I'm not aware that there's crime in Mexico. Sure there is, just like in America, and everywhere else in the world, except maybe Tahiti. There're worse things than being kidnapped and/or killed, such as having to live through a summer in Laredo. Seriously, though, in all the years I've lived in Mexico, and in all the places I've been to in Mexico, never once has anything bad happened to me; and I've always found la policía (the cops) to be obliging and helpful. The demonization of Mexico by the American media, (that in just crossing the border you take your life in your hands,) is way overblown. I'd rather be in downtown Saltillo at midnight, any night of the week, than in downtown Detroit or Los Angeles.

Bad things do happen, though, just like in the States. It was at this very aforementioned flower market that, a couple of months ago, we met Pam and Richard. As Evelyn and I were strolling down one of the long, wide aisles admiring the stalls crammed full of brightly colored flowers of every color and variety on either side, an older Anglo couple passed us by on the left from behind, like a car on the road—I being on the passing side. At that very moment, I was making some comment to Evelyn (in English, about something—I don't remember what—probably something about the flowers—or a particular flower—) and the woman, on my immediate left, exclaimed, in a sort of jesting way, and in a clearly audible voice, without really looking at us, "I think I hear somebody speaking American!" We all stopped. Well, to make a long story short, we all introduced ourselves, stood there and chatted for a bit, exchanged phone numbers, and promised that we would be in contact.

Over a month later, out-of-the-blue one day, Pam called us up. Evelyn, as usual, answered the phone; and the gist of it was that plans were set for Pam and Richard to come to our house in Lomas for dinner the upcoming Saturday evening. It was then that we heard about Richard's "attack."

Pam and Richard are both in their mid-sixties, and have been married for over forty years. They're both of medium height and build; though Richard's thinner than Pam, and, in fact, looks like if he lost about twenty pounds he'd be a beanpole. Pam has an attractive, oval, cheerful face, with striking, sea-green eyes, and wears her silvery hair in a longish, "Beatle" cut; whereas Richard's short, gray hair is thinning out on top. He's thin-faced, clean-shaven and has hazel eyes behind brown glasses. Unlike Pam, he doesn't so much look cheerful, as perpetually worried about something. Richard's originally from Tennessee, and grew up on a farm there. Pam's originally from Ohio, but now lives in Florida. This is to say that they don't live together, as Richard still works as a representative for an American manufacturing firm in Saltillo, which is the same firm he previously worked for for four years in San Luis Potosí, 225 miles to the south, before the firm transferred him, about a year ago, to their Saltillo branch; while, Pam, having taken an early retirement from teaching, lives in Florida. Pam periodically flies down to Saltillo to spend time with Richard, who has an apartment in the city. Richard speaks Spanish. Pam doesn't. Richard, being an ol' Southern boy, has a distinct southern drawl, pronouncing, for example, "Pam" like "Paim," "can't" like "caint," and "our" like "owwah." There're other examples I can't (caint) specifically recall offhand.

Anyway, they came to dinner. Everybody was dressed casually for the occasion, Pam in a short-sleeved, tan dress; Evelyn in a short-sleeved, pale yellow dress; Richard in a short-sleeved, tan shirt and brown slacks, (and wearing the biggest men's gold watch I'd ever seen, whose face was so big it looked almost comical;) and I wore a short-sleeved, white guayabera shirt and blue jeans. We sat at the table with me in my usual spot facing the window, Pam opposite me, Richard on my left, and Evelyn on my right. During the course of the meal, in which we talked about many different things, Richard, at one point, brought up the subject of his "attack." He said it happened when he was living and working in "SLP" (San Luis Potosí, as he put it,) the previous year. He said he was out walking alone down the street one night—just out for a walk—not far from his apartment, at around ten-thirty, when six teenage boys on bicycles suddenly rode up and surrounded him, and proceeded to assault him. They picked him him up, turned him upside down, and shook him so violently that everything in his pockets fell to the ground, including his wallet, the loose change he had on him, his keys, his pen, and his cell phone. Also his glasses. Aside from shaking him, some of them punched and kicked him as he hung in mid-air. Pam interrupted him, "There I was at home in Tampa, sitting on my sofa watching TV, when I received a text message on my cell phone. It was from Richard, and all it said was, 'attacked and robbed on the street, and am now with Jesus—Richard.' I freaked out, thinking these were the only words he was able to text seconds before dying in the gutter!" Richard let out a laugh, and explained, "They threw my keys into the bushes. They took everything else, except my glasses. I made it back to my apartment; but, not having my keys, I knocked on the door of my neighbor Jesús ("heySOOSE"). He let me in, and let me use his cell phone. After giving me a shot of tequila, and calming down a bit, I texted Pam again and gave her a full explanation. I shouldn't have sent that first text, but I was worked up, and not thinking straight. Later, the landlord let me into my apartment, and I hit my bed like the Titanic hit the ocean floor, sleeping until noon the next day."

Poor Richard! While we were having coffee after dinner, Richard received a call on his cell phone. When he stepped out onto the front porch to answer what turned out to be a long call, Pam told us confidentially that Richard was extremely traumatized by this vicious incident, even though he related it to us in a matter-of-fact manner, like he was simply telling us any other story. She said, "He's lost weight, suffers, for the first time in his life, from insomnia, worries about everything—and you must've noticed the facial twitches." How could we not? They were pretty frequent. Pam told us that whether Richard liked it or not, she was going to put her foot down and order him to retire at the end of the year and come back to Florida.

It was enjoyable evening. We enjoyed their company, and could tell they enjoyed ours. We told them they were welcome at our house at any time; and Pam told us the same about the house in Tampa. I've always wanted to visit Florida.

P.S. As regards to crime in Mexico and the United States, I do have some additional comments I'd like to express on the subject, for what it's worth. Major crime in Mexico is primarily what I'd call *"drug crime"*, it's the result of the different powerful and ruthless drug cartels battling one another over control of the drug routes into the United States, the biggest consumer of drugs on the planet. Two other prevalent crimes are extortion and, to a lesser degree, kidnapping. I'd characterize all of these crimes as for-profit, *"business"* crimes, money, and ever more money, are behind them all. In this respect, these crimes are in the age-old *"tradition"* of the Mafia. (Even the attack on Richard was for his money and any valuables he had on him.) What you don't have in Mexico, to any great degree, is the horrific circus of random and senseless shootings that run rampant today all across the U.S. What I mean is the shootings that occur anywhere and everywhere, and against anybody and everybody, innocent women, children, and old people included, (and certainly not for *"profit,"*) such as deadly shootings in kindergartens, elementary, middle, junior, and high schools, colleges and universities, day-care centers, nursing homes, clinics, hospitals, libraries, parks, amusement parks, churches, shopping malls, movie theaters, military bases, veterans homes, courthouses, gas stations, airports, motels and hotels, restaurants, fast-food joints, at political rallies, sporting events, indoor and outdoor concerts, bars, nightclubs, and private parties, road rage shootings on highways, shootings on subways, and, finally, drive-by shootings on residential streets. There're also workplace shootings by disgruntled workers, bombings by right-wing extremists, and terrorist attacks by foreign religious fanatics. And I'm not even including the massive amount of domestic violence. You're not really safe in America *anywhere* today, unless maybe on a remote ranch in North Dakota.

CHAPTER 45

The Beetle

Having finished her breakfast, as usual, before me, Evelyn got up, without saying anything, and took her plate, silverware, and glass back to the kitchen. Having put them in the sink, she unexpectedly made the comment, "I've been thinking about maybe coloring my hair red—not bright red—more like a strawberry blonde—like Belinda. I could buy the color today at HEB. What d'you think?"

"I'd rather not say."

"Meaning you wouldn't like it?"

"Look, Evelyn—you do what you want. You always do. I think it makes Belinda look like a leftover from the Mardi Gras; but maybe it'd look OK on you. Personally, I think people should just keep the color they got."

Evelyn wasn't the least bit offended by my words, and said reflectively, "Maybe you're right." She went down the hall to her room.

As I finished up my breakfast, taking in the melancholy view, her words'd triggered a long-forgotten memory; and one which I'd never mentioned to Evelyn, which was my memory of Valerie Monaghan from back in my single days in Fort Worth. Valerie was the only totally, naturally red-headed girl I've ever known, with long, flowing hair that was really red. As if living up to her "flaming" hair, she was a fiery, party-hard girl; and I had a brief fling with her. (She wasn't only a "party-hard girl"; she was also, actually, just *hard*—I mean, in regards to her character—what some people would've called cynical. She liked to shock.) Sure, we had sex together. After one such bout, I lay there in bed beside her, on her left, and told her how happy I felt, adding that on a scale of 1 to 10 she definitely rated a 10. She considered this for some seconds, then dryly said, with an impish smile, "You men make such a big deal out of chasing after, finally getting, then going ape over a woman's sex organ. It's just a muscle." Leave it to a woman to say such a thing. I'd never heard it put that way before; and there was something so bluntly and clinically depressing about her choice of words that they left me speechless, as well as reachless, I lay there beside her as if in bed all by myself . . . We were on her fancy brass bed in the bedroom of her apartment. To our right, the wide screenless window of her room was open, and a soft breeze entered the room. The sunny Spring day was fading away, and a purplish twilight was beginning to fall. It was as if the great Texas sky was going from titanic to romantic. This was all the light we had, or could still get by with. Suddenly—maybe thirty seconds after her "muscle" comment—something else entered the room through the window, a big black beetle flew/buzzed in and landed on the wall opposite us with a faint plop, whereupon it immediately proceeded to slowly crawl up the wall. Valerie glared at the black bug for a couple of moments as if it had been the Devil himself; then, putting on her panties (at least) as quickly as possible, she jumped out of bed, grabbed one of her black pumps there on the floor with her right hand, went over, and totally *annihilated* the beetle with a ferocious slam of her shoe against the wall (—a real "shot heard round the world"—) using the edge of the shoe to scrap off the remains onto the floor. That was the extent of her "cleaning up" for the moment. This accomplished, she casually dropped the shoe back onto the floor by the bed and calmly got back into bed, snuggling, with a sigh, up beside me. I only commented, with a touch of sympathy, "That poor beetle didn't stand a chance." "No, it didn't," she said firmly. Yes, that was Valerie.

Paula had said, "And I'll make *you* happy. You just wait and see." Would she? Could she? Could I make her happy? Did I even want to, really? Did I even know what I wanted where she was concerned? Perhaps this was nothing but a May/December passion, something which the world tends to look upon with snickering laughter. I remembered *The Blue Angel,* which is a really ancient movie with Marlene Dietrich; but one which deals head-on, and tragicomically, with the subject of an older man and a much younger woman, (though Paula was far above the level of any sleazy cabaret singer.) And *that* doesn't work out at all. As for the "snickering laughter," there was an undercurrent of comedy running through the whole thing with Paula, which I couldn't help but see and feel, even if Paula herself didn't. Mike could see it, too.

I felt a headache coming on. Not finishing all of my breakfast, I got up from the table, went to the bathroom, took two aspirin, and went to my room to lie down in bed for awhile, closing the door. No sooner had I stretched out, than Evelyn, to my irritation, knocked lightly on the door.

"Yes?"

She popped her head in the door and asked, "What's the matter?"

"I have a slight headache. I took some aspirin. I'm gonna lie down for awhile. We can leave in a little while."

"OK," she said softly as she as softly closed the door and went on about doing whatever she was doing.

I dropped off to sleep.

CHAPTER 46

The Sunday Before Monday

Appearances certainly can be deceiving. One of the best examples I can think of is the famous painting by Jacques-Louis David, much reproduced, of the Emperor Napoleon Bonaparte, in military uniform, standing beside his overdecorated desk in his study with his right hand tucked inside his unbuttoned vest, as if he has indigestion. That aside, what about the face of the man who's facing you? The Master of Europe? It's a smooth, soft, round face–even a rather effeminate face—with the slight and obliging smile of a woman, like the Mona Lisa, in this respect. His attempt to look "spontaneous" (perhaps at the painter's suggestion) with his right hand tucked inside his vest and his left leg a little in front of the other only makes his pose look that much more studied. He doesn't look particularly intelligent. He looks like a man who lives in the lap of luxury, has never known hardship or poverty, and who has a very comfortable and spoiled life. Indeed, with his fat face and plump-as-a partridge belly, he reminds me of Roly Poly; and I can imagine him sucking on a piece of candy, or leaving the "sitting" to go take a bubble bath. What I can't imagine is *this man* enduring the rigors, deprivations, and horrors of a military campaign—in fact, *leading* it—living out of a tent, riding through the dust, mud, and snowstorms, dealing with and ordering about battle-hardened veterans, and defeating virtually every army sent against him—and brilliantly, (except, of course, at Waterloo, which he nearly won.)

So it was, on a much more mundane/lower class level,

with Paula. Though, on the surface, she was an unbelievably beautiful and highly-intelligent young woman who was warm, friendly, and charming, and who made you feel like a prince just to be in her company; the more I was around her, the more I began to notice little things that didn't quite fit the picture. That afternoon when we left the park to walk to her apartment for lunch, as we were walking down the street we were accosted by a beggar with long, straggly, brown hair who looked to be middle-aged, though he may have been younger. It was hard to tell exactly, he looked so worn and wretched in clothes that were little more than dark rags, and who looked like he hadn't eaten or slept (or shaved) for days. He didn't say anything, but simply sort of boldly-hesitantly came up to us with his right hand outstretched. I patted my pants pockets. I didn't have one peso to give him. If I had had, I would have given him something. I always do, if I have anything, taking the position that "There but for the grace of God, go I." Not Paula. With only giving him a frozen glance, as if he were a leper or something, she exclaimed, quite rudely, "¡Piérdase!" ("Get lost!") and continued right on talking happily to me. I've already mentioned the stony look (without a word) that Paula gave me when I asked her if those lines of Manuel Acuña meant something personal to her. I haven't mentioned that on that afternoon when I was escorting her from the park to Belinda's office, and she was chattering "away about this and that like a vivacious schoolgirl," one thing she said (with a degree of coldness) was, "You know, I don't see why anyone has to get married and be stuck with some other person—some stranger—*only* for the rest of their life." Though I think this just popped out, she instantly realized who she was talking to, and, letting out a little laugh, self-corrected herself by adding (semi-sincerely, it seemed to me), "Don't take that personally. I really do admire couples who can make a go of it, and who stay together." Paula was truly her own person, all appearances aside, no doubt about it. What was unsettling about her was that she could be both equally kind-hearted and heartless. Obviously—for me, at least—she was there for the asking; but as to how long it'd last, that was anybody's guess.

Around eleven we left the house, (Evelyn driving) and went, as planned, to the flower market again on the northside of town. We strolled up and down the aisles admiring the crowded displays, on either side of us, of beautiful and colorful flowers of every size, shape, and color. The stalls full of multi-blooming rosebushes were especially striking, showing every color of the rainbow, but much more richly and intensely, which would've made Vincent Van Gogh himself stop in his tracks. Overall, the flower market's always a visual joy to see, so over-the-top colorful—even surreal— unlike any other collection of flowers you'd likely ever see all gathered together in one place.

In contrast to all this color, in about the middle of the market, there's an open area, like a square, jammed with utterly plain, off-white, fine cement, large cast objects for sale, including such sculptures as quite realistically cast pigs, alligators, your classic lions sitting on their haunches, similarly sitting coyotes with raised heads and open mouths as if they're howling, swans, turtles, herons standing on one leg, cobras, half coiled and half erect, and falcons, as well as round, square, and rectangular outdoor tables and chairs, birdbaths, and triple-tiered fountains with basins. None of this is presented in any kind of order. It's all just jumbled together. There's no path through any of it, you just have to pick your way around everything. There's not a drop of paint on anything; and this pale, off-white, jumbled "graveyard" couldn't be in greater contrast to the living, luxurious, little world of incredible and amazing color surrounding it. Though not real stone, none the objects are cheap, (except maybe by American standards.) The outdoor tables and chairs, for example, range in price from 6000 pesos ($300) to 10,000 pesos ($500). Actually, for Mexico, I think all of the objects are overpriced—not that you can't always try haggling with the seller and maybe get him to come down a bit. Still, even though I'd love to have one of the cobras, I refuse to pay

1600 pesos ($80), or even 1400 pesos ($70), for it. I ended up not buying anything at the market; but Evelyn bought a medium-sized gardenia bush bursting with very fragrant white blossoms for only 80 pesos ($4).

We walked across the street to the HEB and Evelyn did, in fact, buy some hair color. She didn't buy the strawberry blonde, after-all, but a brown shade matching her natural color. I didn't say anything, but was relieved that she didn't do a Belinda on me. We got a few other things we needed; and shortly were back in the car and on our way back home.

Pretty soon, in heading down the service road which led to the on-ramp to the freeway, we found ourselves, in the right lane, behind a fairly long funeral procession. There must have been fifteen cars creeping along behind the black hearse. When Evelyn was able to move over into the left lane, I observed the procession as we passed it by, and, noticing that each car was full of people, front and back, commented to Evelyn, "Whoever died must have been well-liked, each car is full of people. There must be sixty to seventy people following that hearse . . . I'll be lucky, when I die, if there's *one* car following me."

With not so much as giving the procession a glance, but keeping her eyes on the road, Evelyn said, "What does that matter? After the service at the cemetery, when all those people've gone back home, not once, for the rest of their lives, will any of them ever come back to visit the grave—except maybe, occasionally, members of the family . . . As for you, I'll be there—I hope—I mean, if I don't die first. And I'll come visit you now and then, and put some flowers on you."

I noticed her slight smile as I gave her a look, and said, like a sympathetic friend, "And if it should turn out that way, I'll do the same for you."

"Thanks already," she said quietly. After a few moments, she switched on the radio, and we barely said a word to each other for the rest of the drive home.

CHAPTER 47

Monday-1

Having been dropped off by the taxi at the southern entrance to the park, I arrived at the obelisk-plaza at around twelve-fifteen and took a seat on "our" bench. Typically, nobody else was there, including Paula; but I wasn't unduly concerned, since it took her any number of minutes to leave her nearby office and walk to the plaza. It was a sunny September day with only a slight chill in the air; and it was very still, without a breath of wind, so that the surrounding trees looked more like sculptures than like real trees. I wore a light, green sweater over my long-sleeved brown shirt, blue jeans, and my black tennis shoes.

Time, so-to-speak, ticked on. The very loneliness of the plaza made me, in turn, feel that much more alone. The silent and rigid obelisk in front of me seemed to complete the picture. I mean, a cascading fountain would at least have added some life and sound to the plaza. It was like I was the only living thing there. Twelve-thirty rolled around . . . twelve-forty-five. The result of this was that, after half an hour or so, though I didn't want to admit it to myself, deep down, to my dismay, I just felt and knew that, for whatever reason, Paula wasn't coming. (And she was always there before me.) It was an instinctive feeling; but I felt that my instinct was right about it. Nor did I feel it was up to me to call her on my cell phone. I waited a while longer. No Paula.

Feeling depressed, and even mad (—Who wants to be stood up?—) a little after one I got up and made my way out of the park. Standing there on the curb at the park's southern entrance, facing Bulevar Carlos Salazar, with the intention of hailing a passing cab to take me back home, perhaps it was fortunate (or unfortunate) that no cab came along; for, standing there, after a minute or more, I changed my mind. I decided to walk down the few blocks to Paula's apartment and "see for myself" what there was, if anything, to be seen.

Directly in front of her apartment building, parked on the curb, was a glossy, black, looking-like-brand-new BMW. Looking at it, I deduced that it could be someone visiting Paula, someone visiting one of her neighbors, (or one of her neighbors' car,) or was just parked there by someone visiting one of the surrounding residences. Of course, looking up at the building, I couldn't tell if Paula was in or out. Actually, as far as I knew, she could've been anywhere.

I also noticed, in particular, for the first time, the sign over the entrance to the tortilla maker's shop, which consisted of a fairly short, yellow wooden placard that spelled out, in black letters, "TORTILLAS DE MARÍA." After the word "MARÍA" there was an artistically painted logo portraying a standing and facing white stork, from whose orange beak hung a tied, long, white cloth napkin holding not a baby, but a stack of beige-colored tortillas.

I felt silly just standing there on the sidewalk. It was silly walking down here—pointless. An even sillier thought flashed through my mind, I remembered that famous scene in the movie *A Streetcar Named Desire* where a distraught Marlon Brando stands in front of his apartment building and yells out "Hey, Stella!" at the top of his lungs to attract his upset wife's attention and get her to come down from her girlfriend's second floor apartment; and I had this crazy, passing impulse to do the same thing, "Hey, Paula!" (After all, I was a bit distraught myself.) Of course, I did no such thing. What I did do was walk up the few steps to the ancient front door of the building and tried the handle just for the hell of it, only to find, naturally, that the door was locked.

It couldn't have been more than ten seconds after this attempt than I heard a metal on metal sound, which couldn't have been anything but somebody unlocking the door. I instinctively backed down to the sidewalk. Sure enough, the door opened, and who did I see but Paula herself, holding the big iron key in her right hand, in company with a smartly-dressed young man, on her left, looking to be somewhere in his twenties, and who was a little taller than Paula. Paula only had on a white bathrobe and white slippers; but her companion wore black slacks with a perfect crease down the middle, a long-sleeved, white silk shirt with silver cuff links, and shiny black shoes. He also wore what looked like to be an expensive, big, gold and diamond ring on his right index finger. He had a squarish, clean-shaven, handsome face with dark eyes, and a mass of dark brown hair which was combed (with no part) straight back from his forehead. In spite of Paula's homey appearance, she had on bright red lipstick and her cheeks were lightly rouged. Her hair was fixed the same, with the same iconic ponytail; but on the top and sides, it was a bit mussed up.

If the young man looked at me with a degree of mild curiosity, Paula looked at me like I'd just risen from the grave. Nevertheless, after a couple of moments, she found her voice and spoke up first, "Chris! What are you doing here?"

"You didn't show up at the park. I came by to visit you."

Ignoring what I was really asking, she introduced her companion to me by saying, "This is Eduardo Silva, a friend of mine. Eduardo, this is my friend, Chris Steer, from America."

In admirably polished English, which I couldn't fail but notice, he said, "Nice to meet you, Sir."

I didn't say anything—not that he seemed to care. As a matter of fact, I instantly resented the "Sir," which called out the gulf between our ages, even if he said it innocently enough.

There was a pause. Then he said, without giving her so much as a kiss, in a business-like manner, "Pues, adiós, Paula—hasta la próxima vez." ("Well, good-bye, Paula—until next time"). Paula gave him a little, (and, what appeared to me, ironic) smile, but said nothing. As he descended the steps he said, "Buenas tardes, Señor" and went around to the driver's side of the BMW. Getting in and starting up the car, and without so much as a wave, he drove quickly off down the street.

I looked at Paula. She looked at me. We looked at each other, as serious as sin. I couldn't resist making the sarcastic comment, "And who was that—your stockbroker?"

Without batting an eye, she replied gloomily, "I wish." Then, after maybe seven seconds, her mood suddenly completely changed as she asked me, with a charming smile, "Please, Chris, come up for awhile before I have to go back to work."

I looked at her skeptically. This didn't so much as put a dent in her smile, which she seemed to be *wearing* more than *giving*. Well, like a man having to go through customs, I walked up the two steps into the foyer. Paula shut and locked the door behind me, and I followed her up the stairs to her apartment.

CHAPTER 48

Monday-2 (The Gargoyle)

No sooner had we stepped onto the landing, than the maroon door to our left opened and an elderly couple stepped onto the landing as well, the man closing the door behind them. The old lady held her right arm wrapped around her husband's left one. He was obviously supporting her. The old man, completely bald, who was literally your "little old man," wore a serious expression, and his round face was clean-shaven except for a pencil-thin, white moustache. He was rather elegantly dressed, wearing a black suit, a black tie sporting tiny white dots, and black, well-shined shoes. All in all, he looked like an elderly, but still working mortician. His wife, who was about his height, was something else. She wore a dark brown dress and matching shoes, and wore a string of small, dull white pearls around her neck; but it was her face that instantly drew your attention. It was thin, long, and multi-wrinkled, and made her look a good deal more elderly than her husband. It was—I hate to say it—practically like an old witch's face. Obviously trying to look her best, as they were going out, she'd heavily rouged her cheeks and put on bright red lipstick, which stood in contrast to her short, curled white hair. If this was her attempt to look attractive and young, it only made her look like some chiseled and painted gargoyle. Added to this was the little smile she wore, which looked to me to be nearly a sneer. In comparing her, with her rouge and red lipstick, to the girl I was with, the little frail old lady looked like a ghastly parody of Paula. Paula herself looked at her neighbors indifferently, with no expression; and, not even bothering to introduce me, merely said formally, "Buenas tardes," to which they responded in kind, together, pleasantly, with, "Buenas tardes" as well. I stepped aside a little to allow them to descend the stairs, which they did slowly, arm-in-arm. That line from the Stones' song "Mother's Little Helper" popped into my head, "What a drag it is getting old." Paula opened her door and we entered her apartment.

CHAPTER 49

Monday-3

Once inside her apartment, she informed me that she needed to go put some clothes on, and added, "You can sit down there on the sofa. There're some magazines there. I'll be back soon." She disappeared down the hall. There may have been some magazines on the coffee table, but I had no interest in browsing through them. What did catch my interest, though, were two virtually empty wine glasses in the middle of the table, containing just a smidgen of red wine at their bottoms. I also noticed, over on the dining room table, some bills of money—maybe six bills—lying in an irregular stack, as if they'd just been dumped there. From where I sat I couldn't tell what their denominations were, and I didn't get up to go investigate.

I did pick up one of the magazines, after-all, and had been idly browsing through it for about ten minutes, when Paula re-entered the room. She was carrying her small black purse in her right hand, and she went straight to the table, scooped up the bills, and put them in the purse. Snapping the purse shut, she left it sitting there on the table and came over to where I was sitting. Casually, yet immediately, she picked up the wine glasses while telling me, "I think I'll make some cheese quesadillas again. I haven't had a thing to eat since breakfast; and I'll bet you haven't, either."

"No, I haven't."

"Bottled water again?"

"Actually, Paula, I think I'd like a coke, if you have one."

"I think I do." With a wine glass in each hand, she

disappeared down the hall again.

I couldn't help but notice the general change in her attitude towards me. Though nice enough, she acted like a correct and efficient (and impersonal) secretary more than anything else. (She "wore" no smile anymore.) This "secretary" thing extended to her clothes, since, of course, she would be going back to work before too long. She had on a plain, yellow dress, flesh-colored stockings, and brown pumps. The necklace with the tiny cross was back. The rouge was gone, and the bright red lipstick was gone as well, replaced by a much paler shade of red. Lastly, her hair was as neat as it could be. It was more than all this, though. She'd been just as professionally dressed the day we'd had lunch together and she'd taken my hand, as well as the day we'd kissed on the bench in the park. Now, though, there was a certain distance between us. She'd walked two steps ahead of me up the stairs, and we hadn't gotten physically close to each other in any way. Even more than this, though, she seemed emotionally distant, as if she was preoccupied about something. Being in her apartment with her this time was not like being in her apartment with her the last time.

She brought me a can of coke and set it down on the coffee table in front of me, inquiring, "Would you like a glass with ice?"

"No, thank-you. This is fine." Without another word, she turned and went back down the hall.

I looked at the cuckoo clock on the wall opposite me, about one thirty-five. We wouldn't have much time. I popped the top of the coke and took a few sips. Just as I was sitting it back down, Paula returned with a large plate of quesadilla slices and napkins in her right hand, and a bottled water in her other. Still holding them, she sat down to my left on the sofa, then set the plate and water down in front of her on the table. The cap on the bottled water already having been removed, she took a sip of it, then took a napkin and a slice of quesadilla. I took a napkin and a slice of quesadilla for myself. We ate in silence for half a minute or so, until I said,

"I guess we'll have to eat fast. Look at the time," nodding towards the clock.

"Oh, don't worry about that. Belinda can just wait. Mondays are always slow days." This was the first time I'd ever heard her express any kind of hostility—if that's the word—towards Belinda. Though she sat next to me on the two-sectional sofa, as she had before, she did so like my sister would have, with a good foot or more of space between us. There was another pause as we continued eating and drinking. Then, perhaps realizing that she was being rather severe, she smiled at me and said sympathetically, "I'm sorry about the park. I really was looking forward to it—going to that café with you for lunch . . . Eduardo, like a typical Mexican, called me up at work at the last minute and said he had to see me. So, I saw him instead."

I could've asked her why she didn't call me on my cell phone, but let it drop. What did it matter now? And I was seeing her, after-all. In fact, I didn't say anything.

She continued, as if she wanted to get straight to the truth, for whatever reason, "No, Eduardo is not my stockbroker. Quite the opposite. You saw the wine glasses, and I'm sure the money on the table. You saw the BMW, and the fashionable Eduardo, and you saw *me*." She smiled. "I don't think you need to see anymore, do you?"

Her frankness almost shocked me. "No, I guess I don't."

"What d'you think about it?"

"Why?"

This threw her for a moment. "*Why*? Because I need the money—that's why. Fifteen minutes or so in bed is the quickest way I know of to make that kind of money—short of selling drugs. It means nothing to me. It's over before you know it . . . I'm not married to anybody—and I don't do it every day or night—only every now and then. I don't walk the streets, let myself get picked up in bars, or advertise on the internet. I'm *not* any *prostitute*! (She said this like a person might forcefully answer a judge, on being asked how he or she pleaded, "Not Guilty!") I have a professional job, and live in a nice apartment in a nice neighborhood. I regularly send money home to help out my family in Piedras . . ." She concluded by saying, in a reserved tone, lowering her eyes, "I hope you understand me and don't judge me."

"Oh, I understand you," I said, with a touch of sarcasm. "Who am I to judge anybody?"

Apparently, not much comforted by my response, she said, with some spirit, "You know how much I make working for Belinda, eight—sometimes ten—hours a day, five days a week? In dollars, $100 a week. You know how much my rent is here, in this part of town? $350 a month. Figure it out. And I have to send money back to my family. You have no idea of how poor we really are. Then there's food and all the utilities here. There're things, as a woman, that I have to buy; and, like all women, I like to go shopping. Why shouldn't I? You might say I could get a second job, like a part-time nighttime job as a waitress or something. Yes, and make an extra $25 a week. I *know* my own country. Forget that! And the thing is, if I don't make it here I'll have to go back to Piedras. Go back to nothing."

"I don't see, Paula, why you don't go live in Texas. San Antonio would be a good choice."

"I've thought about that; but I have no car, and no money to buy one. There, you have to have a car to get around. You don't have thousands of taxis and buses like here in Saltillo. I don't know anybody in San Antonio. I'm sure bilingual secretaries there are everywhere. Here, in this town, very few people speak English, even in major businesses. Anyway, I like Saltillo, with its buen clima, and I like this apartment, and I like my job." She paused for a moment, then added, "I like my independence here. And Belinda needs me. She'll probably raise my salary eventually. It's only been six months."

Without really thinking, I blurted out, "You know what, Paula? All you really need to do is to find a financially secure husband and you'll be set."

She gave me a strange look, which I couldn't tell if it was

one of amusement or seriousness, and said, quite openly, smiling, "Would you like to marry me?"

This really threw *me*, and for more than a moment. I couldn't find any words, whatsoever, to say.

She looked at me like a compassionate teacher might look at a helpless, nonresponsive student. "Don't look so worried. You don't have to answer. I know the answer already. I'm just joking with you—though I wish I wasn't. You're exactly the kind of man I only wish I could marry."

"I couldn't divorce Evelyn," I said, in a small voice.

"I think you could, but you *won't*. I guess you have your reasons; but if you still love her so much then why d'you have anything to do with me? I don't think you do. Remember when we kissed in the park? Maybe you don't really know what you want."

"I want to be with both of you."

She smiled knowingly. "That's OK. I've already told you I'd be happy to see you when I can . . . Oh well, you married men are all the same. Eduardo's married. In fact, most of the men I see are married, though not as mature as you."

If this was a compliment, I wasn't buying. "I'm not Eduardo, or I'm sure like any of your other so-called "clients." I'm not seeing you only for that."

Her face reddened and her voice rose, "I know that! What d'you take me for? D'you think I go anywhere, or talk about anything, or discuss Manuel Acuňa with Eduardo, anymore than with any of the others? They're in and out of here in thirty minutes—or less—thank God! I've never been outside this building anywhere with one of them! None of them means anything to me! *Anything*, you hear me?"

This was a side of Paula I'd never seen before. Her back was straight, her face was red, her dark eyes were like burning coals, and her voice could've cut glass.

I tried to calm her down by saying calmly, "OK, OK, Paula, don't"— but she wasn't through, and cut me off with, "You think I *enjoy* it? I do it for the money, only—and I'm not getting rich. No, sir. I do it because I have no other choice

... I only wish I did, with all my heart." She started to return to normal. "And I don't care about marrying anybody. Well ... maybe one person." She made this last remark, looking directly at me, with a thin smile, like someone saying something both positive and negative at the same time. There was a pause. Then, she looked away as she said, matter-of-factly, "Some of these men are really nasty." Considering what she was talking about, there was any number of ways to interpret this remark; but I didn't say anything, and she didn't elaborate. I knew she wasn't quite through; and, sure enough, after some seconds, she said, "I sometimes think and feel I'd like to go join a convent and have nothing more to do with the world." She broke her seriousness, after a moment, with a quick laugh. "Imagine me wrapped up in black like a mummy! . . . But why not? Who's stopping me? Who cares? All of my worries and troubles'd be over if I did that."

Looking at her tiny silver cross, I said, "If you could stand it."

My words were mimicked in her eyes. "Yes, that's the thing."

The cuckoo clock struck (or sang out) two o'clock, which caused her to involuntarily almost jump up from her sofa cushion. I could see that she was now quickly morphing back into the "professional" Paula, and, any second, would be getting up; but I was determined to have my say. "Paula," I said strongly, "please wait a minute. I have something I'd like to say before you get up."

As if she almost welcomed it, she said, "Please, Chris, what d'you want to tell me?" There were no traces of redness left in her face, and her great beauty shined back at me.

"You'll be glad to know, I'm sure, that everything you've told me today has changed nothing. I still want to see you."

"I'm glad."

"I'll go even further. If we do keep seeing each other, eventually, my desire is to have a full relationship with you." I really couldn't believe my own boldness.

Paula was silent and sat very still for a good five seconds

before she said, much *like* a secretary, "I realize that."

There was something about the way she said this that seemed to signify no problema. In fact, it made me feel rather foolish and redundant in even bringing up the subject, like asking a policeman if the gun he's wearing is loaded.

Paula said, with a smile, "Everything'll be fine. Don't worry—but I really must be getting back to work now." She got up.

I accompanied her the short distance to Belinda's office, (not, of course, going inside.). As we talked away en route we made a mutual pact to meet once more at the obelisk—same time, same place—on Friday, and go to that café; and this time she absolutely swore that she'd be there. This time, I'd made the "date" without knowing anything about what'd be happening at the house on Friday, or what Evelyn's plans were, if any. I stood there on the sidewalk and tried to hail a taxi. Two "empty" yellow taxis passed me by without stopping, (sometimes they do this, and I don't know why,) before a bright green taxi, looking like it'd just come out of a Saint Patrick's Day Parade, pulled up, picked me up, and took me home.

CHAPTER 50

"You Ain't Nothin' But A Hound Dog"

I'd just stepped out of the taxi in front of my house when I saw Evelyn entering the block over the speed bump at it's entrance. The green taxi, leaving, passed the white sedan, arriving. "Just my luck!" I said, under my breath.

Evelyn pulled up right beside me as I stood there on the sidewalk; and before even opening the door, she zapped the window down with the button, and asked me, "Was that your taxi?"

"Yes, it was."

"And where were you going?"

"To The Alameda."

"To The Alameda!"

"Yes," I repeated, distinctly pronouncing each syllable, "To The Alameda."

She zapped the window back up, opened the door, got out, shut the door, went up the steps, crossed the porch, opened the front door and went into the house, all without so much as another word or glance at me. After a few moments, I went up the steps slowly, with a heavy heart, and on into the house myself.

Expecting to find her in the front of the house—I didn't. Instead, she'd gone to her bedroom and closed the door. I could hear her moving about the room. I sat down on one of the barstools and lit up a cigarette.

After some minutes, Evelyn came back down the hall. She'd changed her clothes from wearing a tan dress and brown shoes to blue jeans, a light blue pullover sweater, and her white slippers. She sat down on the other barstool next to me, to my left. For some moments she didn't look at or speak to me, but gazed about the dining room and living room as if they were rooms in a museum. She then abruptly reached over with her right hand, took a cigarette out of its package, and lit it up with the lighter. This was ominous. Evelyn rarely ever smoked, unless she was upset or mad about something—but she looked tranquil enough.

I'd turned on my barstool to face her; but, once she had her cigarette, she went back to gazing out at the two rooms. Puffing away, she asked me, "So, you went to The Alameda?"

"Yes."

"Why?"

"Oh, I thought it'd be nice to go somewhere—to get out of the house for awhile."

"All yesterday, last night, and all this morning you didn't say you wanted to go there."

"Oh—well—it was a spur of the moment thing."

"Was it?"

"What are you implying?" It was like I could faintly hear distant thunder rumbling.

Skipping my question, she asked me, "What did you do there?"

I was beginning to uncomfortably feel like I was under cross-examination. "Nothing, really. I walked about and enjoyed the park, and sat and smoked."

"Sounds exciting." She crushed out her half-smoked cigarette in the ashtray. She looked at me. "Guess who I ran into at the dentist's office?"

"Who?"

"Belinda. She'd just stopped by to make an appointment; but she sat and talked with me for a bit while I waited for *my* appointment.

"What a small world!"

"Yes, isn't it? You know Belinda's office is close to The Alameda. Remember the time we went there to take care of your papers?"

"Oh yes."

"And you know that Miss Paula works for Belinda?"

"Yes, I know that."

"Then maybe you can explain something Belinda told me which she doesn't understand—and I don't, either."

My brain raced. What on Earth was she talking about? As if she could read my mind, and was enjoying doing so, Evelyn kept her information at bay as she casually took out and lit up another cigarette. After taking a few puffs, she said, gazing out the window at the distant city, "Belinda said to me that last Thursday she happened to look out of her office window—and what did she see? You and Paula standing close together on the sidewalk, talking. She said Paula gave you a big smile and a long kiss full on the lips, then came on inside. She said Paula was coming back from her lunch break. She said Paula said nothing about anything, and she didn't ask her."

She waited, looking at me, continuing to puff on her cigarette. I waited. It was like at Belinda and Bertie's garden party, you could've heard a fly fly by. I knew not only that I had to say something, but that she wasn't gonna say anything else, for the time being. I also knew that she'd wait for me to open my mouth, even if it took five minutes. It was now up to me.

What could I say? Deny it happened? That would've been like saying that what was in a photograph really wasn't there. Various ideas ran through my mind—like saying that Belinda was making the whole thing up—but that would've been as stupid a thing to say as everything else I thought of. No, the best thing to do was to just "lie low"—*real* low. So Belinda saw what she saw? She hadn't seen anything else, or knew about anything else, and Paula hadn't said a word. On the other hand, I couldn't think of anything plausible to say about the incident. So, I took out and lit up another cigarette, and said nothing.

Evelyn, realizing she had me like a rat in a trap, slowly said, as she crushed out her cigarette, "You don't have to say anything. Because you don't—or *can't*—well, that's proof enough."

"Proof of *what*, may I ask?" I was finally irked into words by Evelyn's superior attitude.

"Proof that you've been seeing Paula behind my back—like today."

I made no reply. The less said the better. This didn't phase Evelyn, though, who said, "I could see it coming at the garden party, the way Paula was all smiles at you. She was attracted to you. I told you so on the drive home. I was already on the trail . . . I never thought, though, you could be so easily led and deceived by a woman half—more than half—your age, you, a man of sixty-two. Women are vain. It must be a great sport for her. I don't know what's happened between the two of you, or how far it's gone; and I don't want to know. I'm not gonna say anything to Belinda. But I know this—and'll say this to you, it's *me* or *her*—*me* or *her*! *Comprende*? You're a grown man and can do what you want. So, do it!" Though she said this strongly, the words that followed were said, after a little pause, in a sudden shift of mood, in a quiet and melancholy way. Staring down at the counter as if staring into a mirror, she said, "You've no idea, I'm sure, of how much you've hurt me, I, who've been true to you from the beginning. After my grandmother, you're the only person I've ever truly loved—or tried to . . . You really have no feelings, no feelings when it comes to me." She looked as if she might cry.

Now, I started, (and was quite ready) to say something, but she didn't give me the chance. She immediately got up off her barstool and went down the hall to her bedroom and slammed the door. I heard her, apparently, leap onto her bed.

CHAPTER 51

"Thinkin' Cap Time"

I wasn't aware that Gigi was asleep, rolled up in a ball, in the right corner of the sofa—invisible to my line of sight from where I sat on the barstool. Now, she made her presence known by getting up, walking a few steps to the center of the sofa, giving herself a little shake, and stretching out her brown and black body so that her tail stuck straight out. This done, she sat down on her haunches and looked about the rooms for a few moments at nothing in particular.

She didn't seem to be aware that I was there at all. Then, she suddenly jumped down and headed purposefully towards and on down the hall, passing me by without a look. Soon, I heard, "Meow!" "Meow!" "Meow!" followed by a harsh, grating sound. Getting up off the barstool and looking down the hall, I saw Gigi, up on her hind legs, scratching Evelyn's door with the claws of her front paws. I was about to correct her by shouting out, "Gigi!" when the door opened just a little and Gigi instantly slithered into the room, whereupon the door was closed.

I went back to where I'd been sitting. I gazed out the window at the great valley of Saltillo, ringed in by the cobalt blue mountains, and the colorful city spread out below. Yes, I reflected, it was a beautiful view—a spectacular view—a once in the world view. Still, it really was just that, a view—a sight—a thing—better than looking out of your window at a prison—but, nevertheless, nothing but a visual delight—and I had other things on my mind . . . I was in a quandary about what to do or say. The effect of Evelyn's "revelation" left me like I was paralyzed. It was like a bolt out of the blue, striking me totally unexpectedly. Of course, it was my own fault. I should never have escorted Paula back to Belinda's office. I mean, how stupid can you be? Now I saw the truth of Mike's remark, "This is a game you're not at all skilled at playing."

I felt sad and mad about everything. Thinking about it, now, in retrospect, I really didn't appreciate Paula's question "Would you like to marry me?" It not only contradicted her "free love" philosophy and numerous anti-marriage remarks, but could even be interpreted as containing a slice of mockery. She knew I wasn't gonna leave Evelyn, and had known it from practically the beginning; but she said it anyway, (and perhaps this is why she said it). Paula was, in fact, deep down, as conventional as all women are when it comes to the subject of marriage, in spite of her unconventional talk and unconventional lifestyle. This didn't bode well for the future. I now had the sneaking suspicion that she'd eventually start pressing me to divorce Evelyn. They're all "sisters of the silk" at heart.

It looked like, now, things were *not* gonna fall happily into place like I thought they were. In a way, I was relieved that Evelyn had gone to her bedroom and "shut me out." I needed time to think, not fight—needed what a friend of mine used to call "Thinkin' Cap Time." I knew Evelyn would give me the cold shoulder for the rest of the day—or so I thought.

CHAPTER 52

The Conversation

I was wrong. I didn't get to have any "Thinkin' Cap Time," right then, because Evelyn suddenly came out of her room and down the hall. She went to the dining room table and sat down in the chair with its back to the window (and the view), and, therefore, sat down directly across from and facing me. She hadn't been seated for more than a few seconds before here came Gigi down the hall as well. Passing me by again without a look, she walked straight up to Evelyn and jumped up onto her legs—all in a continuous motion. Once there, she promptly curled up in Evelyn's lap; and, as Evelyn proceeded to talk with me, she periodically lightly stroked the contented creature.

Unexpectedly and very oddly, I thought, she began by calmly saying, "You once said to me that when you were a baby you were a head banger. You said that once you used your head to bang your crib on wheels clear across the room to the chest of drawers, opened the top drawer, and threw everything out onto the floor."

I smiled. "Yes, that's true—or so I've been told. I don't remember doing it. It was in my Mother's room, apparently."

"I was just thinking about that . . . It makes you wonder."

I gave her a long stare. "Just what are you trying to say? That my *brain* was affected?"

She didn't reply; but, slightly raising her eyebrows, she gave me a look that unmistakably said, "Maybe."

"For your information, my little chickadee, Mother told me she talked to her doctor about it, and he said it was nothing to worry about—that it was just a passing phase—that many babies did that—and that it didn't affect my brain at all. In fact, he told her it was often a sign of musical ability."

"You can't play a single musical instrument. What you do on the piano nobody would ever call *playing*.

"Listen—just what point are you trying to make, if any?"

"You're not normal." She said this like somebody might say, "You need help."

"And I suppose *you* are."

"Well, I certainly wouldn't do something so silly and crazy as what you've done with Paula. A man your age. It's ridiculous."

"You *couldn*'t."

She sat and said right up, "I can get"— but dropped it. She tapped on the table with the fingers of her left hand for a couple of moments.

"Anyway, Paula doesn't think so."

"You don't know what Paula really thinks."

"Look—if you just came out here to argue, you—and that cat—can just go back to your room. I'm not in the mood right now."

" I'll do what I want."

Her remark energized me. "Who's 'normal'? What I've done—which doesn't amount to anything—though perhaps not especially honorable, is much more normal with many men—and many men my age—than you think."

"Is that supposed to be your excuse?"

"No. It's just a fact. Besides, nothing's happened."

"So you say."

It was pointless to go on like this. She obviously wasn't gonna cut me any slack. There was a long pause, during which I noticed a big red, white, and green striped, hot air balloon in the distance slowly ascending from what looked like The Cathedral Plaza area. Finally, she spoke up, "Just remember what I said. There *will* be consequences." Leaving me to ponder over this unambiguous/ambiguous remark, she abruptly got up, uncharacteristically causing a startled Gigi to tumble down onto the floor, letting out a sort of abbreviated "meow!" Gigi, nevertheless, like all cats always, landed upright. Evelyn then haughtily walked past me down to her room, and, apparently from her door, called out "Gigi!" Gigi dutifully responded by racing past me down the hall. I heard the door (not quite) slam shut again.

CHAPTER 53

Happenings

I remembered that line from John Lennon's song "Beautiful Boy", "Life is what happens to you while you're busy making other plans," and I wondered, now, if maybe he meant that sarcastically—even tragically. Certainly, in his own case, it could equally be said, "Death is what happens to you while you're busy making other plans." In any event, you never really know what's gonna happen, at any given moment, which means about the same thing. Belinda didn't have to look out the window at that very moment, but she did. Paula didn't have to appear at the door with Eduardo at that very moment, but she did. Evelyn didn't have to enter the block just as my taxi was leaving, but she did. My plans (and dreams) didn't have to be all messed up, but they were. Then again, I figured what had happened was chiefly my own fault. Like Mike had said, "You didn't have to go," but I did.

Well, things happen, over which you have no control. The question is, what're you gonna do about it—if anything? Even not doing anything is doing something—is making a choice. I vaguely recalled a quote by Robert Browning, "Life is made up of terrible choices," or words to that effect. I didn't consider this as being really true for children; but it definitely was, more often than not, true for adults. Actually, your choices are frequently only "terrible" in retrospect; otherwise, you would've never made them in the first place.

The multicolored balloon, I noticed, was now well up in the sky. It was such a singular sight that it was hard for me to take my eyes off it. It's odd, but seeing passenger planes or jets up in the sky barely arouses my interest, if at all; but seeing a big, colorful, hot air balloon always grabs my attention. And that little manned basket beneath it . . . I wished I was in it right then, just slowly, gently, and peacefully ascending/ drifting away from everything down below.

CHAPTER 54

The Void

With Evelyn incommunicado in her bedroom, along with her small companion, without a hint of any wind outside, without a note from a bird or a bark from a dog, and without any neighbors coming or going on the block, I sat there on the barstool like I had the whole world all to myself, not that this made me feel in the least bit happy. In fact, I didn't feel much of anything, except a degree of resentment over feeling resentful. I wished I was someplace else. I could've watched TV or listened to my CD/Radio player; but in my present mood, that would've been just an irritation. I lit up another cigarette and put my thinkin' cap on.

I thought about Dr. Price, specifically, about something he once told me . . . Dr. Price was a psychiatrist with a last name quite appropriate to his profession, even though he only charged me a nominal fee of $20 an hour, or a session. Back in the late 70s, I was going through a difficult time, both personally and professionally, and actually just picked his name at random out of the Yellow Pages (under PSYCHIATRISTS) as a person who I thought maybe could help me. (I'd never been to a shrink before.) I suppose this act, in itself, showed what kind of sad and lonely state I was in. At the time, Dr. Price was in his sixties and looked it. Clean-shaven and bald on top, he was of medium height and build, and very *correct*, more professionally than seriously. He was always dressed in a neatly pressed, usually dark brown, complete suit with vest, white shirt, and matching tie. Still, this fashionableness didn't offset his obviously well-lived in, craggy face. He never talked about his personal life; so I never knew anything about him except how he acted around me, which was always with unfailing politeness and understanding. Now and then, he might crack a joke in a jokeless kind of way. I didn't see him for very long—only for about two months, once a week. He had an office in Fort Worth. He normally did little of the talking, letting me ramble on for practically the whole hour relating my problems, worries, and memories to him, while he sat behind his desk and listened to me. Looking back on it now, I wouldn't say that he did me all that much good—he only occasionally gave me any advice or council—but there was doubtless a therapeutic benefit in just talking to someone and getting things out of my system. Once, though, (after he was quite familiar with my family history, and towards the end of our sessions together,) he uncharacteristically interrupted my "feeling sorry for myself" by saying something which burned itself into my mind.

I was going on, for the umpteenth time, about my parents and what they'd "done" to me. He interrupted me, with some impatience, by saying strictly, "Chris—you can just stop right there." He'd never done this before, and I shut right up like a clam, quite taken aback, (as he probably knew I would be.) Having my full attention, he said, "Nobody who's ever lived has had perfect parents, and nobody ever will. On the other hand, most people are raised by a set of parents. Just being raised by a man and a woman—*whatever* they're like—has a tremendous influence on a developing child—much more than most people think. You, unfortunately, never had this. Your parents divorced when you were still a baby. You saw your father once a year for a couple of weeks, but that's not the same thing, at all, especially if he was and is like you've described him. And from what you've told me, your mother sounds like she is and was very neurotic, more obsessed with her own unfulfilled needs than with anybody else's. What I'm saying is that you never received the normal love you should have received, and that every child needs. You've had to go through virtually your whole life with this void inside you; and about a third of the population, believe it or not, must live their whole lives with this same void inside themselves. You're not alone, in this respect, by any means. You have to be loved in order to love. If you haven't been, you can still do it, anyway, but it's hard. Endlessly complaining about your parents won't alter the facts. They're never gonna change. You still can. That void will always be inside you, to the day you die; but you can still find love with a good woman and live a reasonably happy life if you really want to. I hope you do; otherwise, I'm afraid you're just condemned to a life of loneliness and frustration—pretty much like the life you're leading now. You've told me all I need or will ever want to hear about your family. Now, you need to forget about all that, and start thinking and talking about what your plans are for the future, and how they can be realized. You can still achieve anything you want to."

Good 'ol Dr. Price. He could've made the same speech—or a variation of it—to Evelyn, whose mother died when she was three, and who once told me, "I was a hundred times more of a daughter to him than my father ever was a father to me. The only thing he ever really cared about was his next drink." Actually, it occurred to me, we did have that in common, though in reverse, If I'd grown up without a father and with a neurotic mother, she'd grown up without a mother and with a neurotic/alcoholic father. The big difference was that while my mother was always there, Evelyn's father rarely was, (like mine.) Then, she had her grandmother. In any case, it was something we had pretty much in common, compared to most people, this void; and, perhaps subconsciously, it was a bond that had drawn us together in the first place, and had kept us together, we really had nobody else but each other, and hadn't from the beginning. When we married, her mother, father, and grandmother were all dead; while, in my case, my father was dead, and my mother and sister, by that time, were hardly involved in my life anymore, or I in theirs. Evelyn had her girlfriends in Monterrey, with whom she kept in contact, and I had Thomas in Fort Worth; but it wasn't the same thing. Yes, I thought to myself, It may have been expressed countless times before by countless people, but it really was loneliness, more than love, which brought us together.

I thought about Paula. Though most people, I realized, would readily condemn her, seeing her as nothing but a slut, I didn't see her that way. I understood why she did what she did; though I thought she was being disingenuous about saying that there was nothing else she could do to earn some extra money. In a big city like Saltillo, where there were thousands of businesses, there was, part-time jobs which paid more than $25 a week—especially with her education. She could do some English tutoring. She could even make some good money by working at some little business over the internet, right out of her apartment. She did what she did because it was easy, took up little of her time, and netted her an immediate tidy sum. No stress. No strain. Paula was young, healthy, and super-beautiful; and she used this to her advantage. I could just imagine her doing this at forty, or fifty, or sixty. Yes, Paula had the self-confidence and—for want of a better word—the *arrogance* of youth, together with a headstrong personality, which enabled her to do more or less what she wanted to. Life hadn't beaten her down yet. She was ready for anything. The sex aside (—and to Paula herself it was obviously looked upon merely *as* an aside in her life—) Paula was really fairly normal, as people go. She didn't carry around any *void* inside of *her*. She enjoyed an apparently loving relationship with her mother and father who I never heard her once criticize. If anything, I think she felt sorry for them because of their ignorance and poverty. She was close to her three sisters, and frequently talked about them. She had educated herself above the norm for Piedras and was determined to make something out of her life, which likely included, as I've alluded to, making a good marriage to an educated man, in spite of all her words about marriage to the contrary.

There's a related meaning to the word "void" when it's used as a verb, which is "to make empty or vacant, CLEAR" (Webster). That's what I felt like doing, forget about Evelyn, Paula, this house, and everything—clear out—and go off and join the French Foreign Legion—Yes, Sir—if they'd take me at my age, which they wouldn't. I knew Evelyn, I knew Paula, (much "better" now, like Mike had advised me that I needed to do,) and I knew myself; and the net result was that I just felt rather indifferent about it all now. Women are not the be all and the end all of existence, except maybe when you're eighteen. I couldn't help but think to myself how things and people are rarely, if ever, like you want them to be with all your sweet desire. They're just the way they are. I noticed that the balloon, having drifted off in a northerly direction, was now getting close to the mountains, meaning that it had considerably diminished in size, so that it looked like a baby of itself. I decided to go outside for awhile.

P.S. I'll never forget another thing that Dr. Price once told me. During one of our sessions together, I was complaining about Thomas, how he got on my nerves, made me lose my temper, and some other things. When I was through, Dr. Price commented, "The difference between you and your friend Thomas is that he doesn't know what reality is. You do, but don't like it." I still feel that way today, for the most part.

CHAPTER 55

My Friend Benito

You can often receive more love and affection—at least, more attention—from an animal, or your pet, (especially a dog—"Man's best friend"—) than you can from any selfish, dysfunctional, cold-hearted human being. For some people, this would include a cat, a rabbit, a horse, or a bird; though birds, like fish, seem to me to live in another, separate dimension. In any event, this comprises a very tiny group of creatures, as most members of the animal kingdom are of a nature that keeps you from getting close to them at all. I can't imagine anyone enjoying a friendship with a grizzly bear, a rhinoceros, or a boa constrictor, or such domestic animals as a cow or a sheep. And the list goes on. Some people like goldfish, or tropical fish. Well, they're nice to look at, and interesting to watch, but there's no bond between you and them whatsoever, except, perhaps a little, in a way, when you feed them. What I never would've believed was that you could have any kind of a relationship with a tortoise, until I met Benito.

Everybody here in Mexico automatically assumes that the name Benito is a tribute to the renowned, and one of the best Presidents of Mexico, Benito Juárez; but this isn't true. At first, I named him Bette, after the famous American movie star Bette Davis, because his oval face, commanding look, and somewhat fierce expression reminded me of her. Only later, after doing some investigation on the internet, did I find out that *she* was a *he* because of his concave underside, whereas the underside of the female is flat. (There's a reason for this, which others may discover for themselves.) I picked the similarly sounding name of Benito. His classification is a Texas Tortoise, a type of tortoise that's found in southern Texas southward into the Mexican states of Nueva León, Coahuila, Tamaulipas, and San Luis Potosí. Though not considered an endangered species, in the state of Texas this tortoise goes by the label of a threatened species, and, in Texas, it's illegal to capture or possess one. He (or his shell, which is of a brownish color,) is about eight inches long by about five inches wide. He has little elephant-like legs covered in scales and ending in black claws, and a retractable, accordion-like neck.

I found Benito one day, about a year ago, when I was returning home through the colony. Benito was crossing the road, but had stopped in about the middle of it, for some reason. I stopped the car on the side of the road, got out, picked him up, placed him on the passenger seat, and took him back to the house with me. I gave him the freedom of the whole yard, the back patio, the front walkway, and the front porch. He became quickly adjusted to his new environment, and for the first few weeks spent much time exploring everything.

Once the sun has risen above the mountains in the morning and is shining down on the back patio, where he customarily sleeps at night in a corner of it, Benito gets up, moves to the center of the patio, and spends a good hour just sitting there, soaking up the sun. Then, he's off and about, usually towards the yard to graze in the grass.

In the beginning he wouldn't have anything to do with me. Whenever I'd get close to him, he'd retreat into his shell, and bar the entrance by pushing his thick front knees together across the opening. Only when I'd step some feet away would he eventually retract his legs and extend his head out again.

What finally "broke the ice" between us is when I started to feed him after having him for about a week or so. Reading on the internet that tortoises love tomatoes, I'd take a tomato and slice it in half, then slice the half into little chunks that he could easily grab, placing the chunks together on the cement somewhere. At first, still wary of me, I'd have to go pick him up from wherever he was and bring him over and set him down in front of the chunks, still keeping some feet away from him as he ate. Tortoises have no teeth, but have powerful upper and lower, beak-like jaws which they use to grab food or rip blades of grass with; and Benito can devour all the tomato chunks in a matter of minutes.

In time, though, and to my surprise, Benito would see me placing the tomato chunks down, and, from wherever he was, he'd immediately make a beeline towards me, as fast as his stubby legs and big bulk would allow him to, which was almost funny to see. Not only that, but as he went about grabbing, crushing, and swallowing the chunks, he'd allow me to gently stroke his head, frequently slightly lifting his head towards me as I did so. It even got to the point where if I went somewhere in the car, like just up to the convenience store by Los Arcos to buy a beer, when I returned, Benito might be waiting for me on the front porch, staring straight at me, whereas when I left, he might have been on the back patio, or off in the yard somewhere. These friendly habits of his have continued up to the present day.

I never truly appreciated the ancient and famous Aesop's Fable of "The Tortoise and the Hare" until I became familiar with Benito's ways. Let me quote from my Penguin Classics edition of *Fables of Aesop*,

> "*A tortoise and a hare started to dispute which of them was swifter, and before separating they made an appointment for a certain time and place to settle the matter. The hare had such confidence in its natural swiftness that it did not trouble about the race but lay down by the wayside and went to sleep. The tortoise, acutely conscious of its slow movements, padded along without ever stopping until it passed the sleeping hare and won the race. Moral, A naturally gifted man, through lack of application, is often beaten by a plodder.*"

This single-minded determination, this refusal to be

diverted by anyone or anything or take a break, this heading straight for your destination as if, like a magnet, it was pulling you towards it—these characteristics are an intrinsic part of Benito's nature. They compensate for his natural slowness. Nothing keeps him from his course. This determination, in a paradoxical way, actually makes him almost "fast." For example, a few months ago, I was watering the potted plants with the hose on the back patio. Benito was there, too. I'd just started to water when Benito decided to go for a walk. He lumbered slowly off towards the yard and disappeared around the corner of the house. My watering over in minutes, I headed for the kitchen door, and didn't see Benito anywhere. Curious as to where he was, I looked all over the yard, but couldn't find him anywhere. Finally, I walked around the house to the front porch and there he was—meaning, in only minutes he'd gone from the back patio, past the long yard, down the front walkway, and onto the front porch because the porch was where he wanted to go and that's where he directly went, obviously not stopping or resting along the way. It also makes me feel special, and even proud, to have Benito, an animal that goes back over three hundred million years to the age of the dinosaurs. Talk about having a link with the past!

The way our house is constructed, we have a square front porch whose floor is covered in Saltillo tiles; and this porch connects with a fairly wide cement walkway which runs past the front windows, turns left, and continues alongside the long western wall of the house, opposite the yard, then turns left again and continues past the rear wall of the house, between that wall and the high stone 'n mortar retaining wall, to the back patio, also covered in Saltillo tiles. In other words, the walkway goes around approximately three-fourths of the house. It's along this walkway that Benito often travels from the back patio to the front porch, or vice-versa, (as he did in the incident just mentioned.)

As I said, I got up off the barstool and went outside. I sat down in my lawn chair on the walkway. The back of the chair practically touches the western wall of the house and is about in the middle of that wall. Benito was a little distance away from me, and more or less in front of me, grazing in the grass. Seeing me, he stopped his grazing and made a beeline towards me, coming to rest on the walkway up against my right brown loafer, as if just being beside me was perfectly sufficient for him. I was touched. His head was just barely sticking out, looking towards the wall; and I said to him, as if he could understand me, "Well, Benito, ol' boy, at least you don't have to be subjected to women's fits. Lord love a duck! What a life! You don't know how lucky you are. I've read that you tortoises have your mating season, but that it doesn't amount to much, maybe fifteen minutes of lovemaking and that's it. For all the rest of the time and the year you and your mate go about your separate and independent ways. I guess I should think about going and finding a female for you one of these days. Maybe I will in the Spring . . . Nobody makes any demands on you, or tells you what to do or what not to do, or where to go or where not to go. No wonder you tortoises have flourished for over three hundred million years. You're never stressed-out. I envy you. In your quiet and unobtrusive way, you're totally adapted to your environment, which no human being is, ever was, or ever will be." I smiled to myself. "It's Man that's the mistake . . . If you tortoises have survived for over thirty thousand centuries, mankind'll be lucky to survive for another ninety years. And if tortoises become extinct, it'll be mankind's fault. Of course, you can't keep mankind down. They continue to "advance" by destroying tortoises' habitats in the process of putting up football stadiums with huge parking lots and sprawling government housing projects."

    As if this was something that Benito didn't wish to hear, he suddenly stuck his head out a little further, made a slow turn to the left, and headed down the walkway. I watched him as he purposefully walked away from me, soon turning and disappearing from view around the corner of the house as he headed down the front walkway, apparently towards the front porch. It made me feel rather sad inside to see him walking away from me like that.

CHAPTER 56

Like An Exile

As I sat there, I wondered where I stood. Staring out at the mountain-surrounded, enormous valley, as silent as death itself, I felt like Napoleon must have felt standing alone on the edge of some cliff on Saint Helena, staring out at the enormous, dead silent Atlantic, in other words, like an exile. The difference was that I wasn't just an exile from my country and career, but from most of life itself, if by life you mean friends, family, intelligent conversation, a busy present, hopes and plans for the future, and even sex (for the most part.) Not only was the void still there, it was worse. I mean, talking to a tortoise! I remembered it was Bette Davis herself who said, "Getting old is not for sissies." She was right on, there.

Señorita Paula. If, as Mike said, "You didn't have to go," it was more than that, and even contradicted that. I had a lovely opportunity literally land right in my lap, and blew it. Yes, that was my problem, and always had been with women, I was such a goody two-shoes, and always such a little gentleman. There was that moment when Paula looked deeply into my eyes and smiled, after saying, "And now, I hope, you have me," following this up by placing her hand over mine. I should've taken advantage of the situation. A little afternoon delight. Now that I knew what she was really like, it would've been an easy seduction. She wouldn't have protested, and I would've gotten what I really wanted—not that that was all I wanted out of her. On top of that, it wouldn't have cost me one peso, I'm sure. So the rain started pouring down in torrents? That would've made it all the more romantic; and Belinda could've just waited an extra fifteen minutes.

The thought came to me that, in essence, that was what Paula really represented, at this stage of my life, to an "exile" like myself, She represented youth, hope, excitement, brightness, a passion for living life to the fullest, a connection to the modern, present-day world, and the ever-promising future—all of those things that I'd grown largely indifferent to, were fading fast, or were gone altogether. The sex was just a fillip.

I wasn't denigrating Evelyn; but Evelyn, like me, was of another generation, was getting old, and was having to deal with much of the same physical and psychological issues facing me that were a result of this. As a woman, she wasn't in Paula's league at all. This was what made Paula like a shining sun to Evelyn's shining moon. And the moon, more often than not, is incomplete, or not full; while the sun is always fully shining in all its strength and glory, even behind the clouds. Anyway, I had to admit that I was, like Evelyn, a moon now, too; and if the sun was of the day, the moon was of the night. This, I realized, said a lot, and meant a lot—more than I wanted to think about.

CHAPTER 57

Intuition

Women are supposedly highly intuitive. Men less so. I think this stems from women's basic, natural optimism, since most of their intuitions tend to be on the bright side. They see things as working out for the best. Men tend to see things as working out for the worst, or as simply not working out at all, or like they wish they would. They're more pessimistic than your average woman. It's a difference in attitude and feeling. For example, if a woman was to win the lottery, she'd be thrilled and excited, but a man would be totally flabbergasted. Still, I'm digressing from the point I'm trying to make. I have some intuition myself; and it told me (negatively) that something not to my liking was about to happen with Paula. I just felt it, or had an "intuitive feeling" about it.

The days up until Friday passed by uneventfully enough. Nothing more was said about Paula by Evelyn or me. I think Evelyn took the whole thing only half-seriously, anyway, and felt that, fundamentally, there was nothing to worry about. After twenty-three years, she knew her man. She even acted especially nice to me, for her. My main problem was how in the world I was going to meet with Paula. Neither Evelyn nor I had any plans to go anywhere, except maybe merely down to the convenience store in the colony, for the rest of the week. I had to think of something.

CHAPTER 58

An Encounter

On Thursday morning, around ten, Evelyn did take the car to run up to the Mini-Lomas, a small, white, adobe convenience store across from Los Arcos, which we regularly frequent to pick up little necessities like cigarettes, (my) beer, milk, tortillas, and other odds and ends. She didn't tell me what she wanted to buy, only that "I need to pick up a few things. I'll be back soon." She'd been gone less than a minute before who should arrive, of all people, than Belinda in her green Honda Civic. She seemed surprised (Uh-huh) that I answered the door, evidently expecting to be greeted by Evelyn. I invited her in. I felt a bit embarrassed greeting her in my old clothes, an old, faded pair of blue jeans, a tatty old yellow sweater, and my decrepit brown slippers compared to her navy blue, long-sleeved dress with a wide black belt, sheer black stockings, and high-heeled, shiny black shoes. Whether it was because Evelyn wasn't there, or because she didn't have any hankering to talk to me, or because she was in a hurry, (though she didn't appear to be in any hurry to me,) she said, before sitting down on the sofa, "I can only stay a minute. I just stopped by because I was in the neighborhood visiting with one of my patients who lives in the colony."

No, Belinda isn't any doctor of anything; but she's made, over the years, a lucrative part-time practice as a sort of quasi-psychiatrist to a clientele of not poor blue-haired ladies, listening to their problems and giving them her advice. How she ever got started doing this I have no idea. She has no degree in Psychology, or any related certificates in anything. I guess she's read a lot of books and magazines about psychology, and has enough brass to pass herself off as a sort of expert on the subject. She also uses a variety of herbs as "cures for all your ills." Belinda conducts her sessions out of a special room on the second floor of her house; but she sometimes goes to her clients, some of whom are too elderly or infirm to easily come to her. Evelyn once had a session at Belinda's house. She was feeling down, and thought maybe Belinda could help her. She told me afterwards that her session with Belinda didn't amount to much. Belinda listened to her, gave her some words of comfort, and a bottle of St. John's Wort tablets.

Anyway, she did politely sit down on the sofa next to me for about eight minutes, and we had a brief chat about this and that. I couldn't resist asking her, at last, "And how is Paula getting along?" and was more than intrigued by her answer, to say the least. Among other things, she said, with a hard smile, "I think Paula has found a boyfriend. He looks like he's just about her age. Isn't that nice? He's tall and handsome and has blonde hair—obviously a gringo—but from America or Canada or wherever, I don't know. His name is Michael. He came by the office yesterday to escort Paula to lunch, and they seemed very close to one another. I haven't found the time yet to talk with Paula about him. I'm glad for her." I just looked at her. Belinda looked like the cat that just swallowed the cream. There was a pause. Then, Belinda suddenly stood up and, with a little smile, said, "I really must be getting back. I'm sorry I missed Evelyn. Tell her I'll call her tonight. So nice talking to you." She opened the front door on her own before I could and walked straight to her car, got in, and drove away.

CHAPTER 59

Stunned

It's a common myth that roosters only crow at daybreak. Not having grown up on a farm, or ever having been around the feathered, colorful creatures at all, I always assumed the same thing, until I moved to Lomas. A number of its residents keep roosters on their patios; and, though they provide a chorus of song at dawn, they also crow, every now and then, throughout the day, all over the colony.

I left the front door open and went back over and sat back down on the sofa, on its left side, where Belinda had been sitting, and which was still faintly warm from her body. I felt stunned, only aware of a rooster crowing off somewhere in the distance, "Cock-a-doodle-do!" The great silence of Lomas enables you to clearly hear some sounds even half a mile away. The rooster *was* in the distance, and it could clearly be heard—even rather loudly so.

It's crowing only lasted for some seconds, and I was soon left alone to the silence of the house and to my undisturbed but disturbed thoughts. *I* certainly had nothing to crow about. I felt like a fool, and like I'd *been* fooled. Can you ever trust anybody—truly believing what they tell you? "I think maybe you have no idea of just how special you are to a woman like me." Apparently, not so special. I remembered something Thomas used to say sometimes when he'd get irritated at me, "You can't accept your age"—a fine thing to say coming from *him*. Yet, when I looked back on it, that was what, in more than a way, Belinda was really saying, or implying, as well, when she said, with a certain sly, self-righteous maliciousness, "He looks like he's just about her age. Isn't that nice?" After-all, it was Belinda who'd seen Paula and I together, kissing, and who was responsible for starting the ball rolling by her conversation with Evelyn.

Still, stunned as I was by Belinda's words, I also felt mad. I wasn't about to let all these women have the last word. Evelyn pulled up in the car. I was more determined than ever, somehow, to see Paula the next day. It seemed that the buds of my intuition had blossomed.

CHAPTER 60

The Finality Of A Friday

Friday dawned, up in Lomas, overcast, windy, and chilly, the cloud cover and the wind making the chill feel that much more chilly. Sweater weather. At the same time, as I stood in the backyard and gazed out across the great valley, I could see that down in town it was bright and sunny, with barely a cloud in the sky. At such times, if it's your intention to go down into town, you question whether or not to wear a long or short-sleeved shirt, or a sweater or a jacket; because once down in the city it can be positively warm, or getting that way; and you can end up carrying your sweater or jacket over your arm, or wishing your long-sleeved shirt was a short-sleeved one. This holds true for some Spring or Fall days; and the month of September was drawing to a close.

And it was my intention to go down into town—specifically to The Alameda to meet Paula at the appointed time. I had a plan. So, at around eleven-thirty, plotting a middle course, clothes-wise, I changed from my old house clothes and slippers into a long-sleeved, white cotton shirt, black jeans, and my brown "cowboy" boots. Telling Evelyn that I was going down to the Mini-Lomas to buy some cigs, I added that I might go on to the nearby HEB, about a mile away, and buy some dessert—maybe a tres leches (three milks) cake, which I love. Now, all of this might take me an hour, or a little longer, which Evelyn was perfectly aware of. Yet, this time, in the frame of mind I was in, I didn't expect to spend more than thirty minutes (or less) with Paula. Forget about going to any café, or going back to her apartment for lunch. I could see her then return to the house roughly within the expected time period. So, at around eleven-forty, I left the house, grabbed a pack of cigs at the Mini-Lomas, then drove Benito-straight to the HEB shopping center, parking the car in its lot. From there I took a taxi to The Alameda. I could always hurry in and buy a cake at HEB on the way back.

After being dropped off, as usual, at the southern entrance to the park, I looked at my watch – 12:15. It was definitely warm in The Alameda, with a slight breeze. The park was also rather crowded with couples strolling up and down the walkways, and children running about. As I headed towards the obelisk-plaza, I thought that, for once, there might be a number of people there. This very thought irritated me. I wanted Paula "all to myself," like the times before.

I needn't have been irritated. As I approached the plaza, I could see, at a glance, that it was deserted, except for the girl with the black ponytail and a tortoise shell hairpin, sitting on "our" bench, on the left, as always. Approaching her again from behind, this time I didn't pause on the walkway for any reason, but walked right up to face her.

"¡Buenas tardes, Paula!"

"¡Buenas tardes, Chris!"

She was wearing a plain, short-sleeved, deep yellow dress and matching shoes, and white stockings. Her shoes were touching each other on the walkway, and she was holding her black purse lengthwise on her lap with both her hands touching over its clasp. She looked very prim and proper, like a prospective teacher sitting across from the secretary's desk waiting to be invited in for her interview with the school principal. She wore what looked like the same thin silver necklace, but instead of a tiny silver cross, it was a tiny silver bee.

I sat down next to her.

After a moment, she spoke up first by asking me, "How are you?"

"Like that obelisk."

She just looked at me, expressionless.

"I mean, the same as always. When you get to be my age things don't change in your life that much."

Whether she caught the deeper (if not sarcastic) meaning in that last remark, or not, I couldn't tell.

She merely said, "Isn't it a lovely day?"

"Yes, it is," I replied. "A little on the warm side."

She said, with a pinch of contradiction, "I've never lived anywhere with such a wonderful climate; but then, I've never lived anywhere except Piedras."

I didn't care to continue this trivial chit-chat. "Paula, there's a question I'd like to ask you."

Her back stiffened, and she looked away. "What's that?"

"Who's Michael?"

It was like her whole body suddenly froze, with her head still looking away. I waited. After about ten seconds she turned to me and asked, "Who told you about him?" then answered her own question, "Belinda, with her big mouth, I bet."

"You're actually completely right. She stopped by the house yesterday morning and we talked for awhile. Evelyn wasn't at home."

"I'm sure she told you he was young, handsome, and a gringo."

"She did. And she said some other things."

I expected her to ask, "Like what?" but she said nothing. A young priest, dressed all in black, passed by us on the walkway, in something of a hurry, without giving us so much as a glance. Finally, Paula said, in a roundabout way, "I met Michael at a party last Sunday. Yes, he's a gringo from Arizona, and works for a big US manufacturing firm there, though I'm not sure exactly what he does. It's something to do with computers in the accounting department. He's tall and handsome, with blonde hair, highly-educated, and, of course, speaks perfect English. He's a nice young man, except he's a little on the aggressive side, which I don't like much. I mean, he's very straightforward. He took me out to lunch yesterday; and before the meal was over, he asked me to marry him, which means he'd take me back to Arizona with him. He says we can be married in a simple civil ceremony there. Maybe he asked me because he isn't going to be here long—only for about two weeks—on some kind of business for his company; and he figured he had no time to lose. I haven't given him my answer yet."

Paula said all of this quite matter-of-factly, betraying little emotion, as if she was giving me the weekly weather report. Significantly, she didn't say anything about what she felt for this Michael, in any romantic sense. Of course, I was stunned by the news, but not as stunned as I was by the news from Belinda. Paula's words didn't surprise me as much as Belinda's did. Perhaps, subconsciously, I was half-prepared for something of the kind. Still, it flew in the face of so much she'd told me; and, if carried out, would be the end of any possible relationship with her. I could've "attacked" her, so-to-speak, considering her previous words and actions, but only asked, "So what are you gonna say—yes or no?"

"If I say 'yes' you have to understand it's no reflection on you."

"That makes me feel better."

Paula didn't miss the sarcasm in my remark. "I'm sorry, Chris. I know what you've wanted. I've wanted it, too. I really have. But—well—this is an opportunity for me I can't pass up, I think."

"Yes, 'opportunity' is the word."

"I *do* have to think about my future."

"I suppose *I* don't."

"No, you don't, not in the same way—and you know what I mean."

"Oh yes, I know what you mean. What'll you tell Belinda?"

"Good-bye."

I almost let out a laugh, in spite of myself. "Well, Paula, in my opinion, you're moving too fast. Then, when it comes to men, you're certainly no ingenue. I guess you know what you're doing." She gave me an odd look, as if she wasn't sure if this was a compliment or a criticism. I asked her, "You say he's here for about two weeks. When does he plan on going back?"

"Not this, but the next Saturday."

There was a pause. Then I said, as matter-of-factly, "Then this'll be the last time we'll be together."

She acted like she didn't want to answer me, fiddling with the clasp on her purse, opening it slightly and, after maybe five seconds, snapping it shut. Then, she said, looking down, "I guess so."

"Can I ask you another question?"

She looked at me. "What?"

I looked directly into her dark eyes. "Do you love him?"

"I don't think that's the point."

I shrugged my shoulders. "Maybe not."

Perhaps she resented the question, for she suddenly stood up. I didn't. Facing me, she formally extended her right hand, which rather threw me. I extended my right hand. We shook hands, she with the same firm grip as she had when we first met, and she said, "I'll never forget you, Chris. I wish you the best of luck here in Saltillo." Before I could say anything, she turned and rapidly walked away down the same walkway on which I'd entered the plaza.

So that was that. I felt a sudden, horrible emptiness, like I wasn't even a person, and about as alive as that obelisk, which now looked more like a cemetery than an historical monument. A solid black pit bull, looking like it held a grudge against the world, appeared on the right side of the plaza and trotted across it. The muscular dog paused for a moment at the base of the obelisk to give it a sniff, then trotted off to the left and disappeared down one of the bush-lined walkways. (Dogs run loose, by the way, all over Saltillo, especially so in Lomas. Apparently, there're no leash laws in Mexico.)

Maybe five minutes after Paula had left, I got up and slowly left the plaza down the same walkway on which I'd entered it.

CHAPTER 61

Cheerful

As I slowly proceeded down the walkway, with my hands in my pockets, there was a a man in a black wheelchair slowly coming my way, maybe twenty feet away. It was being pushed by a woman. I could see, at once, that as far as his legs were concerned, he was a double amputee. The brown slacks he wore hung like two limp rags from his knees down, and, of course, there were no shoes. In looking at him I felt pity for him, not without feeling, I'm sorry to say, a slight revulsion, making me wish that he just wasn't there. He wore a long-sleeved, tan shirt with a dark brown collar. He was on the thin side, with a thin, elongated face. He looked to be maybe in his late fifties, and had graying, longish hair and a long, pointed, graying moustache. Only his bushy eyebrows were still all black. The woman pushing him, who I assumed to be his wife, wore a long-sleeved, dark green dress, and was also on the thin side with a thin face like him, but not so long. Her hair was all steel gray and reached to her shoulders. As far as he was concerned, he reminded me, from the neck up, of pictures (or representations) I'd seen of Don Quixote. As we drew nearer, I was struck by his expression. He wore a happy smile, chattering away, en español, to the woman, as he looked around in every direction but backwards, obviously immensely enjoying his outing in the picturesque park on a sunny day. The woman was more restrained—listening to him, but that was about all. As we slowly passed each other, the man heartily exclaimed to me, "¡Buenas tardes!" which I returned not so heartily; while the woman broke her serious expression long enough to give me a little, kindly smile, without saying anything. As I walked on I thought about what I'd just seen. Here was this pathetic figure of a man, confined to a wheelchair, who couldn't walk, and never would again (—and no telling what else he couldn't do—) and yet he acted so *cheerful*! And here I was feeling sorry for myself over a scheming woman. I won't say that seeing him made me feel better, but it made me put things into perspective. They say that everyone has his or her own "cross to bear." Well, my cross was made out of hollow plastic compared to the heavy one that handicapped man had to bear. Life was unfair; but just acknowledging the fact was hardly any consolation—or excuse. Compared to that man, I really had no reason to feel sorry for myself about anything. I looked up at the sky. It was a brilliant, cloudless blue. What made me feel ashamed, and even amazed, was that this man didn't appear to feel sorry for himself at all.

CHAPTER 62

In Our Yard

When I returned to the house Evelyn was nowhere to be seen. Finally, I looked through the window of the kitchen door and there she was, directly across from me, with her back to me, hanging up the clothes on the rotary clothesline in the middle of the yard. The weather had changed since the morning; and now the clouds were gone and the sun was out, making it feel about as pleasantly warm as it was down in The Alameda. Evelyn was dressed in her "working," plain, white, short-sleeved "peasant" dress, which was of the same shape, but couldn't have been more of an opposite to the "peasant" dress that Belinda wore at the garden party. I mean, Evelyn could've really *been* a peasant; but Belinda looked like she was on the stage playing Carmen in the opera of the same name. I stepped outside and went up to her.

The conversation that followed mainly consisted of me talking to and looking at Evelyn, while she only looked at me every now and then, occupied as she was in hanging up the clothes.

I started off by saying, "I'm back."
"It took you long enough."
"There were long lines at HEB."
"Probably because payday is today."
I didn't say anything. No use pushing a false point. Evelyn commented, "The best time to go is in the early morning. There's hardly anybody there then."
I suddenly felt guilty for going down to The Alameda, and for playing this charade again behind her back. Here she was,

doing her wifely chores like any good wife, while I was out making a fool of myself, as it turned out. I felt sorry for her. All she wanted was just a happy marriage. I asked her, "Do you need any help?"

"Oh, no—I won't be much longer."

"We should have a dryer."

"I don't want a dryer. They're lots of money, and use lots of electricity. This is *free*."

I let out a little laugh. "You're right! I never thought of it that way."

"You see, I'm always thinking about our expenses." She said this almost as if in jest.

"Yes, you are; and I do appreciate it." She gave me a quick smile. "I guess I'm not, and never have been, that good a provider. You should have better clothes, and more conveniences, and enjoy life more."

"I'm not complaining."

"That's the point."

"What d'you mean?" she asked innocently.

"You should. Any other woman would, I'm sure."

"I'm not 'any other woman.' Don't be silly. I have all I need. I don't think our life's so bad."

"It could be better."

"Things can always be better. For now, I'm contented. I only hope you are. I do my best . . . but I wonder when you go running after someone like Paula. I can't help being the age I am." She said this last remark with a simplicity that was poignant.

"You can just forget about that."

"About what?"

"About your age, and about Miss Paula. She's history."

She didn't say anything; but when I said, "She's history," her right hand froze, for a good five seconds, on the clothespin she was hanging up one of her bras on. Then, looking me directly in the eyes, she asked, "You really mean that?"

"I do," I replied, looking as directly at her. She went on with hanging up the clothes, and I just stood there. I thought to myself how here we were, two people, growing old, with a future which was just a continuation of our past.

Evelyn broke the silence by saying, "I remember the first time you said, "'I do.'"

"I do, too. You remember that story I told you about what your cousin Alberto said just before I walked down the aisle?"

"About being throwed out in the street?"

"*Thrown* out. Yes, I do."

"That was so funny!" she exclaimed with a chuckle. "He should never've said that to you. What a liar! Alberto's always been crazy, anyway."

"Yes. There I was, nervous as I was, standing there in the church foyer, waiting for my cue, with Alberto standing beside me. He looked at me with a straight face and said, in English, condescendingly, 'It's an old Mexican custom that once the ceremony is over, the men pick up the groom on their shoulders, carry him out to the steps of the church, and toss him into the street.'"

Paula chuckled again. "Many Mexicans just love to make things up, and play with your mind. I don't know why. It's just the way they are."

"I was *not* amused. It stayed in the back of my mind all through the ceremony."

"Well, nothing of the kind happened at all, anyway."

"No, nothing did. You know, we've never been back inside that church once in twenty-three years, even though we've passed by it now and then on our trips to Monterrey."

"Yes, Nuestra Señora del Carmen (Our Lady of Carmen). We should go back sometime to a service there."

"That would be nice. I'd like to do that."

"Me too."

A strong gust of wind from behind us suddenly tossed all the clothes she'd hung up almost horizontally, before it died away and the clothes dropped back down into their vertical position—it all being over in a matter of seconds. The wind had tossed a pair of her white panties out of the green laundry basket on her left, tossing them a few yards across the yard.

I went over, picked them up, and brought them back to her, which she instantly pinned up. "Thanks."

"De Nada." I replied. ("It's nothing."—more like "You're welcome.")

We chatted for a bit longer until Evelyn had hung up the last of the clothes. Even as she was hanging up the final yellow towel with the clothespins, she asked me, "You haven't had your lunch yet, have you?"

"No, not yet."

She picked up the empty laundry basket with her left hand, turned to me, and said, "I think I'll fix you some tostadas. I know you love them."

"You haven't fixed me those in a long time."

"Well, you've been a good boy lately, and deserve a reward."

"The best reward I've ever had was when I met you."

She was taken aback, even apparently shocked, by this, unused to receiving such a major compliment from me. She slowly broke into a smile, (which I returned,) and said, "I need to fix those tostadas." I followed her into the house.

CHAPTER 63

The Bear

It wasn't long after my delicious lunch of tostadas that I was outside sweeping the front walkway, mainly clear of the brown (or dead) pine needles which endlessly collect on the walkway which runs around the house, as well as all over the yard, from our two giant pine trees. The front walkway is so situated that I can completely see the great valley and mountains to the north, as well as the mountains to the east and west, but not the mountains to the south behind me because the relatively high front wall of the house blocks the view. To see them, I have to be in the backyard or down in the middle of the street. Well, as I was sweeping the front walkway, Baby Diego, in his iconic green overalls with a gray sweatshirt on underneath, came out of his house, and for some moments just stood in the middle of the street looking intently towards the south, unaware, at first, of my presence. When he finally was, he exclaimed, in his simple English, stepping maybe a yard closer towards my house, "Chris! Fire! Here—come here! Fire!" He pointed towards the south with his right arm. I soon joined him in the street and was shocked by what I saw. An enormous, wide plume of grayish-blackish smoke was billowing upwards into the sky from the other side of the southern mountains—specifically, if you were to go in a straight line down our block and to the top of the mountain ridge, then go south maybe five hundred feet or more, that's where it was. The fire hadn't reached our side of the mountain yet, which looked as green and peaceful as always. Of course, Baby Diego and I had the same thought–

would it? "You think it'll come over here?" I asked him. "Quién sabe?" he seriously replied. His wife Berta, dressed in blue jeans and a white pullover sweater, came out to join us. Evelyn, seeing us all out in the middle of the street talking came out to see what was going on, and was as shocked at what she saw as I was.

In studying the thick and wide plume, reaching very high into the sky and tapering off, like an inverted, swirling tornado, I didn't see any evidence of any flames, which I figured meant that the source and the height of the fire was down on the opposite side of the mountains. Baby Diego and I discussed this. Evelyn stood next to Berta and they talked together en español, while keeping their eyes riveted on the gigantic plume. Because it was a good two miles away, you couldn't hear anything, like crackling timber. All you could do was watch the constantly rising, silent plume, continuously changing, or intermingling its colors from the black to the gray spectrum—it being more on the black side right at the ridge. At the very end of the plume, way up in the sky, it was almost white.

We all stood there and watched it for twenty minutes or so; and, in that time, it didn't look it was diminishing at all. If anything, the plume was increasing, both horizontally and vertically, and growing darker, which meant, to our dismay, that the fire was spreading up the other side of the mountain. We all commented on this. Still, what could we do? Finally, everybody went back inside their house.

Typically, there was nothing on the TV or radio about it; but, later on, at around sunset, there was a local news broadcast about it on the TV which stated that the fire was a result of a family camping out in the woods near the base of the mountain, whose campfire, for some reason, had gotten out of control. Local firefighters were battling the great blaze which, luckily, was in a totally uninhabited area. Many local volunteers were helping. They also stated that the elite firefighting helicopter corps from Monterrey, which carried payloads of water, had been called in and were rushing to the fire. One thing they said was that it had been reported that wild animals had been seen fleeing in terror from the widespread, raging blaze; and they cautioned the residents of Lomas de Lourdes to not panic or take any action against any animals they might suddenly find in their neighborhood, like coyotes, bears, or rattlesnakes, but to call the local authorities. They said the fire should be extinguished within twelve hours, and wouldn't reach the colony. Of course, this broadcast was in Spanish; but Evelyn told me what they said.

 Ever since I'd been living in Lomas I'd heard, from various Lomasites, that there were osos (bears) up in the mountains. I'd never seen one; nor did any of the people who'd said so actually seen one for themselves. I considered it more of a legend than anything else.

 A little while after the broadcast I went out in the backyard to have another look-see. The twisting plume was as wide and as high as ever, but it wasn't, overall, quite as dark. While gazing at it, I heard a rustling in the bushy ravine behind me, which was louder than just some bird or rodent, or one of the wild, feral cats. I even thought it might be some person. I went over to investigate. Looking down, I couldn't believe it! A medium-sized, brown bear, with a very black snout, was lumbering along the bottom of the ravine, with some speed, and with evident determination, northwards down the foothill. I looked at it with a degree of awe. I'd never seen a real bear before, outside of a zoo. So what they'd said was true! There *were* bears up in them mountains, after-all! I had an urge to run inside and grab my camera out of its case; but, judging by the bear's movement, I didn't think I'd have the time.

 When I woke up late the next morning, the first thing I did was go outside and have another look-see. It hadn't come over onto our side during the night. The bulging plume was now about half the height it was, though its width was about the same. It also showed little black—even at the ridge—but was now almost uniformly gray. Helicopters were seen coming and going. One of them passed directly over our house (high up) on its way to the fire. By about two in the afternoon, the plume was considerably diminished, and by sunset it was virtually gone from view, with only a few trails of smoke still rising into the sky.

CHAPTER 64

Ending In Arteaga

Arteaga ("AREteaYAHgah") is a small hilltop town (un pueblo) about six miles east of Saltillo, as the swallow flies. (I say "swallow" because these white-breasted birds with their navy blue heads, backs, and long, tapering wings are to be seen all over Saltillo, especially in The Alameda and up in Lomas, and also in Arteaga.) Arteaga, like Lomas, is at a higher altitude than the city, and, like Lomas, is still within the great valley, or encircling mountains. Also, like Lomas, it butts up against the ascending Sierras in the east even as Lomas does in the south, though it's farther from the city itself than Lomas is. The main difference is that Lomas is made up of many foothills, while Arteaga is situated on just one large and very long foothill, as if the foothill had been sliced off in the middle along its length, resulting in a long, flat, oval mesa, on which the town sits, at a right angle to the mountains, with a white Catholic church sporting one right bell tower on one end of the oval (near the mountains), while, maybe a mile and a half away, a large park, containing many tall pines and cypresses, occupies the other end of the oval. The little town itself takes up the space in between these two sites.

A two-lane, brown cobblestone street runs the length of the mesa, from the park to the church. Most of the town's residents live on the sloping side streets off this main drive which mainly contains small shops and stores, a few restaurants, and a number of colonial style millionaire's mansions with extensive grounds. A fairly wide median strip separates the two lanes, all the way down the street, on which stand a seemingly endless row of old, fat-trunked, almond-colored alamo (or cottonwood) trees, interspaced, here and there, with black, wrought iron benches, like those in The Alameda. Far from them all standing erect, most of these enormous trees veer off at every conceivable angle, with the thick branches of a few of them looping all the way over and meeting, then rising, from the ground again. Their countless big, light green leaves provide excellent shade up and down the whole street. They make for a very picturesque and unusual sight, and are Arteaga's main claim to fame, aside from its wonderful, Spring-like climate (in the summer.) Professional and amateur painters have been trekking to Arteaga for years, setting up their easels, and painting these ancient and awesome trees. In fact, one of Evelyn's oldest friends in Monterrey, Angelina Borrego, who's now in her eighties, and who used to be an amateur painter, has an attractive watercolor in the den of her house of one of these trees, which she painted in her thirties.

During the weekends, in every season except winter, Arteaga is a beehive of activity down in the park, which for those two days, becomes (from around noon to around sunset) a huge, outdoor mercado (market), selling all kinds of local goods, one of the most popular being delicious, locally brewed licors de manzana, membrillo, durazno, y mora (apple, quince, peach, and blackberry brandies.) Some of the sellers who set up their tables or stalls are Arteagans, but the majority of them come in with their wares or produce (such as fruits and vegetables, dairy products, homemade desserts and candies, second-hand clothes, leather goods, pottery, rosebushes and flowers, caged birds and chickens, pigs, and even goats) from the tiny hamlets and small farms and ranches in the outlying countryside. By contrast, if you go to Arteaga on a weekday, it's as quiet and sleepy as a cemetery—even more so than Lomas. The only activity in the park is the birds flying about or pecking the ground, or maybe a strolling couple or individual. A fair number of the town's residents are retired people.

We just hung around the house on Sunday. I worked in the yard and garden, and Evelyn cruised the net, mopped the tiled floors of the whole house, and gabbed on the phone. We decided that the next day, Monday, we'd take a basket lunch to Arteaga and spend some time there in the afternoon, just to get away from Lomas (and Saltillo) for a while. Have a change of scenery. Really, on a weekday it's as if you have the whole pretty little town virtually all to yourself. We used to be in the habit of going to the weekend market there, once or twice a month—always on a Sunday; but, over the years, we've gotten out of the habit, as the market's become more and more crowded, so that you have to almost shove your way through all the people to see everything. I don't know why it's increased so much in popularity over the last seven years or so, but it has. Nowadays, every once in a while, we'll go there on a weekday and enjoy walking about the lovely place, usually stopping by one of the small stores off the main drive in order to buy a couple of bottles of blackberry brandy, which we both especially like.

Arteaga, by the way, is recognized as a "magic town." Such small, old towns exist all over Mexico, and are so designated by the government due to their beauty, quaintness, and charm, where you find little, if any, modern industry or architecture; and they're deliberately preserved so as to retain their original, centuries-old appearance as much as possible. The little town of Parras, sixty miles west of Saltillo, and still within Coahuila state, is another "magic town," bigger than Arteaga, and famous for its vineyards and winemaking, not to mention being the birthplace of Francisco Madero, President of Mexico during the Mexican Revolution (until he was assassinated.) Parras certainly is magical in its location, like an oasis out in the middle of nowhere. The town's very green with an abundance of tall pine, cypress, and cedar trees, and emerald green parks and vineyards; while the whole countryside beyond it, where the vineyards end, is nothing, for miles and miles, but low, rocky hills and yellowish desert containing only a minimal growth of scrub and cactuses.

Evelyn and I have been to Parras (once) and toured one of the age-old wineries there. Going to one of these towns is truly like going back in time.

We arrived in Arteaga around noon, (Evelyn driving,) and she pulled up and parked the car near the entrance to the park. Though we both stood there for a few moments and gave the park a quick look-over, (in which there wasn't a soul in sight,) we didn't enter it, but turned and headed in the opposite direction, down the sidewalk bordering the median strip, under the shade of the great alamo trees. We walked slowly along, without talking, I toting the brown lunch basket/hamper in my right hand. I was on Evelyn's right, or on the street side, like any proper gentleman would be, (not that there was the remotest possibility that anything "sudden" might happen.) Evelyn had chosen a simple maroon, long-sleeved dress for this outing, while I was dressed in black jeans and a long-sleeved, deep green shirt. We both wore close to identical brown loafers. Evelyn wore no stockings. In other words, we were dressed casually and comfortably like anyone would be who was just out for an informal, relaxing stroll. It was a sunny and mild September day, and the sky was a very intense, cloudless blue.

After walking for some distance, (so that taking a look back at the park was like looking through the wrong end of a pair of binoculars,) we came to a point where, on our left, there was a black, wrought iron bench facing us between two of the giant alamo trees. I stopped, causing Evelyn to stop, and said, looking at the bench, "Why don't we sit down there and have our lunch." She glanced at the bench and said, "OK." We went over and sat down, Evelyn sitting down on my left a second after me as I set the hamper down on the bench between us.

After a few moments, I pulled back the lid of the hamper and handed Evelyn a white cloth napkin which she placed across her lap. I did the same with the other napkin. The rest of the hamper's contents were two bottled waters, two tuna fish sandwiches in baggies, and two very red apples which

I distributed between us. I shut the lid and we both set our bottled water and apple on it. We settled back in the bench and proceeded to eat our lunch.

Across the street there was a long adobe wall, maybe six feet high, and painted white. From where we sat, it must have extended fifty feet (or more) in both directions. It looked like it had been painted last a long time ago, for the white paint was not so much white as it was a faded almond-color—almost the same color as the alamo trees opposite it. Where the wall met the sidewalk, the paint was pretty much gone, exposing the bare, brown adobe. What grabbed my attention, though, was about the same faded white, colonial-looking, squarish stone mansion directly opposite us, and set back some distance from the wall. Because of the wall, only its upper half was visible from where we sat; and you could see its deep-set, second-story windows. Its roof was flat. The old mansion looked, for all its size, oddly lonely standing back there. The only trees on the property were a cluster of tall pines, off to the right of the mansion, (actually off to its left.) There was no gate (or even a door) in the wall, so that there was no access to the mansion from the street. Talk about privacy! This mansion certainly had that.

Evelyn was unusually quiet, and had been since we'd stepped out of the car; and she apparently wasn't going to initiate any conversation. So, as we ate our lunch, I finally spoke up by saying, "That's some house over there, isn't it?"

"Yes, that's some house."

Detecting a touch of sarcasm in her voice, I said, "It's only a comment . . . I don't know what your problem is. You've been about as talkative as Whistler's Mother ever since we arrived." She said nothing to this, but just looked down at the half-eaten sandwich in her lap. "Look—if you don't wanna talk, then don't." I fell as silent as her. There was a long pause, during which I continued eating. *She* didn't, but just sat there, apparently staring at the mansion, as if she'd suddenly lost all her appetite. I had the instinctive feeling that something was coming.

It did, as she finally broke the silence by saying, (only looking at me out of the corner of her eye every now and then), "Chrisito . . . I've been wanting to talk to you about something that's been on my mind for the last couple of days, but it never seemed to be the right moment at the house. I agreed to come here with you today because I knew we'd be alone here together for two or three hours—in this dead town—and wouldn't have any distractions. Once we got here, though, I began having second thoughts. Why maybe spoil our outing? You have such a fascination for this place. (That touch of sarcasm again.) Maybe I should just keep my mouth shut, after-all. That's why I've been so quiet, if you know what I mean."

"I know what you mean, but I don't know what you mean . . . I suppose this has something to do with Paula?"

"Yes and no. I mean, if you'd never met Paula, and sneaked around behind my back with her, then there'd be nothing on my mind—but she's not the point. Girls like Paula are a dime a dozen. The point is you, who obviously don't value me much—or very much anymore. I'm growing old. I admit it. You are, too, though you refuse to admit it. Yes, it must have been a big boost to your ego to receive such attention from a beautiful young woman like Paula—for what it's worth. I can't imagine any handsome young man paying me such attention, at my age, at all. I guess you men really are all the same. I always thought you were different. I always thought we had something deeper than just that . . . You say that Paula's history. Sure, now that she's rejected you. You can always find another Paula if you want to. The world's full of Paulas. Maybe you'll be luckier the next time." She picked up her half-eaten apple and looked at it. "Like apples on an apple tree, if you don't like the taste of one, drop it, and pick another." She set her apple back down on the hamper.

The silence between us returned. She said no more for the moment, and I didn't know what to say. Her words really surprised me. I thought all this was behind us now, and that she'd put it out of her mind. Apparently not. It made me remember what a (male) friend of mine once said to me, "Women will strongly deny it—but they *never* forgive and they *never* forget."

At length, she ended the silence by asking me, "You have nothing to say?"

"Oh, I can always find something to say, but it may not be to your liking."

"Try me."

"OK . . . You say I refuse to accept my age. If I did, I don't anymore. Paula taught me that. It wasn't a lesson I wanted to learn. I mean, men are wired for desire, more than women are, and"—

She cut me off, stressing each word, "You couldn't be more wrong . . . Men are wired, all right—like Frankenstein," which she said without a shred of humor. I let out a laugh. "Anyway, I don't see how you can say"—

I cut *her* off, "¡Por favor! I told you . . . Can you just let me finish—OK?"

She answered, after a moment, in a steely voice, "OK—do continue."

"Thank-you . . ." A blue swallow suddenly landed on the wall opposite us, and for four or five seconds it stood there, with its back to us, seemingly staring at the mansion, even as we'd been doing, before it just as suddenly took flight, flew up over the mansion, and disappeared. About the second it took flight, I continued, "I was speaking generally. There're plenty of exceptions. Anyway, you put more into my words than I meant, which was desiring something doesn't mean you're gonna get it; and its your fault for desiring it in the first place. You have to be content with less—or, where you and I are concerned, as I see now, with a less that is actually more."

Evelyn gave me a look. "Well, I don't know what to say to that."

"You don't have to say anything. It's not necessary to say anything. Most of the time, all words do, when it comes to expressing your feelings, is confuse everything. People'll say that they 'speak from the heart.' They don't. The heart has no need for any vocabulary. All I can say, really, is that my heart, at last, is in the right place."

Evelyn merely commented, "For somebody who says words aren't necessary, you've got a real way with words!"

I let out a laugh. "Ain't it the truth! Look how much it's done for me!" I exclaimed sarcastically.

"No, no—I think I know what you mean and I'm glad to hear you say it. Maybe you and I are at a new beginning."

"I think we are."

Evelyn tossed her apple away even as I put the caps on our bottled waters and placed them back in the basket. She stood up first. Shooting me a smile, she said, "Come along, Chrisito, let's see if we can buy some of that blackberry brandy." I stood up, and taking the basket in my right hand, with my other hand I took her right hand in mine, and we proceeded to walk on down the sidewalk under the shade of the trees.

THE END

Chris Steer

Author Chris Steer is an expatriate American who has lived in Saltillo, Mexico since 2011 with his wife Evelyn, a cat and a tortoise. He has a graduate degree in English from the University of Texas at Arlington. *In Search of Other Skies* is his first book.

www.ingramcontent.com/pod-product-compliance
Lightning Source LLC
Chambersburg PA
CBHW030318100526
44592CB00010B/481